AWAY ALL BOATS

ALSO BY JOHN N. COLE

Tarpon Quest

Fishing Came First

Striper

From the Ground Up

In Maine

A JOHN MACRAE BOOK
Henry Holt and Company New York

AWAY ALL BOATS

A Personal Guide for the Small-Boat Owner

John N. Cole

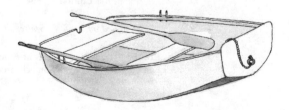

Henry Holt and Company, Inc.
Publishers since 1866
115 West 18th Street
New York, New York 10011

Henry Holt® is a registered trademark of
Henry Holt and Company, Inc.

Published in Canada by Fitzhenry & Whiteside Ltd.,
195 Allstate Parkway, Markham, Ontario L3R 4T8.

Library of Congress Cataloging-in-Publication Data
Cole, John N.
Away all boats : a personal guide for the small-boat owner / John N. Cole.
p.   cm.
Includes index.
ISBN 0-8050-2706-8
1. Boats and boating.   I. Title.
GV775.C59 1994
797—dc20   94-1048
                                                            CIP

Henry Holt books are available for special
promotions and premiums. For details contact:
Director, Special Markets.

First Edition—1994

Designed by Paula R. Szafranski

Printed in the United States of America
All first editions are printed on acid-free paper.

10 9 8 7 6 5 4 3 2 1

For Gertrude,

A blithe and generous spirit

And a lady, in the best sense of the word

Contents

Introduction

This is a book about my life with small boats. It is, as you will discover, a book that is more about a life than it is about boats. But not by much. Boats have been a part of my life longer than any other companion. And they have given me happiness, adventure, and a comprehension of natural elements like the sea, sun, tides, fishes, and storms. Which is not to imply, however, that I am any sort of a marine scholar or small-boat encyclopedia; I'm not. If I were, this would be a textbook about boats; it is not.

It does, however, contain a significant amount of information about boats, especially ones that I owned, worked on, or borrowed. For the most part, these were—and one still is—a particular kind of small boat. Excepting my brief, tempestuous, and exciting affair with a Hobie Cat, and my more languid, brief meeting with a lovingly restored Old Town sailing canoe, each of my other boats was powered by oars—because I have always loved to row—or by some sort of internal combustion engine—because even an oarsman's best work can't propel a heavy boat very far in rough water or against a turbulent tide.

With one exception, every boat in this book was designed to perform a fairly limited family of functions. That exception is the *Emma*, my first boat, a rowboat, a sharpie, a skiff ... the list of regional names for these basic, wooden (most often) small boats is a long one. But you'll know her when you see her. They are still, after all these years, everyone's image of a rowboat, as opposed to a rowing boat, which is quite a different species.

The reason the *Emma* does not fit a single functional category is because I forced her into other lines of work, work she was never intended to do. But, like a lady of the court who falls on hard times and finds herself competing in the streets, the *Emma* adapted. She and I made do with what each of us had. And, like the classic she was, the *Emma* had plenty.

When I say "classic" I don't want to imply a kind of rare excellence. The *Emma* was not an exotic; quite the opposite. She was a relatively mass-produced (for the 1930s) wooden rowboat, put together on what could be called a rowboat assembly line. But she was classic in the sense that she embodied every generic trait that a skiff, or sharpie, or rowboat, should possess. She was an able boat; she could handle the wind and sea with more reliance than most casual observers might expect, given her undistinguished pedigree and utilitarian construction. She rowed well; the energy spent pulling *Emma*'s oars was gratifyingly efficient: one strong stroke would move her forward with impressive acceleration. She was, for her size, reasonably comfortable, although her spare, wooden seats (thwarts) were not cushioned or padded in any way.

If she had a design fault, it was her low freeboard: the distance between her gunwales and the water. If her passengers failed to trim ship and keep the *Emma* level, she could, and often would, ship water over her rails. When I forced her to enter the scalloping trade, this weakness became a flaw whenever I hauled full scallop dredges to the surface and horsed them aboard over the *Emma*'s rail. All that weight—100 pounds or more if the dredge was packed—put her gunwale under and the bay sloshed in. Which is why I kept a bailer handy. After every tow, I'd spend a few minutes bailing, putting that bay water back where it had come from, and the *Emma* would stay reasonably dry and always afloat. She never let me down.

So although I did not choose the *Emma*—I had no choice—for the work she did, she responded to my demands with a wonderful patience. She endured.

The *Emma* taught me many lessons. One of the most important was my realization that most boats will take more punishment than their skippers think possible. Most boats, that is, that are designed and built with some respect for their generic heritage.

So when you decide you want, or need, to become a boat owner, it's an excellent idea to begin by deciding what kind of purpose you want your boat to fulfill. If, like me, you are lucky enough to acquire a boat "because it's there," then you have no choice. But it will also be helpful if you are adequately informed about your "gift boat's" generic history and probable future.

And skiffs, or rowboats, or sharpies, or any relatively stable, relatively flat-bottomed boat that can be easily and efficiently rowed, have a longer generic history than most. They are the descendants of the first animal-skin and wood contraptions held together with rawhide and pitch that floated awkwardly on the waterways of the Middle East 3,000 years ago. Their function today, however, is essentially the same: to move people and products on the water.

When my grandfather bought the *Emma*, he wanted her to be there at the dock ready to take him and my grandmother and perhaps a friend (no more than one) for a row on Georgica Pond. Their home on a point between Georgica and the Atlantic in eastern Long Island was on a part of the pond called Georgica Cove, an arm reaching east off Georgica's main body, which ran north from the ocean back to the Montauk Highway—about four miles. The cove, about a mile long and a half-mile wide, was, and still is, a well-protected patch of brackish water no more than eight or ten feet deep at its deepest. There is not enough room, or "fetch," in the cove for waves to build. It is, and always has been, a fine stretch of water for rowing a small boat. That, plus the Georgica Association's ban on outboard motors, was what started my life with boats.

That was back in the 1930s, but the basics haven't changed. If you live on a relatively manageable body of water—fresh, salt, or brackish—and you'd like to be able to get out on it once in a while just for the joys of being afloat, then you should buy a rowboat. Your best chance of finding one is to ask for a skiff.

There are, of course, a hundred other reasons to own a skiff. Each will make some difference when you make the final decision. Crabbing, clamming, scalloping, oystering, tending fykes, tending eel pots, tending fish traps, fishing for food and/or fun, hauling seaweed, carrying the mail to islanders, or rowing your grandmother to lunch at her neighbor's place . . . there is almost no limit to the jobs a skiff can do, provided none of them is on too large a scale.

Today's skiffs, however, compared to the times when the *Emma* was new, are infinitely more varied, more individual, and, on the whole, a good deal more expensive. The *Emma* almost preceded outboards. Those that were available in the 1930s, especially motors small enough to make sense on any boat under sixteen feet, were cantankerous devices, given to frequent breakdowns and sputtering performance. All of them were pull-started, and you don't know what frustration is unless you have pulled the starter cord on a recalcitrant outboard for an hour or more. Changing spark plugs, adjusting needle valves, and replacing the coil notwithstanding, some of those motors just refused to start. Which is why no one really thought too much about attaching one to the *Emma*'s stern. She got around splendidly as a rowboat; an outboard, in her Georgica life, would have been an affront as well as a problem.

Which cannot be said in the 1990s. It matters not that I recall those early days, that I was the guy who so ineffectually pulled the starter cord for two hours or more. Today's outboards work well, no matter how many memories you bring with you. Knowing that, most skiff designers plan with an outboard in mind. If a person wants to do nothing but row, the designers reason, then let that person buy a rowing shell, which is about as far removed from a skiff as a Grand Prix race car is from a wheelbarrow.

The skiffs of the late twentieth century are fashioned from just about every workable, cookable, and impermeable material known. There are, of course, plain wooden skiffs made from planks and ribs sawed and chiseled from spruce, cedar, pine, oak (for ribs, knees, stems, and rub rails), mahogany, and just about any other tree that's handy. Then there are skiffs made from marine plywood, plastic-coated veneers, Plexiglas, fiberglass, polyesters, and polymers. There are skiffs you can blow up with a tire pump; skiffs you can take apart and carry in a bag; and skiffs of steel, aluminum, and, for all I know, other metals and materials. It's a long list, and the varieties seem endless when you begin to leaf through the dozens of boating and marine publications.

There are, for example, skiff-building kits of varying degrees of complexity. You can buy plans, parts, molds (for fiberglass), and the raw materials you'll need, along with advice on what tools should be the most helpful.

You can find good, handcrafted skiffs for sale in the classified pages of *WoodenBoat* magazine, one of the best reference publications for small boats in the nation. One issue on hand tells me, for example, that I can buy a sixteen-foot Harbor flat-bottomed skiff made at the WoodenBoat School in Brooklin, Maine, for $950. That's an excellent buy for a skiff you know is well made from carefully selected materials. There are other boat-building schools that produce skiffs of comparable value. You'll find them listed in *WoodenBoat* and other small-boat publications.

But perhaps the best way to get your first skiff (I'm pretty sure Macy's doesn't sell *Emma*s anymore) is to inquire at your local marina, waterfront supply shop, or any other place that has a passing acquaintance with the regional marine trade. It's a ten-to-one shot someone will know somebody who builds a skiff or two a year, maybe more. As a general rule, these boats will be your best buy. They will have been built by someone with knowledge of local conditions, and, if the boat builder is experienced, the materials will be those that are available in the neighborhood. That means more value for less money.

There are, of course, other ways to achieve the same goal. Of these, the most practical, and in many ways the most exciting, is the used boat. In any waterfront region—ocean, bay, river, lake, lagoon, bayou, marsh, or harbor—you can find used boats for sale. They are ubiquitous: in front yards, at marinas, at boats-for-rent docks, listed in the "boats for sale" section of the local newspaper's classified ads, and even on the bulletin boards that are found in most rural and suburban supermarkets.

And buying a used boat, especially a small boat like a skiff, is not nearly as risky as buying a used car. For unlike a transmission or brake drum or piston, which are well hidden in an automobile's internal system, small boats have little to hide and no places to hide it. If you can tell rotting wood when you see it, or know corrosion when you meet it, you will be able to evaluate a boat's condition in a few moments of close observation. If you can lift a bow, or sit on a seat, or if you have any concept of the lines a small boat should have, you will have most of the data you need to make a decision. Don't be put off by peeling or flaking paint; in many ways, it's a better signal than a spanking fresh coat that may be chiefly cosmetic, put there to cover up real flaws. And pay even less attention to open seams—if the skiff is wooden—because all wood tends to shrink out of water. Those seams will swell and close once your skiff has been in the water, most likely sunk, for a few days.

Whatever your decision, when your skiff finally reaches your home waters and becomes *your* boat, you'll need to give her the equipment you and she both need to function as a team. Propulsion comes first, and with a skiff you should start with a pair of oars and the oarlocks that will make them work. Once you start shopping for oars, you will realize just how many choices there are when it comes to outfitting a boat, any boat, even one as fundamental as a skiff.

For just as there are scores of varieties of skiffs, there are almost as many kinds of oars. Which doesn't mean that finding a good set that's right for your skiff will be easy. Good rowing oars are fashioned from ash and are difficult to locate. Ash is a heavy, tough wood, and most of the folks who make oars for the mass market must consider it so heavy it will scare off would-be customers. Lighter woods, like spruce and even laminated pine, are the favorites of the few companies who manufacture oars for giant retailers like Sears and Ace Hardware. But these are not the answer, at least not for long.

Oarlocks, which you might anticipate to be a fine example of simple functionalism, have also assumed a varietal diversity of late. Something to do with merchandising, no doubt. In their most basic form, oarlocks can be nothing more than two oak pegs hammered into drilled holes in the boat's gunwales. Called thole pins, the two pegs are set a bit farther apart than the oar's diameter, and they serve to give that oar a fulcrum to press against when the rower takes a stroke. Sometimes the oars are fitted with sleeves that keep them from sliding overboard through the thole pins whenever the oarsman lets go of his oars.

But you won't find thole pins on many skiffs these days, not in these United States where tens of thousands of oarlocks are manufactured of galvanized steel, bronze, brass, stainless steel, and most certainly other metals and compounds that haven't yet imprinted my ken. Each of the different materials can be designed in a dozen different forms, but each has the identical function: to hold an oar in place and to pivot as the oar takes its full stroke, backward and forward. Oarlocks can also fit into drilled holes in the gunwale, but they most often find their home in brackets made just for them. There are metal sleeves that fit into drilled holes, there are brackets that can be fastened to the rail, and others than can be fastened and also removed and carried home if the boat owner is concerned about the possibility of petty theft.

So you can see how an essentially simple mechanism, the simplest that floats, has already become a series of rather complex and personal choices. When you compute the number of decisions that must be made, beginning with the type of material your skiff is fashioned from; the hull's design; the hull's dimensions, color, and trim; and then calculate the variety of oars and oarlocks, you begin to approach the kind of mathematical complexity best turned over to an accountant or, better yet, the accountant's computer.

Which seems to demonstrate the negatives associated with what we label progress. Just a short while ago on the cosmic clock, a skiff was a skiff and—depending on its home region—it was made from one kind of wood, came in one color, and was already fitted with wooden oars and a pair of thole pins. What has happened since those good old days, the same days when Henry Ford produced a Model A with no optional equipment and a choice of just one color (black), is what has happened everywhere: a plethora of choices.

But as long as we stick to the boat, her oars and oarlocks, they are choices that any reasonably sane and even-tempered boat person can manage. Ah, but this is only the beginning, for once you have your skiff and the means to navigate and propel her, you'll need a bunch of other seagoing accoutrements, some of which are required by the U.S. Coast Guard, which, as a new boat owner you will soon discover, will become yet another federal presence in your life.

You'll need an anchor and anchor warp (the rope, or line) to make the connection between the bottom and the boat. You'll have to have life jackets, a signaling device—horn and flares—a flashlight, and a basic first-aid kit. And, depending on the laws in your state, you'll probably need to have the boat registered. If that's the case, you'll want a safe, waterproof place on board to keep a copy of the registration paperwork.

You may, or may not, have to pay taxes on your boat; but you most certainly will have to have a place to keep her. You can put her on a boat trailer, which allows you mobility and the relative security of your own backyard. (But you'll have to license and equip the trailer.) Or you can haul her up on the shore, which means having access to a shore and the means for hauling your boat out of the water: davits, rollers, a winch, what have you. Or, as I did with the *Emma*, you can keep her alongside—and fast to—a dock, either yours or someone else's; if it's someone else's, you'll most likely have to pay a dockage fee. Or you can keep her on a mooring, preferably your own. If it's someone else's . . . well, you know.

In Florida, where there are more small boats than any other state, and very possibly any other nation, most of the small boats are kept in what's called dry storage: cavernous sheds built around multi-storied pipe racks where boats are hoisted to their perches by the same forklift that lifted them out of the water. Which means that your boat will be safe, but that you will also have to inform the forklift operator whenever you want your boat back in the water. Which definitely has an effect on spontaneity.

Becoming a boat person, even on the most basic level, is becoming a different sort of individual who leads a different sort of life. It's a state of being comparable to the difference between being married and being single, or being a parent and being a child. At the very least, it's a life of concern. In most cases concern becomes caring, caring becomes love, and love, at last, becomes an obsession. For boats, as every boat person has discovered, are quite unlike other possessions. They require more giving. Sometimes more than anyone has to give, which is why there are always so many boats for sale.

But you won't be thinking about selling when you acquire your first boat. And if it's a skiff, with oars and oarlocks and every other basic, you will—unless you are very different from everyone else—begin to think motor. For rowing, even with all its pleasures and its excellent physical therapies, has spatial and temporal limits. You can voyage only so far in a given time span. The issue is easily resolved: all that's needed is a small outboard motor. Which is like saying all you need to stay healthy is a heart and liver transplant. Outboards are equally serious. New ones are costly; used ones are even more chancy than used automobiles.

Nevertheless, you will acquire one because your boat tells you to. Which means you will need fuel storage facilities: gas tanks and oil reservoirs. And you will have to have a fire extinguisher; it's a Coast Guard requirement. And because you and your boat can now travel much longer distances, you will need primary navigation systems: a compass, even if it's handheld; and charts, most likely the National Oceanic and Atmospheric Administration issue, price-fixed (at this writing) at $14 each, surely one of the finest bargains in the entire nautical marketplace.

With your new motor you have radically altered the scale and character of your time on the water in your boat. You have activated a process, just as the warming sun and wet soil can activate a small, dormant seed that will become a great maple tree that dominates the forest. You have, if you are not extremely careful, taken your first step along that financially rocky path toward a larger boat—say, one with a small cabin that will get you in out of the weather, put something of a roof over your head. In short, a boat that is a bit more like most of the others that have left you and your skiff bobbing in their wakes as they powered by.

What you will do next is abandon the singularly pure, generic small boat—the skiff, sharpie, or whatever—for a host of relatively impure, and becoming more so, species of powerboats. They begin at sixteen to eighteen feet and move right on up until they near two hundred feet; then you're talking mega-yachts, of which, at $10 million and up, there are more of in this world than you can probably imagine.

When you move on from your skiff, you move away from me and the kind of boats this book is about. How far? Consider this item clipped from the *Key West Citizen*, our local daily newspaper.

Describing the boat being raffled for a worthy cause, the *Citizen*
tells us she's a:

> 26-foot Mako Tournament fishing boat equipped with the
> following: twin 200-horsepower Mercury outboard motors,
> stainless steel props, counter rotation. King loran, depth-
> finder/plotter, King VHF radio, Pioneer stereo with four
> waterproof speakers, full transom, custom T-top. Rupp Top-
> Gun outriggers. Above deck live well, leaning post, 21-gallon
> fresh water with shower. Dive ladder, dual ram hydraulic
> steering, E-Z loader galvanized dual-wheel trailer, built-in
> trim tabs. 200-gallon fuel tanks, remote oil fills, bow rails, full
> instrumentation, custom flush mounting of electronics.

Those "electronics" include gadgets like the new, compact
Global Positioning Systems, a navigational tool made possible by a
network of satellites orbiting about 11,000 miles above the earth.
And soon, there will be a full galaxy of twenty-one satellites to help
push-button navigators learn where they are on any ocean, any lake,
any bay, any river on the planet simply by pushing a button or two
and reading the LCD screen. In addition, the GPS will tell you the
speed your boat is moving and the course she follows. There are also
fish finders, depth recorders, radars, and course plotters, with more
to come from the ever-inventive manufacturers of high-tech boating
accessories, none of which even existed when I first became a
licensed skipper.

These days, once you leave your skiff behind, you enter a world of
increasing complexity and cost, even if you try to keep it simple, as
Brock Yates says in one of his contributing-editor columns in *Boating*, a monthly magazine for powerboaters. Describing his next
boat, the one he's about to buy, Yates tells his readers: "In terms
of equipment [on his 25- to 30-footer], I'll keep it simple. It's
very trendy to set up instrument panels so they appear to have
been yanked out of a B-2 bomber, but the secret is functionalism:

compass, VHF [radio], engine synchronizer, auto-pilot, and a color radar. I'll put on a loran and a GPS too, but I'll save them for long-range cruising."

Well, there you are. If that's what one of the leading boating authorities considers "simple" these days, then, as you'll learn in the pages that follow, my life with small boats is an anachronism. Aside from a compass, a tachometer to tell me how fast the engines were turning over, an ammeter to let me know when the batteries were charging or discharging, and a couple of gauges that informed me about oil and gas levels, I never had any of the equipment that Yates considers basic. And except for my compass, which I have kept on just about every boat, the other instruments were available on just a few of the larger powerboats I operated. A compass is all I have on my current boat; that and a chart and some understanding of the local winds and tides allow me to navigate well enough to get us— the boat and I—where we want to go.

Which is not where Brock Yates and most of the readers of *Boating* want to be. And that's the point. As I said at the start, this book is about a life (mine) with small boats. Each was a boat I loved at the time, each carried me to different, memorable adventures and unforgettable moments.

Each, if you will, was the boat that was there when I needed her. You can't ask for much more than that. It's the boat you need, not always the boat you want, that will prove most fulfilling, most satisfactory. The boats that fulfilled and satisfied me are each in this book. I hope meeting them helps you decide which boat, of all the boats that are out there these days, will be right for you.

Emma

Although there had been many times when my graduation from college seemed a most doubtful eventuality, the miracle of commencement was scarcely on my mind during the weeks that preceded it. All my waking thoughts had to do with boats, and nothing to do with the costs of renting a cap and gown. Even after seven years—three of them spent dealing with World War II from a Flying Fortress in Europe—my roller-coaster campus career in New Haven dissolved to an insignificant mélange of third-rate memories the moment I was offered my first job as a graduate.

It wasn't the sort of job a fellow might have discovered at the Career Counseling Office; nor was it one of those "business" opportunities that so many of my button-down, Harris-tweed classmates had been offered by the horde of Wall Street emissaries who conducted endless on-campus interviews with the best and brightest throughout our last term.

I had suffered no such indignities as an interview. My first job came to me through more accepted channels: from the father of a friend and fellow student. Erhard Matthiessen, the man who made the offer, was one of the few fathers I knew whom I could also claim as friend. For starting with my own male parent, and moving on through the list of nearly every other paternal figure I had contacted during my socially active youth, friendship had seldom been part of our relationships.

Fathers of daughters were particularly belligerent. To a man they made it clear they could see no shred of benefit of any sort accruing from my continued presence on their property or at their daughter's side. When we—the girl of my moment and I—were under the paternal roof, the paternal irritation was palpable. But when I escorted a daughter, any daughter, out from under the roof, that irritation quickly converted to open hostility, fueled by anxieties that would have been flattering had they any basis in fact.

My male friends' fathers were seldom so openly alarmed at my appearance on their doorsteps. They were, with one or two exceptions, cool and often made a point of asking what I had planned for the day, or the afternoon or evening—however long their favorite son might be in range of my hazardous acquaintance. None of my suggestions was received with enthusiasm; some were prohibited on the spot.

By my twenty-fifth year—which was where I was, what with the war and all—when my name so fortunately and inexplicably turned up on Yale's 1948 commencement roster, I had become downright discouraged with fathers. Little good, I had learned from a series of turbulent and harsh encounters, would evolve from any exchange with a male parent, no matter how diligently I remembered my manners.

Except for "Matty" Matthiessen. He was the glorious and happy exception to every paternal pattern of my life. Each time I visited the

Matthiessen home in Stamford, Connecticut, at the invitation of their son and my friend, Peter, Matty's welcome rang true. His tall presence radiated good humor, a zest for life, not authority. His blue eyes danced and his smile banished all troubles. Unlike those grim paternal parents who cast their palls across my adolescence and young manhood, Matty had long since discovered some secret of fulfillment; he was, I knew, a supremely happy man, and the days and nights I shared under his roof were a tonic for my spirits, an affirmation of life that never failed to invigorate my own.

Matty could have asked me to become an account executive with Chase Manhattan, and I would have tried. I would have done anything he asked because he was, and had always been, one of the few among my older generation who gave me such good reasons to believe there could be life after youth.

I would, as I've said, have done anything he asked. But no one, certainly not myself, could ever have imagined that he would invite me to spend my first summer after graduation as captain of the Fishers Island Country Club launch. And, wonder of wonders, I would be paid for the privilege.

There is, and always has been, a great deal of loose talk and overinflated claims about how this or that experience, this individual, or that book, or those recipes can "change your life." Most of those claims are weak. Lives are seldom changed so much by a single event or insight that the change can be called significant. But Matty's offer—which I accepted on the spot—did indeed change my life, set my compass, chart my course, and move me toward a series of discoveries that continue still. For, among other things (and there were many), it marked the start of a forty-five-year intimate relationship with boats, a lifelong affair (notice I deliberately do not say love affair) that has shaped my values, and has introduced me to exhilaration, awe, terror, indignation, ecstasy, and debt, to name but a few.

As has so often been my experience, I realized shortly after my effusive acceptance that there were several intimidating problems I would have to resolve—and quickly, too—before my new job could become a reality.

My history as a small-boat skipper was vapid, to say the least. And yet, as I discovered a day or so after accepting Matty's invitation, without proper credentials my chances of getting past the U.S. Coast Guard's minimum requirements appeared all but hopeless. Because I would be paid for my time at the helm, and because the Fishers Island Country Club wanted all the insurance it could get, their newest marine acquisition would have to be operated by a certified captain, licensed, in Coast Guard language, "to carry passengers for hire."

Which meant that in less than a month I would have to clear every bureaucratic hurdle between my status as a student prince and my wished-for career as Humphrey Bogart in *To Have and Have Not*. Of those hurdles, none was as intimidating as: (1) the Coast Guard requirement that I prove I had considerable experience as a small-boat skipper; and (2) that I take and pass a lengthy written examination (plus a one-on-one interview) at the Coast Guard's Manhattan headquarters on Cedar Street, one of those brief byways in the city's canyoned financial district—the very same place so many of my classmates hoped to be, but for quite different reasons.

If I had learned nothing else at Yale, and I surely had, I had solved a student's most critical problem: how to absorb enough information from the printed page to maintain the illusion of knowledge required by written examinations. Because so much of my stay in New Haven was spent in Manhattan and in making the journey to and fro, my actual on-campus hours had to be scholastically productive enough to avoid my expulsion—an eventuality I devoutly wished to avoid. For given my social appetites, there was no better status than student when it came to having the essential latitude my preferred behavior required. As a senior on the Dean's List, I was allowed unlimited cuts. This privilege, combined with my astute course scheduling, required my on-campus presence primarily on Tuesday, Wednesday, and Thursday.

I had learned the importance of what to read, which accounted for my selection of *Piloting, Seamanship, and Small Boat Handling* by Charles F. Chapman as the text that would allow my transformation from campus cavalier to certified captain. To my credit, I made a superb, indeed the only, choice. Today, the book is in its sixtieth edition and is as close to becoming a bible as the Good Book itself. When I plucked the volume from the jumbled shelves of the Yale Co-op (where I still had credit), the book had half the bulk it has since acquired. But it was then, as it is now, perfectly designed to take a neophyte boatman from ignorance to understanding in a relatively few crisply written and functionally illustrated pages.

With my Chapman at my side, as opposed to Theodore Green's *Philosophy of Art*—the book I was supposed to be reading in preparation for my final exams—I learned the first of what I still know and understand about the rules of the road (at sea), the language of buoys, the points of the compass, fundamental navigation (with compass, chart, timepiece, and common sense), useful sailor's knots, and the language of lights—red, green, and white. "White over white, fishing tonight" is as ingrained in my consciousness today as it was forty-five years ago. And I never hesitate to explain to anyone who will listen what those two white lights on a mast are saying when I can spot them on the horizon.

Charles Frederic Chapman surely never knew it, but his text got me prepared for the most important examination of my life.

But no book could meet the challenge posed by the Coast Guard's requirements for experience. Just to qualify to take the written test, I had to document a minimal amount of time as a small-boat skipper in northeastern coastal waters.

Those waters that I had sailed, rowed, or motored in the entire quarter-century of my existence were limited to Three Mile Harbor, Gardiners Bay, the fringes of the Atlantic off Montauk Point and East Hampton, and Georgica Pond, with my time on Georgica representing more than 90 percent of those hours. I was certain then, as I am now, that Georgica Pond was not included in the Coast

Guard's lexicon of coastal waters. But it, and the *Emma*, were all
I had.

These days, it would be difficult for anyone to visualize the
Emma. They simply do not build boats like her anymore. I am
reasonably certain they did not build many boats like her during the
1930s, when she was first launched.

How many boats that served as well as the *Emma* were discovered at Macy's? But that is where my step-grandfather, Rodney
Burnett, first saw her and bought her as a suprise gift for my
grandmother, Emma Darrow Dodd Burnett. Those grandparents
lived in the last, outermost house on the Georgica side of Apaquogue Road in East Hampton, then a far different place than it has
become. Where media luminaries now abound, families spent their
summers—families of upper-middle-class gentry, but families nevertheless, with traditional opinions of how a summer should be
spent. Fathers (and grandfathers) worked "in town" from Monday
through Friday, and either "drove down the island" on Friday evening or took the Long Island Railroad's notorious Cannonball and
were met at the small white station, with its red rambler roses in
bloom, by mothers, grandmothers, and children in wooden station
wagons, one or two of them with a name like "Dunedin" hand-
lettered in black paint over the varnished panel of the driver's-side
door.

For those children—like my sister and my two brothers and
me—fortunate enough to live on that blessed strip of sandy land,
there was adventure enough at our doorstep. With our neighbors
and friends, the Helmuth, Scott, Keck, James, and Wainwright sons
and daughters, we seldom left our home grounds. Why should we?
On one side we had the open Atlantic, its heaving vastness stretching from the broad, white, warm sands of Georgica Beach across
and across and across until at last . . . Dakar. On the other, we had
the infinitely more benign but no less awesome and mysterious
presence of Georgica, with the main body of its waters spanning a
reach that began just across a slim strand of beach at the Atlantic

and probed perhaps three miles inland, where the tips of the pond's thin, final fingers wriggled through cattails, scrub oak, and pitch pine until they brushed the two-lane, concrete ribbon that was then, and still is, the Montauk Highway.

Often in the late fall and winter, when the Atlantic raged under the brutal hand of a southeast gale, the barrier beach at Georgica's seaward arm would be breached by heedless, surging swells. Pond waters, grown stale under a summer sun, would flush their own instant escape to the sea while that same sea left something of itself within the pond's muddy womb. From those seeds would spring lives not often seen in waters catalogued as fresh by most observers. Impregnated by the fertile ocean, Georgica gave birth to marvelous broods of blue crabs, spearing, alewives, giant silver eels, and sometimes flounder, all the while finding space for its natural children: painted turtles, mummychogs, sticklebacks, and some of the largest, meanest snapping turtles known to man.

Over the years, the *Emma* discovered most of Georgica's secrets. When she first arrived, brought to that outermost house in one of the Home Sweet Home moving trucks, I was too young to skipper the *Emma* on my own. She arrived early in the 1930s, about the time my father grappled manfully with the Wall Street disaster called "The Crash." A stockbroker of verve and optimism, he was slapped hard by the realities of called margins and closed banks. The family quit our duplex at 139 East 79th Street and moved to a large but definitely shopworn place in Glen Cove, Long Island.

For reasons that I have never discovered, my brother Chick and myself were enrolled as boarding students at Friends Academy in Locust Valley, a coed school that took only a few boarders. My brother and I were the youngest—he was nine and I was ten—and although Friends was a gentle and seriously Quaker school, we were quite miserable there.

I'm sure Roddy B (my step-grandfather's family name) and my grandmother sensed our loneliness, for as soon as they opened the Georgica house—often as early as March—they would make a

point of stopping by Friends on their way down the island on Friday
afternoon to pick up one or both of us boys. Those moments when a
teacher came looking for us to tell us our grandparents were waiting
at the school's front entrance were among the happiest of my boyhood. In those days, evidently a survivor of the financial quake,
Roddy B drove a handsome Packard, large, black, gleaming, its
spoked wheels as regal as the wheels on an emperor's chariot. With
Roddy B in the driver's seat and my grandmother at his side, Chick
and I would ride in back, choosing more often than not to sit in the
two plush "jump seats" that folded down and faced backward.
Cocooned in the Packard's humming and secure interior, we
watched each familiar landmark glide by, knowing that as soon as
the "Big Duck" showed up alongside the road outside Flanders, my
grandmother would turn and say, "We're almost there boys." That
Big Duck, I understand, is still there. Whether Long Island ducks—
properly plucked and packaged—are still sold from within its ample frame, I do not know.

I do know that being told we were almost home made the rest of
the trip seem even longer. But when the Packard swung right off the
Montauk Highway just beyond Georgica's westernmost creeks, and
we followed country lanes headed south to Apaquogue Road, when
I could smell the soft salt of the rolling Atlantic, then my heart
would pound and pump joy through every vessel. And when the
Packard slowed for the open, white gate that separated our long,
low, shingled house and its long, narrow lawns from the Campbells'
house, then I loved that house, that ocean, that beach, that Georgica
more than I have loved it any time since. And it is a place, my home
landscape, that I have always loved.

Much of that love was fired by the intensity of the relief I knew
because I had been granted a pardon from those empty Friends
Academy corridors and classrooms that echoed their desolate weekend whispers. And more love flowed from both Roddy B and my
grandmother; both enjoyed their role as surrogate parents and took
from only the best parts. Discipline was all but nonexistent, school

was never mentioned, and some of the most wonderful food any boys have ever tasted came from Roddy B's kitchen where he was the chef, keeper of the ponderous and mysterious coal stove, market shopper, dishwasher, and beverage master—all duties he executed with a delightfully busy, bustling good humor, and with fragments of old songs, whistled arias, and long shaggy-dog stories told over elaborate desserts that made each of his meals an occasion for joy.

He tended the fires, some wood, some flickering at the base of the portable kerosene heaters, that kept the March chill at bay and made that summer place as snug as any north woods cabin. He drove me on his shopping trips to stores that had not yet become supermarkets, stores where he knew each clerk and the proprietor's family, stores where the men and women seemed as happy to see Rodney Burnett return to East Hampton as I was to be with him to watch their welcome.

Every moment of those weekend boons was wondrous. Newly arrived red-winged blackbirds screeched from wavering cattail tops as the males claimed their breeding territories. And on March 23, every spring, the first ospreys would return, soaring in high circles above the Georgica Cove that fronted that house. I would lie on my back on the lawn watching those great fish hawks until one folded its wings and dived, a projectile shot from the heavens into Georgica's waters gleaming under a blinding spring sun. When the bird all but vanished in the white water of its splash, there would be a moment when motion ceased. Then, with labored, slow strokes of its broad wings, the osprey rose from the water, sometimes with empty talons hanging, but most often grasping a silver alewife, the sun flashing on its wet scales. The rising osprey worked hard to gain altitude and bank toward its nesting grounds high in a tree in the woods off to the northwest, on the far side of the Talmadge farm that filled the fields across Georgica from our house with Jersey cows, one fierce bull, and several huge workhorses whose hoofs sometimes thundered behind the fences as the horses themselves surged with spring's adrenaline.

I still dream of that far Talmadge shore and the tremors of excitement that rippled as I approached it, rowing, alone aboard the *Emma*. For it was that boat that allowed me the most joyous of all the joyful adventures of those long-ago weekends in a boy's paradise. Before the Packard was ever driven east along the island for its first trip of the new season, Roddy B had called to have the house opened, the first fires built and lit, and the *Emma* taken from her winter home in the empty garage and gently slid over the wooden bulkhead into the shallow waters of Georgica alongside our short, narrow dock—just two planks wide and about ten feet long. A slim, fourteen-foot wooden rowboat, a "sharpie" as the region's baymen called her, the *Emma* had little or no sheer, she was definitely not high sided, and both her bow and stern were designed strictly for utility, quite without art or grace. But she was a wooden boat, her planking butted at the joints. She needed scraping and painting each new spring, and she needed time sunk there near that small dock so her winter-dried and shrunken seams could swell with moisture and become tight yet another time.

That is where I would find her when I ran to the dock after the Packard braked to a dignified stop at the end of our front walk and I scrambled out, wanting to verify the *Emma* before dark, wanting to make certain she would be there the next morning. And on those blustery March mornings, after a breakfast in Roddy B's kitchen by the coal stove, I would bail out the *Emma* with a bucket, sponge her dry, carry the heavy, ash oars from the garage corner, slip in the galvanized oarlocks, and make ready for my first row across the cove.

It was a voyage of less than three-quarters of a mile, but for a ten-year-old city-bred boy, it was a journey to another world. If the wind blew, I needed to take short, choppy strokes with those cumbersome oars. Or if it was one of those rare moments between weather fronts when the breeze scarcely wrinkled Georgica's silver surface, I would try the long, easy strokes Roddy B had taught me, trying to learn to feather my oars on the recovery. I taught myself to backwater, to spin in a tight circle, backwatering on one oar, pulling on another. And no matter how fresh the wind, in that small cove there was always a lee shore where I could rest on my oars, listen to Talmadge's bull roaring in his pen, or watch for the small, jet-black and vivid yellow heads of the painted turtles, appearing and then disappearing beneath Georgica's gentle surface.

It was on one of those March mornings when the wind blew hard from the northwest and whitecaps salted a slate-gray Georgica that I discovered the ecstasies of sailing. I had to have been no more than twelve at the time; both Chick and I were transferred from Friends after three years there. We were sent to a boarding school in Virginia, many miles from any navigable waters and much too far from Georgica for spring weekends with our grandparents.

But I had my memories to sustain me. More than half a century later, they still do. I built what amounted to a square-rig sail in the garage from a burlap bag separated at its stitches and then tacked to a crude, rectangular wood frame. That assembly was, in turn, fastened to one end of a "mast" that had been inside a rolled carpet delivered by the dry cleaners. It must have been about eight feet long.

When I rowed against the wind, pulling hard with short, choppy strokes, my "sail" lay flat across the *Emma's* seats, below her gunwales where it could not catch the wind. After I reached the lee of the far shore and turned the sharpie around, I lifted the mast into place at the bow and wedged it there with a rock.

Pushing off, I climbed over the *Emma's* transom and sat in the stern with one of those long oars trailing behind as a rudder. As we moved offshore—the new *Emma* and I—the wind buffeted the burlap, but the crude construction held. Gripped there by a fifteen- or twenty-knot northwest breeze, the *Emma* moved faster than I, and probably her designers, had ever imagined she could. Hunched in the stern so I could hold the oar with both hands, it was all I could do to keep the boat from broaching. My "rudder" felt alive in my arms, pushed this way, then that, by the pressures of our swift, hissing progress.

That wind, as are all winds from the north in those latitudes at that time of the year, was cold. And cold winds are heavier, have more force. Georgica itself had just shed its winter ice a few weeks before, and the whitecapped chop that threatened to spill over the transom was heavy too, still thick with lingering winter. Those following seas and the insistent wind, galloping with longer and longer strides as we hissed into open water, pushed at the *Emma* as if she were a leaf in a storm.

My first time, and how memorable. Never before had I grasped the reality of a natural force. Never before had I felt the wind embrace me, pummel me, face me with the comprehension of its dangers, its exhilarating risks and its capacity for generating joy. Awe, fear, even terror were to come later in my life on the water. On that March day I discovered only the excitement of meeting and recognizing a great force that had always been there, but had never

before touched my wind-burned cheeks as it caught the *Emma* and me in its tumultuous embrace.

When the sail ended on our home shore and the *Emma* was shoved by the wind and waves into the fringe of cattails, I clambered forward to move the rock and take down the rattling sail before it tore loose. Then I stepped overboard into muck, labored to slide the boat stern-first into the whitecaps, and waded alongside her until we were far enough offshore for me to climb over the rail, grab the oars, and pull once again for that blessed lee shore across Georgica.

Again and again I made the voyage until my hands blistered, my wet feet chilled, and my stomach muscles ached from the rowing. Throughout, the wind stayed a loyal confederate, never slacking and, every now and then, startling me with a muscular gust, a slap that I feared would surely fracture my ungainly sail. But both of us, the *Emma* and I, held together until I was too exhausted to row one more stroke.

I lugged the mast and sail ashore, hoping that there would be time the next morning—a Sunday that would be the last day of my stay—to ride the wind again. When I came into the kitchen where Roddy B tinkered with his massive stove, and after I sat down before it, feeling the warmth slide into me, he said, "I was watching you out there. You were sailing. Sailing as fast as the wind."

And years later, as my grandmother lay ill in her room with the windows that looked west to the sunsets across Georgica, she would look out over the water, take my hand in her trembling fingers, and say, "It's so lovely. The most beautiful place in the world. I can still see you the day you took the boat out in all that wind. Such a little boy. But you were flying, flying. Do you remember that day?"

And I would say yes, because I had not forgotten it then, nor have I yet.

At the end of my first year at that boarding school in Virginia, just after I had turned fourteen, an upset stomach and a pain in my lower abdomen was diagnosed as appendicitis. I was taken to Richmond and operated on in a hospital there. My Uncle Finley lived in

Richmond and practiced medicine there. He was not a surgeon, but one of his friends who was removed the offending organ. In recognition of my trauma, and I suppose a bit of guilt (they had not been on the scene much of the time), my parents had a small sailboat waiting for me when I returned to that house by the pond in July.

She was a Snipe, a sixteen-foot centerboard sloop my father bought from Ike Halsey, whose garage on Newtown Lane was the largest in town. It housed many station wagons for the winter, supplied them with gas in summer, and, most important, was the only place in East Hampton where Roddy B knew his Packard would get proper care. I never learned the details of how Mr. Halsey and my father came to an agreement on the sale, nor did I fully understand why my parents had decided that a sailboat would be a fitting gift for a convalescent teenager. They had never owned any sort of boat before, nor had they ever seen me sail. Perhaps my grandparents had told their daughter and son-in-law about the day I spent with the *Emma* and that nor'wester.

For someone who knew next to nothing about sailing a proper sloop with jib and mainsail, the Snipe was an almost perfect introduction, and Georgica Pond was the perfect body of water. The main part of Georgica, the water that reached from the ocean to the Montauk Highway, was long enough and open enough to allow for long reaches, especially when the prevailing afternoon breezes from the southwest picked up some speed. And the small channel that connected the main pond to our cove imposed enough navigational and tacking skills to be a fine teacher for an on-the-water trainee.

It was a good while before I developed those skills. For the first two weeks or so, the Snipe and I stayed in the cove while I learned— often the hard way—the difference between coming about and jibing. Once I could navigate west through the channel, I could dock at the Helmuth-Scott boathouse where there were several young men and young women who knew how to sail. They had been sailing for years in the lovely, small catboats they seemed to favor.

And they were generous with their advice and instruction. One or two of the young women even agreed to sail with me on a few of those breezy, smoky sou'wester afternoons. Clipping along with the sails close-hauled and the Snipe heeling sharply as warm, brackish spray flipped into our faces, I began to feel something of a captain's self-satisfaction, especially when my passenger turned her smile toward me.

The Snipe (which was never properly named and thus was called the *Nameless* whenever I had to identify her) stayed around for two more summers, but I never sailed her as much as I did that first one. In one sense, I jilted her for my first boat, the *Emma*.

It was the *Emma*'s utility, her loyalty, her versatility, and her ability to withstand harsh treatment and abuse that brought me back to her embrace. Once aboard the Snipe, I had no options: I could sail or sit there. The old sharpie, however, would adapt to each of my interests, my searches, even my efforts to harvest some of Georgica's natural treasures and sell them off for money.

With wire mesh acquired from East End Hardware (and charged to Roddy B's account), I fashioned eel pots, copied from one I had pulled from the pond. That discovery was an accident. The pot—really a baited trap for snaring eels—had no buoy on the surface to mark it. As I learned later, Everett Rattray, a teenager like myself, but infinitely more skilled at eeling, had a string of eel pots in Georgica. But wary of competition and any possibility of tampering with his livelihood, he allowed only one buoy to mark the entire string of fifteen or twenty pots, and that buoy was on such a short tether that it floated a foot or so under the surface. Everett could find it because he had taken shore ranges when he dropped it. Just after dawn when he tended his pots—so he could be on his way home before any of us "summer kids" finished breakfast—he would row his sharpie to the general location of that hidden mark. Then he looked to the land, lining up the Helmuth-Scott dock with a big scrub pine at the corner of the Talmadge pasture. Once on that line, he'd row carefully along it until he

could just see the chimmney of the Bromley house on the Wainscott dunes. If no one—like me—had tampered with his marker,
he could stand up in his boat and see it there, just where he'd left it
safely hidden from the world by a few inches of water.

I found Ev's marker by accident one afternoon. Drifting downwind in the *Emma*, I stood near her bow, on the lookout for a huge
snapping turtle. I had seen its head, as large as the end of a baseball
bat, on the surface as I rowed. When that head disappeared, I knew
the big turtle would be swimming. They were awesome, those
mighty reptiles, full of menace and mystery, the villains of a dozen
local folk tales about missing fingers, toes, and worse. They had, it
was said, bitten oars off just above the blade; they did, in fact, drag
young swans to their doom. I thought if I could spot this snapper
swimming I might be able to hit it with one of the *Emma*'s heavy
oars. Not that I had thought much of the consequences; one doesn't
at fifteen.

But instead of the turtle, I saw Everett's marker. Curious, I tugged
at it and found that the line from the submerged float was, in turn,
tied to a stouter length of hard-laid manila rope. And that rope, I
discovered, as I tugged it hand-over-hand aboard the *Emma*, was
fast to the first eel pot I had ever seen.

The galvanized mesh of its long, rectangular wire frame gleamed
in the afternoon sun, while within that boxy cage writhed six or
eight good-size eels. They startled me with the violence of their
energies, banging this way and that against the sides of their trap,
sliding as easily as water from one end to the other, making the trap
tremble and shake in my hands. I was panicked at the thought that
those dark brown and silver creatures that reminded me so of snakes
might escape and slither over the *Emma*'s deck, across my feet.

But I was curious, too, as to how they had got where I found
them, and why they stayed. I saw a couple of grisly, water-bleached
chicken heads in the trap, and realized they must be the reason the
eels had entered the box. And then I understood that they had
swum in through the long funnel that was the mouth of the trap. But

even to this day I still can't fully understand why they could not find their way out by swimming back through that funnel, this time starting at the small end. It's a personality flaw of eels—and other fish, too—this inability to exit just as they entered. It's a shortcoming that has cost untold millions of them their lives ever since funneled fish traps were invented thousands of years ago.

Not one word about eels or eel pots had been mentioned in my classroom during ten years of schooling. I was quite unprepared for what I'd hauled from Georgica's bottom on that sunny summer afternoon—unprepared, but totally fascinated.

I eventually put the trap and the string's marker buoy back in the water. But not, as I learned years later from Everett (who had become a good friend) quite where they should have gone. He'd had to use his grappling hook to locate his traps the next morning.

By then I had already begun to pester Roddy B with questions about eels. He knew they tasted good when fried, and he knew that Manhattan fish markets did a big business in pickled eels, but he also knew that neither my grandmother nor anyone else in the family had ever expressed anything but horror at the notion that Roddy B might be planning to serve a bit of broiled eel as the fish dish. "But," he went on, encouraging me as he always tried to do, "I'm sure there is a market for eels somewhere in the town. I'll ask around."

Before he had found that market, I had begun making my first eel traps. I was putting the *Emma* to work for the first time in what had been her rather dignified career. If she had had a voice, she surely would have used it to criticize me for the way I treated her the first morning I lifted my five new eel pots. I had, full of certain hope, brought along a bucket for my catch. And that catch was there, in squirming profusion. What a fertile growing ground was Georgica.

Eels were everywhere, except in the bucket where I had first tried to dump them. That bucket was a minor barrier to their efforts to escape. Within moments the *Emma's* decks were drenched in slime, awash in writhing eels and quite out of my control.

Ashore at last, I found a corrugated cardboard box with a lid and spent the next half-hour or more transferring my morning's harvest from under the *Emma*'s stern seat to a more suitable spot for transport. I found the only way I could get a grip on any eel was to put my slimy hand in a bucket of beach sand before I attempted a pickup. As a result, I ended up with a carton crawling with sand-covered eels that rustled and scraped like dry leaves as they continued their efforts to escape, even though now they had been out of the water for at least an hour.

Roddy B had learned that Ted Lester (of whom, more later) ran a small fish market in Amagansett. He sold retail and wholesale as well, shipping large catches to the Fulton Market in the city. When, on that first morning in my eeling career, I asked Roddy B if he would transport my catch to market in his Packard, he said he would. "But," he said, "Ted tells me they have to be skinned."

"*Skinned*?" Now there was a concept that had never taken any form whatsoever in my commercial plans. Skinned? Skinning an eel, based on what I had seen and felt of the creatures, was surely a contradiction in terms. No one could hold an eel, much less skin it. I was dumbfounded, paralyzed, and thought for a moment of releasing my entire haul and pretending the morning had never happened.

"I'll call Rudy at Dreesen's," Roddy B said. "I'm sure he knows." Dreesen's was the Newtown Lane version of Schaefer's famous market on Madison Avenue where only the finest meats, wild game, and fresh fish were sold. And Roddy B was one of the men Dreesen's welcomed most warmly. "If I had twenty customers like Mr. Burnett," Rudy told me years later, "I could retire in just a few years."

Rudy turned Roddy B's call over to Dave, the Dreesen's fresh fish specialist; then Roddy B handed the phone to me.

"John," Dave said, his voice cheerful but also a bit preoccupied with waiting customers, "take the eel's head in your left hand . . . that's after you cut through its skin all the way around, just behind his head . . . and hold fast. Some folks put a nail through a board and jam that through the head. Then take a pair of pliers in your right hand and loosen a flap of skin where you made the cut. Once you get enough so you can get a good grip with the pliers, give it a good yank, pull away with your left hand, and the skin will come right off, like a glove turning inside out. Got that?"

"Yes," I said, not wanting to hear more details. "Thanks a lot, Dave."

"Anytime," he said, and hung up.

I found a pair of pliers and went back to my box of eels, who were still animated enough to wriggle a bit when they felt my hand groping for a grip. My efforts with knife and pliers were shameful, humiliating, and served only to suffuse me with guilt; how could I have initiated such a brutal process? I persisted just long enough to skin one eel. The rest I carried back to Georgica and released. They had definitely lost their pep, but not their apparent immortality. After fifteen minutes or so, the entire haul had vanished into the cove's muddy depths.

I carried the headless, now pale blue eel carcass to the kitchen and asked Roddy B if he would cook it for my dinner. He obliged, cut the eel into two-inch sections, sautéed them in lemon butter, and there they were, a kind of atonement, on my dinner plate.

I would have eaten them no matter how they tasted, but they were sweet and delicious. The dinner, however, was not incentive enough for me to take the *Emma* eeling ever again. She had done her part, and would again. I knew that. But I could not bring myself to contemplate another skinning session, no matter what the Fulton Fish Market was paying for eels.

Much later in my life, eels returned to our family, but that's another story and involves another boat.

Blue crabs—we called them blueclaws—were right up there with eels as a Georgica resource. That same summer of eels was also a banner year for crabs. Some unseen and unfathomable act of nature had combined oceanic and Georgica forces to produce a bumper crop of some of the largest blue crabs ever seen on eastern Long Island. Many of them were more than a foot from shell tip to shell tip; and when those monsters extended their claws, they

protected a span of almost two feet. Both Chick and I understood
the value of size when it came to blue crabs: more crabmeat per
crab, less picking to get it.

Sensing there was money to be made selling fresh-picked crab-
meat, we organized and began operating a crab harvest venture,
with the *Emma* serving once again as the fulcrum of our entire
effort.

Loading her with crab traps, lines, two crab nets, and several
gunnysacks to hold our catch, we rowed the *Emma* west out of the
cove toward the Georgica Gut, the place where the pond and the
ocean came closest, the place where only that narrow strip of sand
separated the two. Also part of our cargo was a bushel basket filled
with fish heads, chicken heads, and other assorted offal donated
from behind the counters at Dreesen's.

We set out baited traps and baited lines, enough so we could

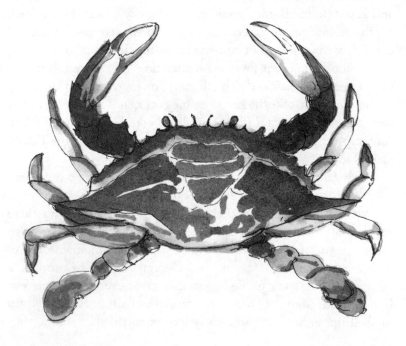

simply move from one to the other throughout the morning and early afternoon. By the time we got back to our starting place, there would be a crab or two munching on the bait, ready for netting.

By two o'clock when we rowed the *Emma* home, we had stuffed three of our gunnysacks full of crabs. We filled a galvanized garbage can half full of water, built a fire beneath it, and when the water got boiling hard, we dropped in the crabs and left them there until they turned red.

Then came the picking, the work part. But because the crabs were so large, even that was less arduous than usual. Soon we had a couple of big crockery bowls mounded with white, delicious crab-meat. Once again, the Packard was our delivery wagon. Roddy B drove us and our product to a restaurant we'd called, a place on the Montauk Highway just over the Wainscott line. The chef there, a woman, was delighted with what she saw when we put those bowls on her kitchen counter. When we left, we were counting our money.

The mere act of holding folding money in my hands sent my mind into orbit. By the time Chick and I finished supper, I had a master plan that would make us blueclaw kings. We were primarily catchers, not cookers and pickers. After all, we had the *Emma*; she was our key. If we could, I said to Chick, build a kind of crab corral, a place where we could pasture our catch the way the horses and cows were pastured at the Talmadge farm, then we could concentrate our energies and equipment on the crab harvest while the harvesting was good. When bad weather arrived, then we could round up our captive crabs, cook them, and, perhaps even with some hired help—possibly our sister Jane—do the crab picking all at once.

I wish, now that I look back on my boating life, that more people had argued with me more often. My reasoning was so often so full of holes that it's difficult now to comprehend why anyone, even my lovable brother Chick, failed to object to my ramshackle schemes.

But objections were never to be. The next day, with a roll of chicken wire and a bundle of oak stakes (purchased from our friends at East End Hardware), we built a large crab corral on a shallow, sandy point just to the west of our dock. The point was then under about six inches of water, which seemed about right for crab grazing and shallow enough to be properly fenced with our chicken wire.

The next day, we dumped four or five gunnysacks full of crabs into our new corral, and the following morning we made plans to row back to the Georgica Gut and come home with even more.

One of the late summer's first nor'easters changed those plans, and then some. It blew, wet and raw, for two days. We spent our time indoors, building shelters in our big room above the kitchen, reading Street & Smith's *Wild West Weekly*, acting out Sonny Tabor's gunfight or one of Kid Wolf's encounters with the bad guys. We played hearts and, when we had exhausted every diversion, we tussled with each other until we exhausted ourselves.

When the sun returned on a southwest breeze two days later, we made plans for more crabbing. First, though, we took a look at our corral. It had become a crab catastrophe.

No one could have persuaded me that captive crabs would fight with each other, with even more grim purpose than two brothers trapped indoors by a summer storm. But those blue crabs had done their level best to do each other in. The corral was littered with carcasses, severed claws, and wounded crabs. And either the nor'easter or one or more of the largest crabs had breached our chicken-wire barrier. What few crabs had survived the battle had departed the battleground.

We spent the morning putting the point back the way we had found it: without stakes, without fences, and without a single captive crab or crab carcass. We cleaned up the *Emma*, stowed our crab nets in the garage, and, by silent but mutual consent, declared ourselves out of the crabbing business.

That was not, however, as some might surmise, the last of our wretched adventures with that loyal and long-suffering boat.

Toward the end of the summer of '41, our last summer before we both became college freshmen and then went to war before we could finish our first year on campus, Chick and I still spent much of our time at Georgica. Not as much as we had when we were younger; now we could drive our own car (we shared a Model A bought for $50), we played tennis, we went to the club beach where we were properly awkward in the presence of young ladies, and we even spent time sailing in races at the Devon Yacht Club. But our hearts belonged to our home landscape, the place that had held our growing in the cupped hands of its impressive natural presences, the place that still promised adventure, the place where we were always at ease with ourselves.

We still rowed the *Emma*, often with a young lady or two sharing the stern thwart, out of the cove and west to the Georgica Gut, where we would picnic, swim, toss a football, or simply lie on the warm sand pondering our pleasant past and present and worrying a bit about our uncertain future. It was on one of those days that I spotted a shark finning just beyond the surf. There was no question about the creature's identity. Not only were the top of its tail fin and the tip of its dorsal classic shark fins, but a true shark shape—dark, shadowy, and about six to eight feet long—was clearly visible in the blue-green ocean shoals no more than ten feet deep.

A couple of our friends, probably Walter and Sonny, were with us and all of us were excited by the presence of such an awesome visitor in waters where we had been swimming most of the day.

We chattered, watched, joked about swimming out through the surf to grapple with the shark, and, as the creature seemed reluctant to leave, finally worked ourselves up to the notion of harpooning the shark from the *Emma*, just as we knew swordfish were harpooned every summer in the waters off Montauk and Block Island. While the *Emma* waited, faithful as always, on the Georgica side of the beach, I ran back to the Helmuth boathouse where I knew I could find an eel spear—a long pole with a forked, barbed, three-tined fish spear on its business end.

When I got back, the shark was still finning, cruising the Gut's shoals as casually as a Sunday stroller in the park. With the help of a couple of driftwood logs we used for rollers, we hauled the *Emma* across the beach and made ready to launch her through the Atlantic surf, which, fortunately for us and our boat, was exceptionally well behaved on that windless afternoon. It was, however, very definitely the first time the *Emma* had seen ocean duty, and each of us was quite aware of the risks we imposed on what was, by then, an aging sharpie.

With me at the bow and Chick amidships, we slid the *Emma* seaward and held her there in the surging ocean wash. Beyond us, perhaps thirty feet or so, the shark fins continued their heedless meander. When the waves lapped at our chests, we both clambered into the boat and Chick went right to work at his oars, taking long, deep strokes, pulling hard to make sure we cleared the surf line quickly. Even a small breaking sea, caught just wrong, could swamp us.

Chick, who a few years later would pull an oar on the Princeton one-hundred-fifty-pound crew, got us offshore in good shape. Before either of us was quite certain what we should do about it, we were just a few feet from the shark. Swimming effortlessly alongside us, it looked a great deal larger and meaner than it had from the beach. I was sure its eye, which looked as large as a black tennis ball, was fixed on me. It was an implacable eye, and I all but gave up the quest then and there. But we were young, very young, men. Our peers watched from the beach. Once committed to the notion of harpooning our awesome visitor—a suggestion I guess I was the first to propose—I could not simply withdraw.

"Swing the bow around," I yelled, and Chick followed instructions. That maneuver dropped us back, a bit behind the shark.

"Now pull ahead slowly." Chick did.

I raised the eel spear, remembering the illustrations of Captain Ahab in *Moby Dick*.

The *Emma*'s bow eased up and then passed the shark's tail, slow, undulating, and impressively unafraid. In a moment I stared down at the shark's broad back and the tall, stiff dorsal trailing its delicate wake.

A length of rope, the *Emma*'s painter, was fast to the top of the eel spear handle; its other end was looped around my wrist. I knew that as soon as I stuck the shark, it and I would be linked by a strong, six-thread manila line. I wasn't sure that was what I wanted to happen.

But, with the same sort of reckless bravado that was to get me in trouble so many times, I brought the spear down in one convulsive thrust aimed square at the middle of that broad back.

I've never been certain of what happened next. I wasn't then and I'm not now. A completely unexpected explosion of violence paralyzed my senses and reactions.

Pricked by the eel spear's barbs, the shark ended its contented afternoon with a convulsive roll, so strong and so quick that before I could react in any way, the eel spear handle was slammed against the *Emma*'s gunwale, slammed so hard that it broke in two with a loud crack.

I was left holding the broken top half with its line still looped to my wrist. The shark's sudden maneuver had also pulled the barbed tip of the spear from the creature's back. The splintered top of that half, held upright by the weight of the spear, bobbed like a disembodied flag pole on the surface.

The shark was nowhere in sight. We had the broken eel spear and a prominent gouge in the *Emma*'s rail to tell us we had met it and lost.

"Boy," Chick said, "that happened fast." He went back to his rowing, headed us toward the beach, then paused. "I guess it's a good thing that spear broke loose. That shark might have yanked you overboard."

I thought so too, but I said nothing. I was properly awed by the the most violent demonstration of wild quickness and strength that I had yet witnessed in my young life.

There was more violence to come. As we soon learned, coming ashore in a small, flat-bottomed, Macy's rowboat through the

Atlantic surf, even on a relatively calm day, is more difficult than launching through and over that same surf. A following sea, when there is no resistance to hold a stern in place, will push the boat broadside unless the oarsmen are experienced and strong. Chick was strong, but quite without experience.

Almost before we could comprehend what had happened, our attempted landing became an accident. Pushed by a breaking wave, the *Emma* broached and tried to roll over. Chick had no time to slip his oars free of the oarlocks and as the boat heeled over, the inshore oar dug into the sand, caught there, then cracked loudly, split by the strain. Yanked from its fastenings, the oarlock ripped free, taking its screws with it.

As we tumbled into the wash while the sea slammed the *Emma* against our shins, we began yelling at each other, both of us near panic at the thought that our boat might suffer even more humiliation and injury.

With help, we tugged her toward the beach. She was heavy with water that had sloshed over her gunwales, but we got her high enough to bail her out. Then we rolled her across the sand back to the Georgica she never should have been asked to leave.

With just one oar, the *Emma* had to be paddled home. It was a long trip and I did all the paddling. Between them, Sonny, Walter, and Chick had quietly determined that I had been the instigator of the reckless quest that had wreaked such pointless havoc.

Our summer—and our innocence—ended soon after. I repaired the oarlock, bought a new set of ash oars (at East End Hardware), and took a last look at the *Emma* before my trip to New Haven. There, at that modest dock, swinging just a bit in the southwest breeze before sunset, she looked as she always had: long for her size, low-sided, narrow, but gray, patient and eternally loyal, the boat of my boyhood, adolescence, and very young manhood.

I said a kind of good-bye then, but seven years later I was saying an enthusiastic hello again. For the *Emma* became the key to the U.S. Coast Guard's requirement that I come up with some evidence of small-boat experience. Without the *Emma*'s help, there was no way I was going to be issued that bit of official paper, my authorization to "carry passengers for hire," my ticket to my first real job—well, the first real job I really wanted.

It was, I'll have to admit, my college experience as a liberal arts major that was key to my successful utilization of the *Emma* as my passport. If an English major learns anything, he learns how to take a kernel of truth and expand it to a pasture of bullshit. Which is what I did with my *Emma*.

That incident with the shark became "navigated coastal Atlantic waters." My eeling converted to "frequent commercial fishing trips," and my rows around Georgica with those young ladies, and even the grandmother for whom the boat was named became "cruises on the waters in and adjacent to the town of East Hampton, including Gardiners Bay and Three Mile Harbor." That was stretching things a bit, because the *Emma* had never been trailered to either of those lovely saltwater bays. But I had been taken bluefishing by Chief of Police Harry Steele in his Jersey skiff, and we navigated both the bay and the harbor.

With references from two friendly adults—older brothers of my friends and contemporaries—my *Emma* essay satisfied the invisible Coast Guard authorities who read it. Their communication that told me so was one of the first, and last, from any government agency that filled me with relief, joy, and gratitude to my great friend *Emma*.

After that, I needed only to pass the written exam—a piece of cake after I had read my Chapman. After all, I'd been passing exams at New Haven with considerably less study.

On the first Monday of the first week in June 1948, I opened the official envelope that held that bit of paper that certified me as Captain Cole ("for vessels up to 65 feet in length in northeastern waters of the Atlantic coast"). No wonder I lost interest so quickly in the notion that I had to hang around for commencement. I'd already been assured I'd get my diploma, and that was not the bit of official paper that interested me.

On the Tuesday after I got my captain's papers, I left New Haven for the Matthiessen home in Stamford. The next, and one of the most important, small boats in my life waited for me in Stamford Harbor, and I could hardly wait to meet her.

But I had not forgotten the *Emma* and all she had meant to me and done for me. Nor have I ever.

The Launch

She was brand-new, an eighteen-foot Chris-Craft designed and built in the grand manner: teak decks, bright mahogany work gleaming with several coats of spar varnish, a graceful hull with lines that had memorized the old Gar Wood speedboats of the thirties, those single-purpose extravaganzas skippered by playboys in yachting caps and a girl or two in a swimsuit along for the ride. Peter and I stood on the Muzzi Boatyard dock high above Stamford Harbor, looking down at the boat that had, that bright June morning, become my responsibility.

From above, she looked like a miniaturized version of a larger cruiser. Forward, she had a tiny trunk cabin, then a windshield and a small wheelhouse that opened onto an afterdeck with built-in bench seats along both rails. Just astern of the wheelhouse, two large, boxy engine covers with removable cushion tops provided another place for passengers to sit. She was rated for six passengers plus her skipper—me.

A twin-screw boat powered by two ninety-horsepower inboard Klamath gasoline engines, the launch was designed for speed. I always thought, with her delicate lines, her rather grand teak and mahogany, that she was built for a career on Lake George or Lake Placid—any of those Adirondack watering holes surrounded by towering summer hotels framed by shaded verandas where stockbrokers and their ladies rusticated in Panama hats and linen suits as snow white as the launch's pristine hull.

Mr. Muzzi, a stocky, deeply tanned middle-aged man with black eyebrows, had followed me and Peter down the dock, carrying his heavy metal toolbox. "The gearbox on the starboard engine needs adjustment," he had told us. "It's making too much noise when you throw it in gear." That was a noise I knew I never would have

recognized. I had been intimate with just one engine in my life: the four-cylinder power plant in the Model A, which was then and still is a masterpiece of functional simplicity. Spark plugs, carburetor, fuel pump, coil—they were all out in the open, able to be understood, able to be repaired, even by college kids.

That engine had taught me what I was looking at when Mr. Muzzi raised the engine cover, opened his toolbox, and went to work with a wrench. With no concept of his purpose, I could not help, nor did I offer. I knew that anything I said would only reveal ignorance, so I said nothing. Peter and I sat silent on the stern transom, exchanging looks but nothing more.

Taking a set of ignition keys from his pocket, Mr. Muzzi stepped around the open engine hatch to the wheelhouse. The launch was outfitted with a classic ship's wheel, finely fashioned of wood and brass with eight small handles protruding like spokes from its rim. That wheel was supported by a dashboard of circular gauges ringed by stainless steel that shone silver against their mahogany background: rpm indicators for both engines, fuel gauge, ampere meters for both generators, oil pressure gauges, and, on top just above the wheel, mounted on the small shelf between the wheel and the windshield, was the launch compass, a globe with a transparent hemisphere that magnified the compass-face letters and numbers that have guided navigators for centuries.

I have never understood why Mr. Muzzi did what he did next. Starting the starboard engine, he moved its chromed throttle lever slowly forward, increasing its rpms. Once he had the setting he wanted, he stepped back toward the stern, leaned down into the open engine hatch with a wrench in one hand. He was, I assume, about to make some sort of adjustment he could monitor by the sound of the engine.

We never knew what that adjustment might be. Within seconds of his move into the the darkness below decks, the engine stuttered for a split second, the same split second that Mr. Muzzi uttered the most terrible moan, a sound of shock, surprise, fear, and pain.

He rose to his knees, his right hand a bloody mess cupped in his left.

His tan face bleached to pale, shaking he surged to his feet, blood dripping steadily to the decks, and trotted to the stern. Clutching his wounded hand to his belly, he stepped up to the ramp that led to the dock and trotted toward the small office building at the dock's inshore end.

The engine kept running, its sound filling our ears. I eased around the open hatch and turned the key to "off." The engine quit. Peter and I looked at each other. I'm sure my eyes were as wide as his, and my cheeks as pale.

"God," he said. "What happened. Did you see his hand?"

"Yes. It's a mess." We both kept our eyes on the office door at the end of the dock. In moments it opened, a man stepped out to hold it wide, and Mr. Muzzi, his right hand and arm wrapped in a white towel, came out and trotted across the parking lot to a car. The other man followed and jumped in the driver's seat. The car got out of there in a hurry, headed, we were sure, to the emergency room at the nearest hospital. I never saw Mr. Muzzi again, and I never learned just how severely his hand had been injured. But I knew it was bad; I have always thought he must have lost a finger or two.

Stunned and queasy from the sight of so much blood on the deck, Peter and I closed the engine hatch, found a mop on the dock, and tried to clean up.

We were alone there on the launch for half an hour before anyone came to tell us what to do next. While we waited Peter began talking about omens, and how blood on a new ship was definitely not a good omen. I had to agree. How could it be? So, I wondered to myself, does this mean my summer is cursed?

I was relieved when another man, one of the yard's hired mechanics, arrived. He picked up the tools Mr. Muzzi had left scattered on the deck and said we might as well go home. He would have to wait to find out, if he could, what adjustments needed to be made. The short shakedown cruise that Peter and I had planned to take would have to be postponed. We drove back to the Matthiessen home, talking about how this day that had started with such promise had become such an unpleasant memory.

The cancellation of the shakedown cruise was definitely a bad break. There was no leeway in our schedule. Matty had already gone to Fishers Island, and he expected us to arrive the next day. As the man in charge of every aspect of reopening the Fishers Island Country Club for its first full-service season since the war, he was not going to be pleased with any delays, especially those that involved his son and his friend with a reputation for irresponsibility.

When we got to Muzzi's the next morning, we both wished for another day. Drizzle eased steadily from low clouds, and a mist wavered over Long Island Sound. Visibility from the end of the Muzzi dock was little more than a half-mile. I was hoping someone would tell us the launch was not ready, that there were still mechanical problems waiting to be diagnosed and repaired.

That was not to be. We were told the launch was seaworthy. Mr. Muzzi, we were also informed, was still in the hospital, but would be released soon. No one wanted to tell us how badly his hand had been hurt.

Peter and I got out the only chart aboard the launch, one Matty had given us. It covered Long Island Sound waters from City Island to the west to Plum Island in the east. Fishers Island was not on it, but Peter had sailed those waters since boyhood and could guide us from Plum Island.

The line we drew from Stamford to Plum Island was almost due east and covered about sixty miles, according to our reading of the chart's scale. If we averaged twenty knots an hour—a fair cruising speed for a small boat with two big engines—the voyage would take between three and four hours. If we left before 10:00 A.M., which was our plan, we calculated we should reach Fishers by 3:00 P.M. at the latest. We phoned Matty and told him that.

We idled out of Stamford Harbor about 9:30 A.M. with both engines running at less than 500 rpm. Chris-Craft had mastered the science of designing exhausts that made all of its engines sound like torpedo boats. Listening to that glorious, rumbling burble, that creamy sound of restrained power, as we cleared the channel set my adrenaline in motion. But as we passed the final "No Wake" marker and I advanced the throttles to about 1,800 rpm, just enough to get that modified V-hull up on a plane, I felt more anxiety than excitement.

Riled by an erratic breeze from the southeast, low clouds plumped with drizzle swung even lower. Often, peering through the dripping windshield, I could not find the line between sky and sea, even though I could still see a half-mile or so. While Peter watched for buoys, I kept my eye on the compass and made sure I stayed on a course just a few points north of east.

About 10:30 the sky brightened, the breeze shifted to the southwest, and for perhaps a half-hour the visibility improved, as did my spirits. But not for long. In one of those meterological quick-change events so typical of New England, the warm sun together with the wind shift and colder water spawned a surface fog bank. Quite suddenly, Peter and I found ourselves wrapped in white cotton, a blanket of fog made more brilliant and blinding by the noon sun, which was now shining above the fog. I had the feeling that if the launch had a very tall mast, I could have climbed high enough to get above the cottony blanket.

How I wished I could. I had not expected such dense fog. I had taken no bearings before it closed down. I had only a general notion of our position, and now, with scarcely enough visibility to see the bow, I had to throttle back to idle speed. If asked, I would have had to admit that I could see no way out of our predicament until the fog lifted and I could get a visual sighting of either the Connecticut or Long Island shore. Peter was well aware of the problem, but neither he nor I had a word to say about it. Both of us kept quiet while I kept my eyes on the compass and tried to keep the needle squarely on our heading.

An hour went by, one of the longest of my life. We were still locked in and we had still seen nothing. There was no radio, no electronics of any kind aboard that brand-new boat. And when I shut down the engines to see if we could hear a bell buoy, we heard nothing. The notion that we might be cursed began to seem a likely possibility.

It became a reality when I noticed the fuel gauges. We were running out of gas.

The list of navigational and seamanship mistakes I made that day is a long one. Near the top was my failure to calculate how many hours of operation and at what speed those engines would run on what amount of fuel. I wasn't even sure the gauges were accurate. On an untested, untried boat, I should also have made a manual check of our fuel tanks with a properly marked dipstick.

We were, as Peter and I both realized, about to lose all power and begin drifting in a dense fog. Not a healthy prospect in any waters, but surely more dangerous on the busy waterways of Long Island Sound, waters heavily traveled by plenty of large, commercial vessels, tugs, and barges.

I shut down one engine, ran the other at idle speed. It was, I thought, the only action I could take.

If the skies had not cleared, and suddenly, it would have been a delaying tactic, nothing more. But in a wonderfully miraculous way, the fog vanished. One minute we were enveloped, the next we were blessed with landscapes on our north and south. But they were not those we expected to see.

I recognized the Long Island shore to the south: we were somewhere between Port Jefferson and Greenport. We should have been off Plum Island, forty miles east.

Running slowly on a good visual bearing, I noticed the compass needle turning, even though I traveled a straight line. I was face-to-face with my second great mistake. Our compass had not been calibrated or adjusted; something on board was causing the malfunction, some metal presence that disturbed the proper magnetic orientation of the needle. I'd taken a boat to sea without a working compass, and I'd encountered zero visibility, the one condition that makes a compass critical.

We had been running in a large, pointless circle.

"We've got to get some gas," I said to Peter, who nodded rather grimly, I thought.

I steered straight for the Long Island shore. We had, in my view, no options. If we made the beach, one of us could jump overboard and wade ashore, find the nearest road, and hitchhike to the nearest gas station. To my way of thinking, on that memorable day, it seemed a rational plan. I was too ignorant of the risks involved to worry much about them.

The beach we approached as we ran out of gas was, like so many of Long Island Sound's beaches, stony. With large, weathered boulders shoving their shoulders above the cobbled beach every fifty feet or so, I needed no chart to tell me there were likely to be similar boulders offshore, underwater. Boulders that could bend a propellor shaft or splinter a plank if the launch happened to hit one at the right angle.

Easing toward that unknown shore, I came as close as I dared to going aground. Then I eased back offshore a few feet and Peter dropped the anchor. I cut the engine and the launch drifted slowly toward the rocky beach, pushed by a gentle breeze that had swung more to the west.

We were lucky, to say the least. When we got as close as we could, Peter dropped off the stern into waist-deep water and waded ashore, holding his wallet high over his head. He would, we had decided, walk inland until he found a road, then hitch a ride and return with enough gasoline to get us to Fishers. If one learned nothing else at Yale, one learned the supreme arrogance that bred our kind of confidence.

I watched Peter vanish into the scrub oak and pine on that unknown shore, and went up to the bow where I hauled in enough anchor line to pull the launch a bit farther from the rocks. Then I went back to the wheelhouse to wait.

It was about five o'clock, already two hours after we had told Matty we would arrive at Fishers. But we had almost three hours of daylight left on that long, June day. And the weather had apparently decided to behave. The evening was clear, almost windless, and full of the promise of a splendid summer sunset. Nevertheless, as I sat there so alone, forlorn and consumed with shame at the consequences of my blunders, I could find no redemption in the glories of a June evening. I was consumed with anxieties about what could happen if the wind began to blow from the northwest, and I searched constantly for any sign of Peter's return.

And then he was there, walking toward the boat with a five-gallon can of gas in each hand. There was one more, he told me, in the truck that had driven him back from the filling station he had found.

He waded out, holding one gas can in both hands above his head, a move that required strength and balance. After two more trips and then another two back to the road with the empty cans (and his wallet), the launch had fifteen gallons in its gas tank—enough, I hoped, to get us home at last.

Running on just one engine, we followed the Long Island shore past Greenport until we reached Orient Point, and then Plum Island. After that, we began the crossing between Plum and Fishers, the place where Block Island Sound and Long Island Sound waters meet. Even on a pleasant June evening, those waters are turbulent, tossed by the energies of conflicting currents. It is no place to run out of gas.

If the launch was cursed, I thought, the crossing from Plum to Fishers might never be completed. We would finish our day drifting on Block Island Sound in the dark of a moonless night.

That final eight miles from Plum Island to Race Rock just west of Fishers was one of the longest voyages I have ever taken. When we passed Great Gull and then Little Gull Island to the south, we could at last see our destination. The lighthouse at Race Rock was sharply profiled against the darkening eastern horizon, and the green and sandy heights of Fishers' west end rose beyond it. Houses, the Coast

Guard station, roads, and even automobiles took shape as we approached. The gentle breeze had swung all the way to the northwest, bringing a kind of autumnal clarity to a soft, June evening.

With Peter acting as pilot, pointing out channel buoys and a myriad of markers, we cruised along the island's north shore toward East Harbor and the dock that waited for us. I prayed over and over that our single engine would maintain its comforting rumble; I dreaded the stutter and cough that would tell me we had run out of fuel, twice in one day.

It was 8:30 when we rounded the red buoy off Hungry Point, then slowed as we entered East Harbor. Our trip that we estimated would take less than five hours had taken more than eleven. I was relieved beyond measure to see the launch's new mooring float just a few feet beyond our bow, but I was sheepish and chagrined at my stupid mistakes—errors that could have had much more serious and costly consequences. I had hoped Matty would be anywhere but on the dock waiting and watching, but there he was, tall against the twilight sky, above us on the high pier.

"I was getting worried," he said. "I was just about to call the Coast Guard."

Peter smiled, looked up, and said, "No need to worry. We had fog and a problem with the compass, among other things." He laughed, but said no more. Matty joined the laughter. The two, father and son, had an easy, open relationship. And Matty, who had to be a bit concerned about his choice of new skipper for his country club's new launch, never said a critical word.

There had been no curse, only carelessness and ignorance, a dangerous combination at sea. If anything, I had been blessed with good fortune and good friends. Otherwise, I would not have made it through that first day as a duly licensed captain.

The lessons I learned so dramatically turned out to be the first of many. That entire summer was a learning experience, and some of the lessons were costly. For while I might have learned to study well enough to pass a Coast Guard exam, I had never learned to navigate a powerboat. That process required on-the-job training, trial and error, and a great deal of good luck.

As a marine classroom, I was soon to discover, there must be few locations more demanding than the waters around Fishers Island, especially those to the north, between the island and the Connecticut shore. There may be other stretches of coastal water more clotted with rocks, islands, hammocks, clumps, shoals, and reefs, but I know of no other that has so many of each in such a relatively small space.

Fishers Island Sound is less than four miles wide (from the island's north shore to the Connecticut side) and it's a bit more than ten miles from the entrance to New London Harbor on the west and Watch Hill to the east. These were the waters I would need to navigate most of the time. But to do it safely I would have to avoid, among other obstructions, North Dumpling, South Hammock, Pulpit Rock, South Dumpling, Seaflower Reef, Horseshoe Reef, Vixen Ledge, Black Ledge, Ram Island Shoal, Cormorant Reef, Eel Grass Ground, Red Reef, White Rock, Latimer Reef, East Clump, Middle Clump, and Seal Rocks, to name just a few. In addition, as you might expect in such rocky, tidal waters, there were lobster pots by the thousands, each marked (in those pre-Styrofoam days) with a hefty wooden buoy, often tugged a foot or more beneath the surface by the tides that so continually ripped around the island. Because they were invisible when they were underwater, those pot buoys were a menace to turning propellors. At just the proper depth to be caught by the churning blades, the buoys and their tethering manila lines would wrap around the shaft, bend prop blades, and thump so hard against the hull that they could splinter the planks above them.

In brief, my home waters that incredible summer were a small-boatman's nightmare. And then there was the fog.

That was my first and last full summer on Fishers, so I have no way of knowing if every June, July, and August there are as foggy as they were during the summer of '48. Like many of the other young people with seasonal jobs at the club, I lived in a rambling summer-house on Barley Cove. The place had somehow been acquired by the country club; I never learned the details. It was perfect for its purpose, and I should have enjoyed it more. But each morning I awakened, I would lie there and listen for the foghorns. There were several within range of Barley Cove; I knew each by its signal. And when they sounded, one after the other in their overlapping dirge, I knew that I would be spending my workday on the launch hunched over my compass, my charts, and the pocket watch I kept on the shelf beside the compass.

For I had learned the principles of dead reckoning: first penciling my course on the chart; then annotating it with the proper compass headings (compensating for variation and deviation); and then also adding the time—at 1,500 rpm—it would take the launch to get from one buoy or one light or one marker to the the next.

It was tense work for a relative novice with trusting passengers aboard. I would leave the red nun on my stern as we cleared East Harbor, staying glued to my compass (properly adjusted ever since that first voyage) until my watch told me it was time to look for the next buoy or listen for the next bell. Often, those strong tides would sweep me off course, but throughout that entire foggy summer, I never once became lost. I had many near misses, but no times when I had to shut down because I just plain did not know where I was. Today, almost fifty years later, that sort of navigating has been all but superseded by electronic direction finders, radar, and other computerized systems even small motorcraft can carry. As for me, I've always been grateful I learned the way I did, although there were times during that summer I wanted out of that awesome classroom that was Fishers Island Sound.

Like the evening Admiral "Bull" Halsey—wartime commander of the U.S. Pacific Fleet—brought his daughter to the dock and asked me to take her to Watch Hill. I knew it would be dark before we could get across the sound, and I knew the approaches to Watch Hill were some of the most tortuous on the coast. The narrow channel began just east of Stonington and wound around for more than a mile through mudflats and marshes. There was no room for error, none.

"You be careful, now, skipper," the admiral called down as we left the dock. *Careful* was not the word for my tense and cautious navigation across the three miles between East Harbor and Stonington Point. And then there was the channel, in the dark and through the ground mist creeping across the marshes. We made it to the Watch Hill Yacht Club dock, but once my passenger disembarked safely, I stayed right where I was for the night.

Oh, that fog. How it deviled me. On another morning a young girl and her mother, both wearing their finest summer dresses, were brought to the dock by the girl's father. I was to take them to the Montauk Yacht Club, where they would attend a wedding. They had made arrangements for the trip a week ahead of time; for them, it was the event of their season.

If I had not known that, I might not have left the dock. Fog had taken hold overnight and was not about to let go. Montauk Point was twenty miles due south across the deep tidal waters of Block Island Sound. Without visibility, I could drift less than half a mile and be just far enough east to miss Montauk Point. And when I did that, I would be crossing the Atlantic headed for North Africa.

But I cranked up the engines, eased away from the slip, and turned due south when we reached East Point and the Wicopisset Passage. In minutes, the point was lost in the fog. While the mother and daughter sat quietly, and, I suppose, anxiously, in the stern wearing slickers to protect their lovely new dresses, I stared at my compass and my watch. Because I knew the tide was falling, edging me east, I edged back, keeping the launch a degree or two to the west.

At 1,800 rpm, the trip would take an estimated hour and a quarter. That, let me tell you, was one long and lonely hour. And its final fifteen minutes seemed to last a lifetime. Just as I was about to shut down to listen for the horn at Montauk Light, the launch slid out of the fog into brilliant summer sun, just as quickly as that. And there, just a hair or two to the west, were the two riprap breakwaters that mark the entrance to Montauk Lake, the small, busy harbor that shelters the Montauk Yacht Club and the greatest number of charter and party boats squeezed onto one spot of water this side of Hong Kong.

I wanted to yell, to celebrate, to shout my relief and my thanks for the blessed solar energies that had destroyed my enemy fog at precisely the right time. Instead, I acted as if I'd expected nothing less and cruised confidently to the Yacht Club dock.

By late afternoon when the wedding and the reception had ended, my two ladies returned for the trip home, happy and now wearing summer dresses that no longer looked brand-new. With the sun shining and a moderate breeze from the southwest, the run to Fishers was a piece of cake. I kept the engines piping at about 2,800 rpms, and their sound was loud enough so the passengers could not hear me singing to myself.

There were those good days, plenty of them, during that summer of my learning. It was a splendid time simply to be young and alive. Most Americans were in full recovery from the war years, feeling good about their country and themselves. Prosperity was no longer just around the corner; it was on the same street and everyone could see it coming closer. And the men and women and their well-kept children who summered on Fishers Island were surely more prosperous than most. They spent those blissful days celebrating their good fortune and, whenever the foghorns were quiet, I joined that celebration with enthusiasm and the endless energy of a young hedonist.

Which sometimes, even in perfect weather, got me into trouble. Those lithe, tanned, long-legged daughters of those prospering parents and their equally tanned and self-confident gentlemen escorts and brothers soon discovered that their club's Chris-Craft had to be the best waterskiing boat on the island. With 180 horsepower ripping at full throttle, a skier traveled at more than 30 mph—very fast for those days and fast even today. When I wasn't ferrying briefcased brokers in summer seersuckers to the railroad station at Stonington, or meeting the Friday trains at New London, I carried a welcome cargo of swimsuits squeezed around the perfect shapes of the island's loveliest lasses, plus their seasonal entourage of acceptable young men. "Captain, Captain," they called to me as my heart shook and sweat trickled down the small of my back.

On a Sunday afternoon, I towed a young Rockefeller male (I forget his first name) clear across Fishers Island Sound. He rode a single ski, and did it so well no one, least of all the lasses, wanted him to stop when we reached Stonington. So I roared into the Watch Hill channel, which soon led to Watch Hill Harbor, where I made a wide, full-speed turn past the vast school of great yachts moored there, then headed south, back through the channel as my skier waved to one and all.

"Captain, Captain, that was super!" echoed through my evening as I lounged on the porch at Barley Cove, a southside cool in my hand and warm in my gut. Lovely girls, all the gin I could drink (and did), the touch of salt on my skin, the sun in the sky, soft nights that never seemed dark, and dawns that brought more of the same— "Captain, Captain"—how could days, weeks, and months like that fail to ruin even a good man, which I definitely was not.

Two days after the Watch Hill boat show, I was called to the office at the Fishers Island Country Club—a huge stuccoed and slate-spired mansion overlooking its golf course to the north and South Beach on its other waterfront side. In my numbing innocence, I had no reason for apprehension. I imagined an important member wanted personal consultation on a fishing trip aboard the launch.

The man who waited for me introduced himself as Sam Allen, an attorney. He was white-haired, hearty, and nonthreatening. As I was to learn later, he was the senior partner in a Wall Street law firm. Today, he would be billed out at $300 an hour, or better.

Mr. Allen spent about fifteen minutes explaining the document he had in his hand. It was a formal complaint against the club, objecting to the club launch that had sped through Watch Hill

Harbor "in a reckless manner," which caused a wake that in turn upset a tea service then in use on the fantail of one yacht in that school of yachts I had circumnavigated so deftly.

The plaintiff, as Mr. Allen pointed out, was quite within her rights. The most basic and universal rules of the road for boats of all shapes and sizes require them to hold to idle speed inside all harbor limits. Full throttle is most assuredly the other side of idle speed.

Looking at me with his sharp, Yankee-blue eyes, Mr. Allen said, "Matty doesn't know how to treat this. It certainly demonstrates carelessness, at the very least, on your part. And," he continued with a sigh, "the lady tells us you broke $650 worth of fine china. I'm not sure how the club is going to pay that." Long pause. "Have you got any suggestions?"

At last I began to sense the depth of my troubles. For the first time I began to understand that my job, my glorious job, might be on the line. Good-bye, Captain.

"I, uh, I, I definitely did the wrong thing. I know that now," I said, although such knowledge had never occurred to me on that fateful Sunday afternoon. "I'll write a letter of apology. And I'll send the $650 along with it."

"You will?" said Mr. Allen, surprised.

"Sure," I said, "I'll do it right now. I'll go get the money." Which was another benefit of that spectacular career. The launch had been such a success, and my arrangements with Matty as to my share of the take (two-thirds) so generous that I was loaded. I was buying cases of champagne for the folks at the house on Barley Cove, and I still couldn't spend my income fast enough.

"I'll have to talk with Matty," Sam Allen said.

"I'll be back with the letter and the money in about half an hour," I replied, knowing I should clear out while the going was good. When I got back, with cash and an appropriately abject apology, Mr. Allen looked over both and said, "We'll see if this is acceptable."

It was. A couple of years later Peter told me Matty had decided to fire me when he got the complaint. But after he heard about my response, he changed his mind, just. I never knew I had come so close. Hey, what's so great about a tea set, anyway? In a few wonderful days, I'd forgotten all about it.

But I was to try Matty's patience yet again. It's a wonder that man endured that summer and continued to smile his brilliant smile. It was put to the test one morning when Willy Witt was to take me and some of the other young workers at the club on a fishing trip aboard Matty's fifty-foot Huggins. Like the launch, that superb boat—built at the same yard that had designed and launched the navy's fastest subchasers—had two large engines. Which was one reason Matty named her the *Double Trouble*; the other had to do with his own frequent misadventures as her skipper.

She was a lovely piece of work, strip built with one-inch southern pine squares steamed and fastened to a design of flowing curves that flared into a high bow, then swept back to a low stern cockpit, a perfect deck for deep-sea fishing. She had a spacious cabin and a fine flying bridge above it, which is where I stood on that fateful morning.

Willy Witt, older than I but a bit younger than Matty, was beside me at the wheel. A year-round Fishers Islander, he trained hunting dogs there, specializing in setters and Brittany spaniels. Now and then, he would work for Matty at this job or that; like so many islanders he had many skills and was an experienced boat handler. As the *Double Trouble* warmed up, her two mighty engines throbbing, he looked at me and a smile lit up his weather-beaten face and his sea-blue eyes. How lucky I am, I thought, to be headed for a day's fishing with this man and aboard this boat.

Willy slipped the controls into gear and idled away from the East Harbor pier. Our course to Montauk Point would take us around East Point and through Wicopisset Passage, the same course I had taken with the wedding guests. About one hundred feet offshore of our East Harbor berth, a green-can buoy marked the prescribed channel.

"Okay to cut that buoy?" Willy asked me as he shoved both

throttles forward and the *Double Trouble* buried her stern and surged ahead with a roar.

"Sure," I answered. I had done it countless times in the launch.

Willy swung the wheel and we banked toward the buoy's far side. Just as we reached the marker, there was an impressive thump that shook the boat from stem to stern. And that was instantly followed by a nerve-shattering grinding of metal and wood. Willy, holding his right wrist with his left hand, quickly switched off both engines. Then he looked at me, those blue eyes wide with shock. It was one more terrible moment I'll never forget.

"Lift that deck hatch," Willy said, pointing to the afterdeck. I slid down the ladderway from the flying bridge and opened the hatch. Seawater poured into the *Double Trouble*'s hold. We were sinking.

"She's taking water," I yelled.

Willy restarted one engine, heard the grinding sound, and shut it down. He started the other. This one sounded rough, but operable.

Turning the crippled boat back the way she had come, Willy idled her toward shore until she ran aground just a short way from where her voyage had begun, but a long way from the high hopes we had shared those few minutes earlier. Willy shut down the engine, still holding his right wrist with his left hand. "There," he said, "it's near high tide. When the tide falls we can tell better about the damage. Maybe we can fix her enough so we can get her to the boatyard."

Shit, I thought, as I watched seawater begin to flood the cockpit, *now what have I done?*

What I had done was make yet another fundamental mistake. I had often cleared the big rock just inside that buoy because the launch didn't draw more than two feet, even with her stern down at high speed. Matty's much heavier and larger boat, with its stern buried by the surging thrust of those mighty engines, pushed down close to five feet, maybe even six. However much she "sat down" when her throttles were opened, it was far enough to allow the *Double Trouble*'s propellors to slam hard against the top of the rock.

At her speed, the rock crushed the starboard skeg and pushed the turning prop right through the stern planking, wrecking not only the prop, shaft, and stern, but also stripping the gears in the engine's transmission and opening a hole in her stern planking, a hole big enough to sink Matty's pride and joy in less than an hour. I had created yet another disaster for one of the men I loved and respected most in the world.

Willy's right wrist, I learned later, had been fractured when the wheel he held spun as the starboard rudder and skeg slammed into that rock. But he came back with Matty that afternoon and put enough of a plywood patch over the hole in the *Double Trouble*'s stern to allow her to be towed safely across Fishers Island Sound to the boatyard in Stonington, which built draggers and had a ways large enough to haul out Matty's wounded boat. I never learned how much the whole mess cost, but it was a hell of a lot more than $650. Shaft, skeg, hull, rudder, propellors, and more had to be repaired or replaced—a big job, to say the least.

But Matty never scolded or criticized me. Now there was a tolerant man. And it was I, not Willy Witt, who told him that I had said it was okay to cut the buoy. Willy Witt was too much a gentleman—too much a man—to try to shift blame or make excuses.

He died of a heart attack working one of his dogs in a field trial long after that summer became history. The dog had just come up on a point and Willy stood behind it, shotgun in hand, ready to flush the bird. That was as far as his life got. The next moment he was stricken, falling. But as he went down he remembered to break open his double-barreled gun, making certain there would be no accidents.

A part of my summer of 1948. A summer school packed with painful, but unforgettable lessons. Since then, in forty-five years of small-boat ownership and operation, I have not: run out of gas, cut another buoy, failed to properly adjust my compass, ignored the rules of the road, or been cited by the Coast Guard for any violation. Which does not mean I haven't gotten in more trouble at sea, I have. But not those troubles.

And as the summer neared its exhilarating end with a parade of September's crystal days and elixir nights, the launch and I became good friends. After Labor Day, after most of the summer people had returned to their city and suburban homes, the launch and I stayed on, stayed to share those days with one of those fine tanned and laughing ladies. I had, at last, become a friend of the person I had wanted to be, the "captain" that my papers claimed me to be. Through trial and error (more errors than trials) I had become a boatman. At last, I had progressed from the *Emma* to navigation of open water, to reading charts and understanding my compass, to boat handling and boat maintenance. All that, and those brilliant last days of summer washed away the gall inflicted by those harsh lessons learned.

I could take the launch through the Race in the teeth of a nor'wester, knowing how to cope with the chaos of the chop created by swift, ebbing tides. I could run at night by stars and lights. I could even run with some confidence in the fog, although to this day I'd rather not.

I had come to like my job, my first job, and to love the man who gave it to me, and took such a risk. That job had got me invited aboard some of the finest yachts in the world. I had been a passenger aboard Jock Whitney's torpedo-stern, four-engine (and Rolls-Royce engines at that) superyacht, the *Aphrodite*, its sixty-foot, jet-black hull rising on a plane as those engines roared and moved us at more than thirty knots from Fishers to Port Washington between breakfast and lunch. She was a wooden boat to end all boats, and I understand that years after Jock's death she has been restored and still reigns. Because of the awe I'll always remember as her passenger, I am grateful she's afloat and cared for.

And then there's the dinner I had aboard the *Aras*, Hugh Chisolm's graceful and classic extravagance built just for him at the Bath Iron Works in Maine. Named after his wife, Sara, the *Aras* was a yacht designed in the grand manner. The son of the man who arrived in the Maine woods late in the nineteenth century and

founded a papermaking empire on the banks of the Androscoggin
in Rumford, then a hamlet, now a mill town complete with towering
smokestacks, the Hugh Chisolm I came to know was a friend of my
father's. Then a portly fellow in his sixties, he cruised through his
summers aboard the classic vessel papermaking had paid for.

I was aboard the launch when the *Aras* tied up at the deepwater
end of the Country Club dock. I had no idea it was Hugh Chisolm's
boat, nor had I ever met the man. I was, however, much impressed at
the yacht's extravagant elegance and the skills of her captain, who
docked in a decidedly cramped situation without a moment's hesitation or any sudden surges. A few minutes later as I stayed busy
polishing the launch brightwork, a round, smiling, rather cherubic
white-haired head leaned out over the dock some eight feet above
me and called down, "Are you John Cole's son?"

I said I was and the voice from above picked up in volume and
authority. "Well I'm Hugh Chisolm, a friend of John and Helen's.
Sara and I would like you to join us for dinner this evening. Come
aboard about seven."

It was a request, an order, and an invitation. But even if I'd had a
reason for declining, I would not have missed the chance to see
more of that yacht. She had the kind of elegance that had vanished
with the arrival of income tax and the Great Depression. Close to
seventy feet, she combined a snow-white hull with teak decks and
the satin mahogany that framed her deckhouse and salon. Her ports
were rimmed with golden brass, her rails fitted with brass hardware,
and her canopied, carpeted afterdeck furnished with chairs, glass-
top tables, and a chintz-covered sofa that looked as if it belonged in
a mansion.

But nothing I saw above decks, including uniformed crew mem-
bers in outfits Gilbert and Sullivan would have envied, prepared me
for the luxury below. When I arrived for dinner, we had one cocktail
on the afterdeck and then went down a banistered companionway
to the grand dining salon. Hugh and his wife—a tanned, handsome
woman with snow-white hair—were joined by five other guests and

myself. But the long, superbly set table with Chippendale chairs at each place could have seated twice our number, and comfortably. Fine, heavy silver, delicate china, and crystal wineglasses combined with the salon's mahogany paneling to give the space a kind of baronial splendor.

Shortly after our first course—chilled crabmeat as I recall—had been served by two stewards in what, in those days, could have been described as black Eisenhower jackets, our host at the head of the table picked up his silver knife, held it handle side down in his right hand, and began rapping it firmly and insistently on the table: rap . . . rap . . . rap . . . rap. Conversation died as all heads turned toward Hugh Chisolm. *Now we are going to hear a toast*, I thought to myself, although I also considered it a bit early in the meal to begin such ceremonial activities.

But it was not a toast, nor any such studied announcement that the yacht's commander-in-chief wished to utter. He merely wanted silence while he talked. I was so swept away by the gesture—which I had never witnessed before, nor have I since—that I cannot recall what Hugh Chisolm had to say, except to remember that it was merely a sentence or two of comment on a statement that had been made by one of the guests. When he finished, the silence continued for an uneasy span until Sara Chisolm resumed her small talk at that long table's distant end. For the rest of that superb meal, each guest, myself included, kept an eye on our host's right hand. The moment it held a table knife upside down, all conversation ceased while each of us waited for our master's voice.

After I had made my proper good-nights and thank-yous, after the final brandy on deck, I eased the old Packard that had been my grandfather's along the island's narrow, tarred roads toward my room in the beach house on Barley Field Cove, dreaming of how I might behave were I the captain of such a splendid vessel. Through the long winters I would cruise the Caribbean with a fishing skiff in its davits on deck and a cluster of glamorous guests on board to keep me company. But I would not, I knew, ever need to pound my knife handle on the tabletop to make myself heard. For one thing, at that stage of my life, I never thought much about saying anything that could be construed as "important," not during dinner, anyway.

Like so many Americans during that rollicking, optimistic, and hedonistic summer of 1948, that first true postwar summer, I wanted only the enjoyment of the moment, the roll in whatever seemed pleasurable at the time. I had been lucky. I had survived a shooting war in which I was included among those shot at, quite often and with little regard for my well-being. It was not until that unfettered and glorious summer as the skipper of that nonessential but quite delightful launch on that determinedly high-spirited and playful island that I found a way to celebrate my good fortune, my being alive, being on the water, having an identity, running a small boat through the fog, into the chop, across dark waters under the stars, past the shoals, reefs, rocks, and clumps into safe harbors where lovely ladies waited. O captain, my captain, what a summer that was.

Jock Whitney and Joe Pulitzer (called "Old Joe" on the island to differentiate him from his son and namesake) were two of my passengers who changed my life by granting me the promise of gainful employment after that summer finally became October and not even I could find a reason to stay on. Joe Pulitzer, whom I carried most often as an angler who loved to do battle with the large bluefish that frequented the waters off Race Rock, was sincerely interested when he asked me what I would do when my summer job ended. And when I replied that I wanted to be a journalist, a newspaper reporter, he suggested I try the *St. Louis Post-Dispatch*, his fine newspaper.

Which is how I ended up in St. Louis a month or two after my last, chilly day on the waters of Fishers Island Sound. But a week or so after my arrival, printers at the *Post-Dispatch* went on strike. Many good and experienced journalists were laid off; no new, inexperienced, would-be cub reporters were being hired.

I worked, instead, as a stock boy at Scruggs, Vandervoort, and

Barney, one of the city's largest department stores. And I got that job with the help of Frank Mayfield, a college classmate whose father ran the store. I was not, in anyone's opinion—including my own—a born retailer. But I had fun in St. Louis, a great party town, went to the zoo and to the St. Louis Blues hockey games. But after the holidays, even St. Louis hunkered down for the winter and I returned to Manhattan.

I found a job there as a writer–public relations man with a small, new outfit started by two experienced men-about-town: John McLain, who wrote a column for the *New York Sun*; and Harry Sobol, whose brother Louis wrote another, different sort of column for the *New York Journal American*. My newest employer was News Contacts, Inc., financed by Jock Whitney, a good friend of John McLain's as well as the man who had given me that memorable ride aboard the *Aphrodite*.

As it turned out, my first job as a Yale graduate, my splendid summer behind the wheel of the Fishers Island Country Club launch, the job that had rendered my father apoplectic, was my stepping-stone to two more jobs that could, if I had let them, have launched me on a proper business-suit career. Working for News Contacts clients like the Stork Club and the New York Racing Association, however, required me to spend many days talking to jockeys and watching horses race at Belmont Park, and just as many nights chatting with Walter Winchell, Dorothy Kilgallen, and Sherman Billingsley at the Stork Club, at that time the city's most notorious watering hole.

Most of my evenings ended early in the morning as I walked the sidewalks toward home, where I could get just enough sleep before post time at Belmont, where, as you might guess, I often watched the races from the Greentree Stables box, cheering on Whitney and Payson horses. My job was the envy of my more dissolute friends, of which I had several. It also led to introductions to some of the city's most glamorous young ladies, who were properly impressed with the good tables I got at the Stork, the Colony, the Drake Room, the Barberry Room, and any of the other first-class drinking and dining spots on my News Contacts client list. It was at that marvelously dissipated point in my life that my father made the now oft-quoted observation: "John, the only two things you care about are fishing and fucking."

He was correct about both, but more on target with fishing. Before the next year was out, I quit my job, quit the city, and went to join my friend Jim Reutershan in East Hampton. I had passed along the captaincy of the Fishers Island launch to Jim the summer after I left. He, in turn, had come to Manhattan where he worked briefly in the fine furniture trade. There must have been something about that Fishers Island job that generated rebellion and dreams of a life on the water, because it was rebellion and dreams that brought Jim and me together on the shores of the Atlantic on a superb, late October day in 1950. We vowed we would never leave the waters we loved, that we would find a way to make our living on the seas around us. And with no true idea of how to begin, and almost no money to begin with, we got started.

Our first acquisition was also the first dory in my life. Like the *Emma* and the launch, that dory was a boat that moved my life to yet another level of consciousness.

That Dory

We named that dory the *Blue Peril*. Because she was blue when we bought her for twelve dollars. And because the first knowledgeable, working commercial fisherman who looked at her said, "She's a peril, ain't she?"

She must have looked so to anyone who knew dories and took a living from the water. For me and Jim, she was our ticket to a new life.

That, I'm certain, has been a dory's role in many lives through many centuries, for they are among the most ancient and honored small boats of the world. There is an early (1497) Dürer print that includes a small wooden boat with classic dory lines, although the dory's verified history does not begin until the eighteenth century, when French and Portuguese cod fishermen on the Grand Banks off

Newfoundland launched dories from the larger schooners that were their mother ships.

There are excellent reasons why the design has survived and prevailed over five centuries. The first is seaworthiness; the second is simplicity. The two, of course, complement each other, but there are few other examples where both are so fortuitously joined. A washtub is a simple, utilitarian design, but almost impossible to row. A wooden dory (and I've yet to see a fiberglass or plastic dory) has three bottom planks, six side planks, a stem, a transom, five frames, two to four plank seats, and oak rails. Except for the seats, transom, and frames, every structural piece of that wood is curved, or should be.

The three bottom planks include the center piece, which has straight sides; the two pieces that join it port and starboard have their outboard edges curved from bow to stern so that, once joined together, the three bottom planks make a long oval, narrower at both ends than at its center. The narrowest, almost a point, is at the bow where the stem attaches. The stern end is just a bit wider, and it is there that the narrow, bottom end of the transom connects. When the frames, angled outboard, are fast to this deck, three planks on each side are bent around them, each overlapping the other just a bit. These planks not only curve around the frames but also curve up a bit at both bow and stern. It is the plank seats that help push out a dory's sides, and the way the planks are fastened that bends them up at the ends.

And there's more. The three bottom planks are also forced to bend upward at both bow and stern—not much, perhaps a couple of inches. That's enough to impart what boat builders call sheer. In the dory's case, especially when one is being launched from a sand beach, that sheer helps prevent the suction grip of wet sand that can often make a heavy, flat-bottomed boat all but impossible to move.

A proper dory at rest has what sculptors call dynamic tension—built-in stress that pulls one element against the other in a kind of contained set of opposing forces. To me, a proper dory is as lovely as any sculpture. The curved wood tugs against itself, yet holds the entire boat in a perfectly balanced form that flows as the sea itself, each wave of each plank joining the other in a rhythm that matches the ocean's.

Like Leonardo, the early artists who created the dory had a superb understanding of how to combine form and function. The narrow bottom and the flaring curved sides not only allow the boat to move easily through the water, as she must if she is to be rowed, but also make it possible for the dory to stay afloat and stable while she carries loads that would sink other designs of equal and greater size. The secret is that narrow bottom and those flaring sides: the more weight loaded onto a dory, the more she sinks into the water; but, at the same time, because those flaring sides generate more and more resistance to sinking, the more the dory resists. The end result is a loaded boat of exceptional stability, like one of those doll toys with a round weighted base: every time they are knocked over, they right themselves.

And still more. A dory's relatively high sides (just the opposite of the *Emma*'s), its sheer, its narrow bow and stern, and its low center of gravity not only are designed for heavy loads but combine to

create one of the most seaworthy designs ever tested by the worst the North Atlantic can dish out. It is the roughest stretch of water in the world—cold, windswept, and dangerous. The story of Howard Blackburn, the Gloucester cod fisherman who was lost in a squall and not able to be picked up by his mother ship, has been told a thousand times. Rowing sixty-five miles through wintry, stormy seas in weather so cold his hands froze around his oars, Blackburn and his dory survived five days and nights alone on the wild Atlantic. His landing on the Newfoundland coast has long been considered a kind of miracle, as well as an unimpeachable verification of the dory's seaworthiness and the Gloucesterman's stubborn courage.

The *Blue Peril* when Jim and I got her would not have lasted fifteen minutes on a flat-calm sea. For one thing, she had a gaping hole in her port-side planking. Unlike the larger dories used along eastern Long Island beaches by commercial fishermen who launched those boats to set and tend nets, the *Peril* was a small dory. While the standard size was about fourteen feet on the bottom (as measured from the bottom of the transom to the bottom of the stem) and about seventeen feet on top, the *Peril* was a short twelve feet on the bottom. She had never been designed for work in the open surf, but had been built as a smack dory to be carried aboard a dragger and launched only in an emergency or when she was needed to make on-the-water repairs to the dragger's exterior hull.

In the service of the Montauk Point dragger that was the *Peril*'s mother ship, she had never been needed for anything. Year after year she rode on her perch atop the dragger's wheelhouse, her bottom on the flat, level roof, her port side rubbing against the dragger's utility mast. Riding that roof in rough and choppy seas, that dory rubbed and chafed her port side against that mast until she had worn a hole clear through her middle and topside plank. At the same time, the pounding she took while her bottom rested on the hard planks of the wheelhouse roof had knocked her silly. Every bit of sheer that might have been built into her had been pounded straight. What Jim and I had to do was make an oceangoing surf dory out of a small wooden boat that not only had never been designed for that work but had been so badly treated that she was no longer seaworthy in any waters, including Georgica Pond.

Without Jim Reutershan's skills, patience, and good humor, the *Peril* could never have been repaired and resuscitated. Three years older than I, Jim had piloted a P-40 fighter plane for the Army Air Corps before I was old enough to volunteer. He was back home after flying hundreds of combat missions in the skies over North Africa and Sicily, back home with medals, captain's bars, and a job training new pilots in combat skills. Unlike me, however, he had been born in East Hampton, gone to its public schools (and then Antioch College in Ohio), and grown up with the sons and daughters of men who made their living as commercial fishermen, carpenters, mechanics, charter boat captains, electricians, and musicians and artists as well. Along the way, he had acquired the sort of knowledge that I had not: he knew how to make things go, how to make what he needed, and how to make the best of any given situation with his combined hard work, ingenuity, and a certain dashing self-confidence when it came to taking chances. Many times, more often than not, his gambles paid off.

He understood how men could take a living from the rich waters around Long Island's easternmost tip. He also believed he could come up with new techniques and improvements that would give him—and his crew—an edge.

But, like me, he didn't have much money. Like me, he had left his job in the city without much forethought. His yearning to be on the water, to be in a boat, was stronger than his generally dependable common sense and Yankee thrift. Which is why we ended up with the *Peril*. Jim was convinced that he could repair and modify her so she would meet our needs. He was almost right.

We brought her to the East Hampton Main Beach on a flatbed truck borrowed from Percy Schenck, Jim's uncle and the town's leading wood, coal, and oil dealer. Gene Winberg, the man who lived at the Main Beach and was its caretaker, was a friend of Jim's and agreed to let us use space in the large, rambling, and empty (in October) beach house for our tools and material. The *Peril* rested on the porch of the beach house and as we worked to give her a second life, we could look up at the ocean we wanted to live by, sail on, and take fish from. Perhaps it was the exhilaration of those clear, sparkling Indian summer days and the breath of the sea in my face, the white sand warm under my feet when we broke for lunch at noon, that gave me the patience to endure the miserable, painstaking, often humiliating, but always instructional job of becoming Jim's shipwright apprentice during the long, all-but-endless days of reconstructive surgery we performed on that inanimate but appealing patient: our very own dory, our first dory, our own *Blue Peril*.

There was not one inch of her cedar-planked, spruce-bottomed, oak-framed self that could be called healthy. Every inch of that wooden boat needed care, some more radical than most. We began with the most grievous wound—that hole in her port side. Because we were most reluctant to tamper with fundamental structures—we were neither skilled enough nor experienced enough to try open-heart surgery—we based our recovery work on reinforcement rather than fundamental renewal. With this as our basic approach, Jim opted to cover the hole on both sides with a layered wooden patch. This was accomplished with quarter-inch waterproof plywood sections cut to fit the shape of the dory's existing planking—two paired plywood panels for both holed planks.

These sections were thin enough to bend to the planking's existing curves and were large enough to overlap the hole by at least six inches on its fore and aft sides. When the patches had been painstakingly shaped so they fit perfectly, we covered their inside planes with marine caulking and then fastened them to themselves and the dory with hundreds of small brass screws. With Jim on the outside of the boat and me inside lying in the dory's bottom holding the plywood patches in place while he drilled screw holes, we put those screws in place one by one, by hand. No power tools for us. Each screw hole had to be countersunk, and each screw perfectly true so

it would attain maximum holding power with its short threads. At
the end of my second day at this job, a blister as broad as a golf ball
had blossomed in the palm of my right hand, cultivated there by the
ceaseless pressures of a recalcitrant screwdriver handle.

When we finally finished, including covering the countersunk
screw heads with waterproof plastic wood, and sanding both sides
of the patch until the whole was smoother than the *Peril*'s original
planks, we moved on to the rest of our patient. With raw strips of
white oak purchased from Frank Barnes at East Hampton Lumber,
we covered both rails, soaking the oak over three days so it would

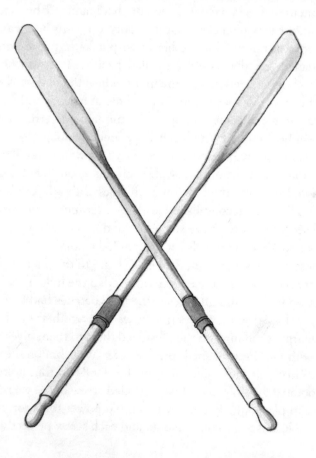

bend more easily. Then we cut marine-plywood triangles, twenty of them, to bolt over both sides of the knees of the five oak frames, port and starboard, where they joined the sides and the bottom. We cut a small triangular piece of oak and pressed it tightly into place behind the top of the stem at the bow—more reinforcement. And then we turned the *Peril* over and screwed three long, thin oak strips the length of her bottom. As long as we knew she had negative sheer, we wanted to do what we could to keep her from suctioning into place on wet sand.

And when we had finished all the orthopedic surgery we thought might help make the *Peril* seaworthy at last, we sanded her down by hand, inside and out, right down to the bare wood, as Jim kept reminding me. Only a few specks of ancient caulking and filler remained to remind us of what that dory had once been. But one of Jim's best virtues—and he had many—was his quiet humor. When, at last, we had finished sanding, finished applying our primer coat, and finished putting filler where it was needed, Jim came back from a trip to East End Hardware with a gallon of Interlux Bimini Blue, a yacht paint that no dory the length of Long Island had ever worn. We covered her with two coats, inside and out, thwarts and all. And then, about three weeks after we had begun our project, the *Blue Peril* was alive and well, ready to go to work, ready to look just like her name. As a final touch while the paint set hard, we put a couple of four-by-four timbers under her bow and stern and a sandbag inside, amidships. We hoped the counterstress would restore a half-inch of sheer, but, in my opinion, she stayed as flat as she was.

Election Day was almost upon us, the day that traditionally marked the final peak of the striped bass coastal migration along the inshore Atlantic rim south from Maine and Massachusetts, Rhode Island, and Connecticut. Every striper from every estuary, river, and bay was on the move toward Montauk Point, where those giant schools turned west and followed the beach on their way to New Jersey and from there south to the Chesapeake. We had the *Peril* ready, but we had no gear to load into her, no seine, no gill nets, no

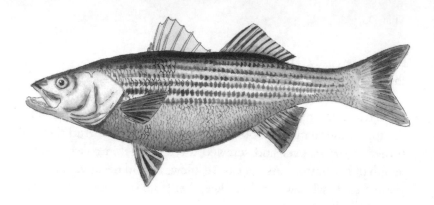

nothing. Gene Winberg, however, had several gill nets, each of them aging but serviceable. Like all nets in those days, these were knit from cotton twine and needed much care. Unless they were dried and properly cleaned after a few days in seawater, the organic twine would begin to rot. Gene's nets had not been ignored, but neither had they been cared for as well as they might. They were, in fisherman's parlance, tender, meaning the twine could be parted by a relatively moderate tug.

Our gill nets were not the best, but they were there. They gave us a reason for launching the *Peril* through the surf, a way to justify the endless hours we had spent bringing her back to a useful life. And they gave Jim and me, at last, a reason to believe our aberrant lurch from our city careers to our new fishermen's lives was an oceangoing reality and not merely a metropolitan dream.

There are days on eastern Long Island during October's final week when movement toward winter is suspended by the arrival of one of the season's rare autumnal highs, a gentle front coaxed along by civilized breezes from the northwest. On such days, the sky is brilliant blue and cloudless, the air crystal pure, and the joy of living outlined so clearly by the delicate elements that no one asks questions of their gods. Even the Atlantic behaves on such days, and it was on one such afternoon that Jim and I loaded our borrowed gill net into our dory and rolled her from the upper beach to the wet sand at the rim of the sea.

Tamed by steady breezes off the land, the surf could hardly be
called waves. Wavelets is more accurate: slight, short seas no higher
than a man's knee—perfect conditions for our initiation. I wore no
waders as my more authentic counterparts would have; I was still
the boy who had spent his summers swimming in this ocean. At the
Peril's bow, I eased her off her roller and tugged her down the gentle
slope of sand awash toward the white water of the well-mannered
breakers. Neither Jim nor I had ever launched a dory through the
surf; she was much heavier, more cumbersome on land than the
Emma. So I stood there, the Atlantic swirling around my knees,
feeling the *Peril*'s bow rise and fall in my hands. The sea had given
her life at last.

Jim stood at the dory's stern, his hands gripping the top of
her transom, his china-blue eyes looking straight out to sea. Once
we got beyond the breakers, it would be his job to set the net;
mine was to pull hard enough on our new, heavy, nine-foot ash
oars to get us there once Captain Jim had picked just the right time
for our launching. That "right time" would come between sets of
oceanic waves, a pause in their rhythm that ocean fishermen call a
"slatch." It's a word, even though it may not be in your dictionary.
And it's a word that lives depend on. In rough seas, launching a
dory when there is no true slatch and the swells are misread can
bring disaster.

On that introductory afternoon, however, we had little reason for anxiety. The small seas breaking around my legs were
too well behaved to make trouble, even for inexperienced dory-
men. Jim knew this, but he made a ceremony of our inaugural
launch.

"Not yet. Not yet," he called from the stern.

Then, "Okay, Johnny. Get ready."

And after that the words that I would wait for and hear so often
over the next seven years: "Get in, John."

That was my command to move fast, clamber over the dory's rail,
get into my rowing seat and unship my oars, sliding them out

through the oarlocks, holding them above the water poised and
ready for that first crucial stroke.

"Now, pull, Johnny, pull!" Jim yelled as he pushed our dory
straight ahead, into the face of the waves.

Dropping my oar blades into the water as I leaned far forward,
the oars back toward the bow, I dug deep into the wash, scraping the
oar tips on the sand on that important first stroke, the one that
would get us moving. With Jim pushing one last time in waist-deep
water as he clambered over the stern, I took shorter strokes, hard,
but choppy.

The *Peril* was light and lightly loaded. She had been so long on
the beach that her hull had dried like bones in the desert. As I
rowed, she shot ahead like a cork on the surface. But she was just as
quick to tip. "Tender"—the same word used to describe half-rotted
cotton twine—is also used to describe a small boat that is tippy,
unstable. Dories of every sort, when they are dry, are tender. If you
stand in one, or shift your position from port to starboard, the dory
responds in exaggerated fashion. Its gunwale dips alarmingly; the
rail almost goes under. More unsettling is the human tendency to
pitch with the boat. Off balance, a man can fall, even go overboard
from a dory with the *Peril*'s modest freeboard.

"Some tender, isn't she, Cap?" Jim asked and laughed because
that's just what a visiting haul-seiner had said when he had stopped
by a few days before to visit and watch us work. He had known just
by the look of the *Peril* that she would be unsteady until she had
soaked for a while in the sea.

I gloried in the fact of our flotation. I didn't worry much about
our boat's minor faults. We were on the water. Each stroke of my
oars sent the *Peril* darting ahead. The entire majesty of the Atlantic
heaved ponderously beneath me with planetary rhythms. Offshore
there was only ocean, miles of it, between us and the blue-on-blue
horizon. And beyond that, Dakar. Boats had brought me full circle,
first the *Emma* and now the *Blue Peril*; each had swept me across the
surf to the awesome mysteries of the open sea.

This time with a purpose, as Jim made clear. "Ready to set the net," he said. "Hold her straight offshore."

We were not far beyond the surf when he dropped the first anchor, its ten fathoms of line tied to the net's inshore bridle. As the line fetched up, Jim began guiding the twine over the stern—the stern and rub rails we had sanded so carefully to make certain there would be nothing that could impede the net's passage or catch its meshes.

I needed to pull harder to be sure the net kept slipping overboard. As it hit the surface, the lead weights along its bottom line pulled the twine toward the sand some fifteen feet below us. Corks on the upper line pulled toward the surface so the net stretched like a curtain hung from the waves.

After what seemed longer than thirty fathoms, 180 feet, we reached the net's far end and the offshore anchor; its marker buoy and line went out, with me pulling now as hard as I could to straighten the net as much as possible. When the offshore line came taut as I leaned into the oars, Jim paused, tugged, and dropped the anchor.

"There she is," he said. "Let's row back along her and see how she looks."

I rowed the *Peril* carefully, paralleling the straight line of corks. We could see the top two or three feet of our net, its meshes hanging open and straight, waiting for a fish to push its nose through the two-inch diamond, pushing until the twine slipped past its gills, then held it there, helpless, trapped, unable to go forward or back.

"Work," Jim told the net. "Okay, Cap, take us ashore," he said, leaning back along the transom like a prince aboard his barge, his smile almost breaking through.

There was nothing I wanted on shore. My day sang because we were fishermen now, in our dory, tending our nets. So I disobeyed my captain and, like a horse freed from the stable, rowed west along the coast, toward the Gut, past the dunes of my youth and their rambling homes, one of them still my family's.

Gliding with each stroke of my oars, the *Peril* rode the ocean like a leaf. Dry she might be, tender too. But she was sound; no leaks beyond the seepage normal for a wooden boat that had yet to swell. And she rowed well, so well she spoiled me for the larger, more cumbersome, albeit more seaworthy dories that I would soon be rowing as my new career progressed. But on that day I was redeemed. I had my place in life and that place was on the bow oars of a dory that rode the surf like a song.

I rowed almost to the Gut and back before we came ashore, easily in the flat seas of a windless, early sunset. Departing with the sun that created it, the day's warmth vanished and the chill of an autumnal night nipped at us as we put rollers under our dory and heaved as we pushed her up the beach above the farthest tide line.

That night was long. At supper in Jim's kitchen we chattered about the fish that were already hitting our net. "Thump, thump, thump," Jim said, "they're banging that twine while we're sitting here. We're making money as we eat."

It was exciting talk. Catching fish for a living seemed to me the best of all possible worlds. I could not sleep, waiting for the dawn.

And when it arrived, a clear, cool, and windless second edition of the previous day, we were in the same kitchen drinking hot coffee and munching on doughnuts. We were silent because Jim's widowed mother was asleep in her nearby room, but if we could have talked, it would have been more of the same dreamy optimism, more of the fisherman's constant companion: visions of the big haul.

At the beach, the *Peril* waited. In the east the first of the sun showed beyond the Atlantic as we launched our dory, this time to tend our net, not set it. As we looked along the wavering line of dark corks, we could see breaks in their sequence where corks had been pulled beneath the surface—a sure sign that there were fish in our net.

As I backwatered to the inshore end, Jim leaned over the gunwale, picked up the cork line, and worked his way down until he had both the cork line and lead line in his grip. As I worked to keep the dory at right angles to the net, he would pull us along its length, picking out fish as they came aboard.

"Hello," he said, before he had hauled back more than a few feet. A small striped bass hung from the meshes, a fish just large enough to be a keeper. Our first.

Working it free, he tossed it on the *Peril*'s deck. At thirty cents a pound, the then-wholesale price for small stripers, we had earned our first fifty cents.

We had eight more stripers in the dory when we finished running the net. The job had taken a while because sea robins, with their spiky heads and shoulders, dogfish, crabs, and skates had also got tangled in our twine. Trash, fishermen called them, but trash that had to be freed.

The sun was high, already warming the day, when we came ashore, leaving our net to fish another twenty-four hours. We took our stripers to Gene Winberg's small kitchen, where we called Rudy at Dreesen's and were told he would buy our catch, but first we had to clean and fillet each fish. We were prisoners of the market; nine stripers was not a catch we could box and ship to Fulton, and at ninety cents a pound for fillets, Rudy was paying us better than market prices. We had about fourteen pounds of fish; we got $12.60 from Rudy, sixty cents more than the *Blue Peril* had cost when we rescued her from abandonment. Jim kept $4.20 for himself, gave me the same, and put the final share in the "boat" account, the reserve we would build to cover expenses. How hopeful we were.

That afternoon, the wind moved around to the northeast, and blew harder as the evening neared under increasingly cloudy skies. When we got to the beach the next gray morning, the surf was too choppy for us to launch. The entire ocean moved west, pushed by raw, merciless winds from the east. We rolled our dory to the edge of the white water, but I could scarcely hold her against the slanting seas and we gave up.

Rain arrived that afternoon, the cold, steely, stinging rain of a true nor'easter, a rain that rides the whipping wind and pushes home the

truth of the winter soon to come. Along the east-west beach, the
Atlantic flowed like a river beneath the wind, undercutting the sand
until steep banks rose at the sea's edge. And just offshore, that
easterly "set to the west," as the fishermen call it, dragged our gill net
from its moorings and carried the twine along with its dogfish,
skates, crabs, sea robins, and perhaps a striper or two down the
beach in a ball. Two days later, after the blow, we found it all but
buried under the sand about three miles west of the Main Beach. We
had lost our anchors, and the net we retrieved was beyond repair.
Our fall fishing was over, and we tucked the *Peril* under the Main
Beach boardwalk for the winter.

A long winter, but a good one. In the early mornings, Jim and I
would drive the Model A to one of Uncle Percy's woodlots where we
cut and loaded the oak logs he sold as firewood. He paid us fifteen
dollars a cord, and we cut at least a cord a day. In the afternoon,
we'd go back to the Main Beach and work on hanging our new haul-
seine, the net we would set from the *Peril* in a semicircle from the
beach. We hoped we would set it around more stripers than we
could land. It was those dreams that kept us going through the
winter.

In late April, when the Atlantic had settled down and spring had
arrived on the East End, we began our haul-seining efforts with a
brand-new, one-hundred-fathom seine and a crew of four: myself,
Jim, Peter Scott, and Gene Winberg, who could not always make
the morning hauls because of obligations to his job. When Gene
could not be there, Bumps Leddy, the village police chief's brother,
took time off from his job as an estate caretaker to give us a hand.
Like Gene, Bumps was a barrel-chested bear of a man, stronger than
any two of us.

Each of the five Lester haul-seining crews that fished the beach—
headed by the Lester brothers Ted, Bill, and Old Frank, and Old
Frank's sons Harry and Francis—had haul-seines that were at least
three hundred fathoms. But they also had much heftier dories to

carry them and trucks with winches to help haul their long nets. We had the *Blue Peril* and no winches. We hauled by hand.

We did not catch many fish until May, and then we got just enough to keep us going. But our dory, that peril of a dory, did its job. It carried our seine and it carried me on the bow oars, Peter amidships, and Jim in the stern, setting seine. One morning in early May we made a set near the Gut, less than a half-mile from the spot where Chick had rowed the *Emma* on the great shark chase. A storm at sea had built great swells—huge waves we could not see but which, nevertheless, were on their way to break on our beach.

One great hissing wave out of nowhere caught us as we were ending our set and trying to come ashore. Jim yelled, but there was nothing to be done. That wave rolled us over, and for a moment I was trapped in my heavy waders beneath the *Peril*, caught in salty turmoil and darkness, not knowing which way was up.

Bumps Leddy, waiting on the beach to catch our dory's bow when we landed, waded into the waves, picked up the *Peril*'s gunwale, and lifted it, a feat of strength that probably saved my life. I felt Bumps's big hand grab at my shirt as he yanked me clear and stood me up. It had all happened too quickly for me to be as awed as I should have, but later I realized what Bumps had done. And I also learned that we should study the ocean and its behavior more carefully before we launch a dory into its heart.

Later, in May, we got our big haul, on the beach just to the east of Sonny Wainwright's rambling, white house. There were stripers everywhere. Peter, Jim, Bumps, and I were yelling as we tossed them thrashing higher onto the beach.

It was a haul to remember, a catch that hooked me on commercial fishing for the next seven years. And an experience that marked the start of my love for dories that has lasted a lifetime.

Captain Kidd

Once we began fishing, my life became all fishing. There was no other way to survive. I never would have made it through that first spring season with Jim and the *Peril* if I hadn't moved in with my grandparents when they opened the house on Georgica. Roddy B was such a gentle, generous soul. By that time, my grandmother was seriously stricken with Parkinson's disease, and Roddy B got very little sleep because he cared for her so diligently. He had every reason to be short-tempered, but he never greeted me with anything but a smile. He was genuinely excited by our fishing stories; he talked with us over coffee in his kitchen about boats, nets, and the migratory wanderings of the fish of eastern Long Island waters. And when I was pressed for cash to buy essential equipment, that oddly dapper but always considerate gentleman would "lend" me the money.

Not much: ninety dollars for my share of the haul-seine; twenty-five dollars for repairs to the Model A, small amounts but critical to my survival. But by October, Rodney and Emma had closed the house and returned to the city. I was quite on my own. The house was shuttered, my support system dismantled, and those wonderful Roddy B meals were no more. It was those I missed most.

We fished through the fall with erratic success: a few good hauls, many dry ones. But I had a backup occupation. In September I modified the *Emma*—yes, that *Emma*—for use as a bay scalloper. There is no more delicate or delicious shellfish, in my opinion, than the adductor muscle of the northern bay scallop. And the early 1950s were bonanza years for the tasty bivalve, a species that has since all but vanished from Long Island waters in spite of diligent conservation efforts.

Those efforts included strictly enforced catch limits and restrictions on catch methods. Only sail or hand power could be used to propel scalloping boats and the dredges they pulled. The larger boats sailed; sharpies like the *Emma* were hand-powered by a simple but effective system: an anchor fast to a long line was dropped and the boat powered away until all that line, at least 100 feet, was paid out; then the motor was shut down, the two dredges (or more if the scalloper was a Samson) tossed overboard, one from each side; then the scalloper went forward to the bow and hauled back the anchor line, hand over hand, pulling the boat and its dredges back to the anchor. As those steel and net dredges scraped along the bay bottom, scallops (if any there were) flipped back into the net bags. At the end of the tow, the full dredges were hoisted over the side and their contents dumped onto the culling board. There the scalloper bent over his catch, separating live scallops from hundreds of old and empty shells, seaweed, crabs, periwinkles, small fish, and all sorts of strange bottom-dwelling flora and fauna that made scalloping a continuing surprise. Just about everything came up in those dredges.

Hand-powered scallopers were limited to five bushels a day, and the bay constables were diligent enforcers. If the scalloping was good, even I, a beginner, could catch my limit and be ashore by two or three o'clock—provided, of course, we'd got on the water just after sunrise. But the catching was the fun part; then came the opening. Northern bay scallops—not to be confused with the southern, or calico, scallop—have a large, butter-colored adductor muscle, the one that opens and closes their shells. It is this part of the scallop that is its delicacy; the rest must be discarded, along with the shells.

To extract that muscle, you need skill and a scalloper's knife. I had the knife but no skill. I needed to hire a professional opener, or else stay up all night. Several of the Lester wives and sisters could open scallops fast enough to constantly keep one empty shell in the air. Which meant they picked up a closed scallop in one gloved hand, sliced it open with the knife they held in the other, and in the same motion flipped the top shell toward the big garbage pail at the end of their work table. With almost the same stroke of the knife, they would slice the muscle free of the bottom shell, flip the meat the other way into a clean, gallon container, and toss the bottom shell toward the garbage pail. And while that shell was still in the air, they'd have their hand around the next scallop and their knife moving toward its target. It was a wonderful thing to see.

If the scallops were fat, a bushel in the shell would yield a gallon of meat and a bit more. At prices that ranged from eight to ten dollars a gallon, on those days when I could get my five-bushel limit and after I paid my openers their two dollars a gallon, I would be taking home between thirty and forty dollars a day—about two hundred dollars a week for a six-day week doing what I liked best, being on the water. In those days, that wasn't bad money. Two hundred dollars in the fifties would equal about six hundred in the nineties. It often occurred to me that a handful of scallops taken from one of those gallons could be served at the Colony, my old luncheon spot, and the lucky diner would be charged about twice as much as I got for the gallon. But he wouldn't be living my life, and that's what counted.

At long last, after two decades of effort—much of it misguided, to be sure—the *Emma* and I were making money. In my thirtieth year I had somehow managed to prove myself, to take a living from the sea, to move myself onto a level of skill that allowed me to be called a bayman without condescension. And I was doing it aboard the *Emma*, the Macy's storebought rowboat that my grandfather had ordered off the floor so he could row my grandmother the length of Georgica Pond so she could call on her friend Mrs. Wolf, Sonny Wainwright's grandmother.

No one from those charmed times would have recognized my *Emma*. She had a ten-horse Johnson outboard fast to her stern. Outboards were not even allowed on Georgica. For another, she had my culling board laid across her gunwales amidships. And there in her small, narrow bow, more than one hundred feet of anchor warp lay piled, one end of it fast to a heavy, rusting grapple that Francis Lester had pulled from his gear-packed cellar and given to me to use. But most of all it was the detritus of the sea—the smashed barnacles, the clumps of seaweed, the rotted lumps of squashed sea squirts and stepped-on scallops—that changed the good, old, faithful, long-suffering *Emma* from a proper grandmother's rowing skiff to a working, sloppy, wet, and stinking scalloping sharpie. And that was only the beginning.

Scallop season ended in December, and haul seining, in spite of oft-told tales of that one big haul just in time for Christmas, was not worth the effort after Thanksgiving. Many of the Lesters began cod fishing: taking their dories miles offshore and setting trawls baited with skimmer-clam chunks. Even if the *Peril* had been a larger, more able dory, I would not hazard a December trip far out onto the Atlantic. That took more courage and skill than I possessed.

Most other baymen opted for clamming: digging or raking hard clams—*Venus mercenaria*—from area inshore waters. The majority worked Montauk Lake, which in those days had a soft bottom, much of it covered by a green, single-bladed underwater grass that was responsible for the good clamming. Those dense blades of grass sheltered larval clams as they made their transition from tiny free-swimming newborns to shelled bivalves the size of pinheads, that then dug their way into the soft bottom and began growing. Because it had been a freshwater lake before it was opened to the Sound to create a splendid harbor, Montauk Lake was rich in natural nutrients and had just the right salinity and tidal activity to make it an exceptional shellfish environment. That was then. These days, so I'm told, the lakeside construction of summer homes, motels, restaurants, and marinas has generated runoffs that have altered the critical balance so essential to hard-clam fecundity.

But when I trailered the *Emma* the twenty-some miles from East Hampton to Montauk Lake, there were still plenty of clams to be had, if you could dig them from that tenacious bottom. There were three digging options: scratch raking, tonging, and bull raking. Like most clammers, I had each of the three distinctly different implements needed for the job, but I never learned how to do well with any of them. Scratch raking meant wearing waders and walking out into water up to your waist or a bit farther. The scratch rake was indeed a long-toothed rake with an attached wire basket and a longish wooden handle with a short horizontal piece about halfway up the handle shaft. If I gripped that crosspiece firmly with both hands and rested the top of the long handle on my shoulder, I could, if I worked at it, put enough pressure on the underwater, business end of the apparatus to dig the rake's tines into the rocks, shells, and mud deep enough to dislodge clams from their tight little homes, provided I could yank the rake back toward me with enough force to dislodge my quarry.

It proved to be exceedingly hard work, and intensely uncomfortable in December. But then, as I was soon to learn, there is no easy way to go clamming for a living.

I went from scratching to tonging, always in search of major results with a minor effort. Tongs are a complex implement, worked standing up from a boat, preferably as far out over the gunwale as you can lean without falling overboard (which has been known to happen to tongers here and there). Imagine a pair of ice tongs with straight, twelve-foot wooden handles. Then forget the single tongs and add two pronged rakes in their place, each about eighteen inches wide. Add a wire basket atop the opening and closing jaws of the two pivoting rakes and you have a device that I found about as difficult to operate efficiently as a spade with no handle. What I was supposed to do was open and close the upper end of the wooden handles. This, in turn, opened and closed the toothed, raking jaws at the lower end and popped clams into the wire basket.

Hey, a physics teacher could tell you how clamming tongs are supposed to work, but I never met a physics teacher who could make money clamming. No one I ever saw, except for the third-

generation baymen who worked alongside me with damnable efficiency, could master a pair of tongs. I either dug them so deep in the bottom I all but capsized the *Emma* trying to yank them free, or, if I did snag a clam or two, it slipped out because I could never shut my tongs properly before I hand-over-handed them straight up from the bottom.

When I told Francis Lester of my troubles, he suggested a bull rake might serve me better. "All you need bull rakin' is a strong back and a weak mind," he said. Then he laughed as he added, "The weaker the better, they tell me."

I was eminently qualified cerebrally and, in those days, physically. But first I had to find a bull rake. They were not easy to come by. They seemed to be inherited by generational baymen like Francis and Milt Miller. They were just part of the gear that seemed to breed

in the dark corners of their cellars and turn up whenever it was needed: gear like fikes and whitebait seines and eel spears and clam baskets and scallop nets, dredges and knives and oarlocks and bay seines and corks and leads and wire baskets, cod hooks and blue-fish spoons, crab nets and eel pots and trap stakes and bunts and gill nets and trammel nets and sturgeon nets, bilge pumps and wader patches and wheel bearings and cotter pins, cotton twine and seine needles and a half-dozen different kinds of six-thread rope: hard-laid, tarred, soft-laid, and salvaged from some wreck they'd found washed ashore on a beach that only they could navigate.

But I was born handicapped; I had no such cellar. I had to take the ferries to Greenport and walk to East End Supply and buy a bull rake. Those demonic devices were never mass produced; the ones sold at East End Supply—a genuine headquarters for the region's commercial fishermen—were made by a blacksmith who lived near Riverhead. Bull rakes are large; that's the first impression they give. They are welded from spring steel. The largest—with thirty-two teeth, which is what I ordered—costs two dollars a tooth, a major investment. It looks like a garden rake on drugs. The teeth, if they were straight, would be about a foot long. But they are curved in something more than a half-circle—say, about two hundred degrees around. And they are spaced precisely an inch apart because a clam less than an inch thick was illegal in those days. The teeth are welded to a single piece of straight, steel stock, each tooth precisely fitted so the sharp, tapered, business ends of those teeth line up like thirty-two steel fingers sprouted from that steel bar. Because they are spring steel, the teeth can flex, which is what they do when a bull rake has been worked deep into the mud and then yanked, inch by inch, through that bottom.

The yanking is done by the strong-backed witless clammer aboard the *Emma* on the surface of Montauk Lake. He is connected to the bull rake by a long, thin yellow-pine pole—say, about twenty-two feet long. It has a ten-inch handle mounted crosswise at its upper end. That's the handle the clammer yanks on.

When he's tugged his guts out through his asshole and into his waders, he breaks the bull rake free of the mud and tries to pull it hand-over-hand up to the skiff. Because it's full of deep lake mud, black and pungent, the rake—heavy enough on its own, empty— weighs more than one hundred pounds. When, at last, it surfaces, the clammer swings the long handle back, horizontally, so the weight of the rake ends up a few inches outboard of the gunwale, counter- balanced, you hope. Then, as gently as possible at first, the clammer begins to slosh the rake back and forth in the water, washing out the mud bit by bit. As silt clouds the bay, clams too large to slip through the rake's curved tines begin to show up, looking lovelier and lovelier as they lose their mud coating. Sometimes there can be thirty or forty clams, almost a half-peck in one haul.

Sometimes. But not too often in my case. No, what happened to me most often at first was more on the downside of bull raking: my pole would snap in two just as I tried to lever the rake up to the gunwale. Then the rake would splash back into the water, lose all its clams, and be hauled back by its safety line empty while I went about fitting it with a new pole. I always carried at least three in the boat, and there were days when I had to drive the Model A all the way back to East Hampton to get more poles from Frank Smith's lumberyard.

On one of those days as I returned in the blackest of moods, I backed the Model A down onto the gravel beach on the west side of Montauk Lake. The *Emma* waited there, loyal and patient as always. My bull rake with its fractured handle rested on the rocky beach beside the sharpie. In my haste to get back on the water, I backed too far and too heedlessly. The "A" fetched up a bit and when I got out to study the reason, I discovered I'd backed over my own bull rake, pushing several of its sharp tines through my right rear tire, already almost flat. Distorted by being run over, the rake's critical shape had been bent into a caricature of the graceful curves that made it function. In a few seconds I had ruined my day, damaged a tire, rendered myself immobile, and crushed my $64 rake beyond repair. I had to jack up the "A" where she stood, take off the wheel, roll it out to the road, and hitch a ride to a filling station in Montauk Village. And, because the tide was rising, I had to hurry.

When I got home—well, where we lived that winter—my new wife asked me how I'd done that day, a question she asked with some apprehension every evening when I returned from my outings aboard the *Emma*. We lived in a small summer cottage on the tip of Louse Point in the Springs, a place given to us for the winter by generous Joe Liss, a writer of big-time television scripts who was a friend of my friend Peter Scott. From the windows of the tiny house, I could look out over Acabonac Creek and Gardiners Bay, a splendid view during the summer, but a bit intimidating in February when salt ice ringed the shore and north winds huffed across the harbor. The place had no heat other than a Franklin stove that I kept red-hot with cannel coal. The stove was too small to hold a fire overnight, and we often awakened to find our fresh water reserves, hand-pumped from a well outdoors, wearing a cover of ice. No wonder Cynthia asked about my progress as a clammer. We lived on the brink of survival, and I was about to drop off the edge.

With that thought in mind, and facing daily battles with my (new) bull rake, I began to think about easier ways to make a living. But I would not give up my life on the water. So I began to take a scholarly interest in hard clams, using Aristotelian principles of logic. (See, I learned something at Yale.) I reasoned that it might make my life a great deal more enjoyable if I could find a way to grow my own clams—a notion that only a true innocent could take seriously.

Which led me to the library and a book titled *Marine Products of Commerce*, which in turn led me to Dr. Victor Loosanoff, a marine biologist (and Yale graduate) who directed the U.S. Fish & Wildlife Service, Department of Marine Fisheries Research Laboratory in Bridgeport, Connecticut, just across the sound. Dr. Loosanoff, I learned from the literature, was developing methods of spawning and hatching and growing hard-clam larvae in the laboratory, where he had successfully kept them for a year, when they could be transplanted to a proper marine environment. By the time they were a year old, their survival rate in the wild would be high.

Wow. Someone had already had my idea! I worked with Dr. Loosanoff for a week in his lab while he patiently showed me the basics of hard-clam husbandry. I hadn't been back more than week, when I ran into S. Kip Farrington, author, big-game angler, friend of Hemingway, and manager of the Maidstone Mugwumps softball team, for which I played right field every summer Sunday. I was not a big-league right fielder, my teammates called me "Awky" (short for awkward), but Kip had a spiky sense of humor and not only kept me on the team but became my friend.

He was also a friend of another big-game angler, Joe Gale, a Manhattan Buick dealer who had made millions selling cars after the war. Joe, for reasons I never quite understood, had leased Gardiners Island for two years, and when I told Kip about my work with clam farming he quickly suggested I continue my efforts on Gardiners Island. I think Kip really believed I knew what I was talking about. As he did when it came to hooking, fighting, and landing giant bluefin tuna, Joe Gale took Kip's advice on many other topics, including clam farming, a shellfish technology so avant-garde in 1953 that I was its only in-the-field practitioner.

But if location was the key to success, then there could be no better spot than Gardiners Island. With three protected, saltwater tidal ponds on its south, west, and north sides, each 100 percent unbothered by runoff, each biologically pristine, and each owned outright from bottom to top by the lords of the island (some of the only such riparian rights in the nation), those diligently protected waters were ideally suited to my experimental efforts.

I would have moved to Gardiners even if the ponds weren't so suitable. The place had always fascinated me. When we were in college, Sonny Wainwright and I would take off from the East Hampton Airport in his small Cessna and land on the short, grass airstrip on the island's south end. We would bring our shotguns, jump out the moment the plane stopped rolling, flush some of the stocked pheasant from the sumac and barberry alongside the run-way, drop two or three, pick up our birds, and be taking off by the time an angry Charley Raynor, the gamekeeper, had heard our shots, jumped in his Jeep to catch us, and maybe even shot us (he had a black reputation, indeed).

Yet during my clam summer, Charley was my boss, but the island was our adventure. Cynthia and I lived in a farmhouse that had been there since before the Revolutionary War. A checkerboard etched in the floor had been carved by a British soldier during the War of 1812. The island's colonial history began in 1639, when Lion Gardiner bought its 3,350 lush acres from the Montaukett Indians (for ten bolts of cloth). He had left Europe after the Low Country wars and came to America as the officer in charge of building a fort at Saybrook in what would become Connecticut.

But the island's most notorious legends were told about Captain William Kidd, the pirate who plundered ships of every nation from the Caribbean to Charleston and beyond. Those legends repeat tales of buried treasure on Gardiners Island and more tales of plunder shared by Bill Kidd and John Gardiner. Few of them were proved, but gold coins were reported washed ashore on the sand spit called Gardiners Point on the northwest end of the island, where later a fort, now in ruins, was built.

I had grown up listening to those legends, and had camped overnight at the old fort, before the war and before it was used as a practice target by navy dive bombers. I had been taught to swim by Fanny Gardiner, and had heard more stories about that island's ducks, geese, turkey, and deer. So whether or not my clam experiment had a chance, I wanted the opportunity to live for a while on that fabled shore.

Our adventure got off to a great start when I learned that my duties included becoming the skipper of the *Captain Kidd*, the forty-two-foot Nova Scotia utility and fishing boat that Joe Gale had bought and had delivered by two Novi tuna fishermen. Built strictly for work, she was a broad-beam, high-bow, low-stern vessel with a trunk cabin and the sweeping lines of a Maine lobster boat. Her cabin was far forward, which made for a wide and spacious after-deck, quite unobstructed and covered with loose-fitting spruce planks in case they had to be taken up for work on the propellor shaft and steering linkage. Like so many Novi boats, she was built primarily of spruce, a soft wood, but readily available on Nova Scotia's coast where just about every man over twenty could build a boat. They built them cheap, they built them big, and they built them so easily that they didn't worry too much about how long they might hold together. When they had done their work, another would be built.

The *Captain Kidd* had a converted Buick engine (perhaps one reason Joe Gale bought her) freshwater cooled with copper pipes running from its radiator the length of its hull and back. In frigid Nova Scotia waters, the system worked well. In Gardiners Bay during the summer, I had to be careful about overheating and boiling away my coolant.

Other than that, she was an impressive boat, the largest I had ever skippered and I felt great at her wheel. She had a shift lever (forward-neutral-reverse) that looked like a track switching mecha-nism for the Long Island Railroad, a three-foot stalk of steel that stuck up through the deck on the boat's starboard side just inside the wheelhouse. Her single propellor was huge, pitched to take a deep bite. With serious reduction gears in place, that prop turned slowly, but chewed into so much water that the *Captain Kidd*, once underway, had a lovely, ponderous, gliding momentum. She was easy on fuel (another Novi trademark), and because her hull was so gracefully rounded and curved, she moved through the Gardiners Bay chop as if she were greased.

I made the trip from the island dock to the commercial dock at Three Mile Harbor about twice a week, picking up groceries and supplies for the clam breeding station I was setting up in what had been a small granary at the island dock's inshore end. Tides move forcefully around the clock through Three Mile's deep and narrow channel, and I loved bringing the *Captain Kidd* alongside the dock's high pilings and its tarred bulkhead. With her big single screw, she had to be maneuvered quite differently from the twin-screw launch I'd handled at Fishers Island.

The *Captain Kidd* behaved like a lady with slow reflexes: if you tapped her knee with a hammer, you'd wait about a minute for her foot to kick up. But once I got the knack, I could make her dance. I'd ride a flood tide up the channel, swing wide just above the dock, head into the tide, spin the automobile steering wheel mounted on the cabin bulkhead, throw that huge shift lever into reverse, and punch the throttle up to about 3,000 rpm. That big, beamy boat would shudder as her prop took hold, and if everything worked, she'd slow, stop, and slide almost sideways until she nudged the dock with barely a thump. As the summer moved through July and August, I got better and better at that maneuver; I began to hope people would be snapper fishing from the dock—as they often did—so I could show off.

In addition to setting up the breeding station, which was not as complex as it sounds, I had to make scientific observations of the Gardiners Island tidal ponds. I took bottom samples, tested water for purity and salinity, took water temperatures at different times and tides, and also did a bit of clam digging (scratch rake) to get some idea of the natural fecundity of the waters we hoped to use as clam-growing greenhouses. I loved the work, if you could call it that. I didn't. Being able to wander alone over the hills, fields, and towering forests of that fascinating island was my idea of a great way to spend a day, or a week, or an entire summer.

Often I jumped deer in the brush where they had laid up for the day hoping to escape most of the summer heat. They would scramble to their feet and take off with those high, popping leaps, their white tails rising and falling like gently bouncing dandelion seeds. Pheasant were everywhere, and, in the woods under the arching beech trees, I saw turkeys every now and then, the tom in front of a stately procession of hens who picked up each foot and put it down as if they were practicing a cheerleader's strut.

And Charley Raynor, who I thought must have learned that I was one of the airborne poachers, gave me other chores. During August's warmest week, I had to clean out a henhouse that looked to me as if it hadn't been tended since those British prisoners had been pardoned. I dug through about three feet of solidified chicken shit and wondered what the assignment had to do with my clam-farming experiments. But no one argued with Charley.

The large, fertile clams that spawned millions of eggs and sperm whenever the water temperature reached a bit above 70 degrees Fahrenheit (about 22°) did their thing in the controlled temperatures of my small but productive breeding station. If all the fertilized eggs that I helped hatch had become littlenecks I could have loaded a string of barges and retired on my Fulton Fish Market checks. But those eggs needed time to become swimming larvae, and then the tiny seed clams that we hoped would populate the Gardiners ponds.

While the metamorphosis was under way, I had considerable free time and spent most of it as far from Charley as I could—which meant I was "doing research" at the northernmost tip of the island, where I checked on the life cycle of the clams in Bostwick Pond. I noticed that every day, in every corner of that sizable tidal pond, green crabs were doing a job on young clams. I'd first see the crab digging into the mud and sand, then reaching in with its claw, almost always coming up with a dime-size clam. Once on hold, the clamshell would be crushed and its insides daintly transferred from half-shell to crab mouth. I made a note in my lab journal that the first step toward a successful clam farm might have to be a green crab eradication program.

In September, Joe Gale came up with another way to tap the island for a portion of his rent money. He invited his city friends out for what was called a deer hunt, but was little more than a deer shoot. Those creatures had never been hunted and were just wary

enough to keep from being stepped on when I surprised them in
their day beds. But I had to stay out of the woods and under deep
cover during the early autumn weeks when those metropolitan
nimrods blasted away, slaughtering deer right and left.

Charley Raynor appointed me the official deer dresser, and each
day he would ride the island roads in his flatbed truck, loading it
with dead deer. Once he had a truckful he'd dump it near the
outbuilding that I called the slaughterhouse. It had a crossbeam
with two hooks so I could hoist a deer carcass, tail up, and catch its
two hind legs on the hooks. Then I'd slice the deer's belly from tail
to stem and reach in with both hands and haul out guts full of
grapes, acorns, and grass that the once lively creatures had ingested.
Not my favorite job, but I wasn't saying no to Charley.

When I had the day's deer dressed and cleaned, I'd haul them
down to the dock and toss each carcass onto that broad afterdeck of
the *Captain Kidd*. At midnight, or thereabouts, when very few folks
on the mainland were up and about, I'd take the *Captain Kidd* across
Gardiners Bay, up the Three Mile Harbor channel to the head of the
harbor where a truck waited. In the dark just before dawn, I'd help
load the truck and then, around three in the morning, make my
wonderfully solitary way back to the island. Meanwhile, the deer
were headed for the venison chefs at Luchow's and the "21" Club.

It was on those nights that I most loved the old *Captain Kidd*.
With that big prop flopping over and her sweet hull gliding across
the dark waters, she would carry me on a timeless journey under the
dazzling equinoctial stars of September. With a touch of frost on
the northwest wind, and often the whistle of gathering wildfowl
on the breeze, those solitary nights had a kind of enchantment about
them, as if I could steer that boat forever across that sweet saucer of
a bay on an endless voyage toward the dawn.

But that was not to be. As the summer ended, so did a realistic
notion of continuing my work in the clam lab. The building was
unheated; ice would soon cover much of the tidal ponds. I said
good-bye to the *Captain Kidd*, that magic island, my infant clams,

and the security of what was almost a regular job. We could afford to rent a small place for the winter, a place in The Springs, just down the road from Jackson and Lee Pollock, Joe Liebling, Barbara Hale, Julian Levy, Harold Rosenberg, Tino Nivola, Bill de Kooning, and a bunch of other artists and writers who became our friends and somehow encouraged me to keep on trying to make a living fishing, even though I never got good at it.

The *Emma* and I went back to work, this time at a different sort of clamming, and as winter became spring, my career was boosted by the start of serious relationships with two new boats in my life.

The following summer, a much accredited marine biologist from Rutgers spent three months on Gardiners Island studying the feasibility of clam farming there. The primary conclusion of his 110-page report was that little could be done with the ponds unless the green crab population was eliminated.

So much for science.

Work Boats

After the Gardiners Island interlude, I had to go to work, real work. My days aboard the *Emma*, the *Peril*, the Fishers Island Country Club launch, and the *Captain Kidd* had brought me some money, but it was an aside, a fringe benefit of days that I considered spent in the pursuit of pleasure. If we labored fourteen or sixteen hours in soggy boots and soaked oilskins for a few pounds of fish, or a bushel of cherrystones, I never thought about whether our catch would bring enough cash for groceries, gasoline for the Model A, and perhaps a bottle of Gilbey's London Dry gin, which I was in the habit of drinking straight, on the rocks, in those days when my body seemed impervious to whatever punishments I might bestow.

I never thought about much of anything because I was living a dream, my dream of ecstasy on earth. Which meant I could either be on the water in a boat small enough to communicate wind, wave, and wonder; or I could be in the water, feeling its pressures against the skin of my waders, nudging its bottom with my feet, witnessing the fine surprise of a sand-covered skate blossoming in alarm at my step and flying into the violet darkness of the offshore depths with a ripple of its pale wings. Such natural extravaganzas were the currency of my sustenance, and as I acquired them day after brilliant day, the real due bills of life were accumulating at home with devastating frequency. But to me, debt was an alien presence in the corner of the room, beyond my comprehension or my concern. The notion that I owed was, in a kind of blind madness, not able to be translated to action, or even anxiety, by my conscience. One of the gears that drives responsible maturity was missing from my makeup.

But by the early 1950s, my wife was doing her best to impress me with the gravity of my moral omissions. Our son would soon be born. The long-forgiving merchants in the stores where she traded were pressing her to stem my flooding debts. And on those evanescent days when I would sway in tune with the northwest wind across Gardiners Bay, or surge with the swells that caressed the ocean beach, she would be home dreading the knock on the door or the summons of the telephone.

There were abrasive discussions of surrender, a return to desks, executives, and no matter what price had to be paid, the possession of a regular paycheck. But I would not surrender my life with the water; I would never deny my mistress. What I promised, and what I did, was to recalibrate my time with her. What I tried to do was what I knew others had done. After all, there were commercial fishermen on Long Island's East End who paid their bills, sent their children to school, visited a dentist, and kept a relatively new automobile, along with a pickup truck, in their driveway. I could, I promised Cynthia, be like them. At the time, it was a promise I thought I could keep.

I got off to a good start when I joined Captain Ted Lester's haul-seining crew. Uncle to Francis, brother to Frank, Bill, and Happy, uncle to Harry and Richard and Bill, father to Stewart, husband of

Jenny, and a relative of scores of Lesters whose forebears had settled eastern Long Island shortly after Lion Gardiner acquired his island from the Indians, Ted Lester was the most energetic, quick-tempered, impulsive, hard-driving, stubborn, and hyperactive fisherman of a notable fishing clan with almost three centuries of absorbed fishing knowledge accumulated in their collective subconscious. Of the Lesters with haul-seining crews on the beach (Ted, Bill, Francis, and Frank), only Captain Ted would take on "foreigners," a term that classified anyone not born to an eastern Long Island fishing family of at least three generations. Ted, his brothers explained, accepted volunteer foreigners because, his detractors and competitors claimed, he could subtract a larger share of the catch proceeds for himself and his equipment.

I never discovered any such imbalances. Ted supplied the truck that towed the gear and powered one winch, another vehicle with the second winch, the longest—more than 300 fathoms—haul-seine on the beach, and the heaviest, largest dory I had ever seen. It was my job to row that dory's bow oars while Captain Ted stood in her stern, setting the seine, grasping handfuls of twine and coils of the net's lead line, flinging them overboard with each stroke of our oars. If I, or my companion oarsman amidships (either Clarence Midgett, a generational fisherman, or Peter Scott or, later, Peter Matthiessen, both foreigners like me) missed a stroke, caught a crab, or, worst of all, popped an oar out of its place between the thole pins, Ted would quickly make it plain that we'd better get our shit together, and the sooner the better. Each morning when Captain Ted arose from his bed—usually an hour before dawn—he had only one plan for his day: to catch fish. It was the rocket that powered him, that kept him moving, literally, for fourteen to sixteen hours at a stretch. And he expected no less of his crew, nor would he condone it. If you could not keep up with him, Captain Ted left you behind.

My part of keeping up meant helping to launch that monster dory, rowing it through the surf, helping to beach it, and then, after I had helped to haul back the seine and sort and toss our catch into Ted's truck, loading the dory onto her trailer and then clambering back into her stern where I worked with a partner to reload the seine and make everything ready for our next set. Ted, being the man he so definitely was, wanted our reloading time kept as brief as possible. As the truck's only driver, he pulled us along the beach a bit faster than our reloading speed, so we always had to horse the heavy waterlogged and sand-covered seine into the dory, or else watch it straighten out behind us as Ted tried to tow us, dory, and unloaded net to the next dot in the ocean where he believed he could smell a pod of fish so large it would make us all wealthy men.

With a net close to a half-mile long, the setting, hauling back, emptying, and reloading process took almost two hours, provided nothing went wrong. When I fished with Ted, he liked to make at least six sets a day—close to twelve hours of hard work, provided nothing went wrong, which it so often did. And then, at the long day's end, we would return to Ted's packing house to wash, weigh, pack, ice, and box our catch. Up at four in the morning; home, if we were lucky, by nine in the evening. Few workers behind those desks that I dreaded worked seventeen hours, sometimes for very little money, or none at all. Yet I considered my "regular job" with Captain Ted's crew a step toward maturity as well as a labor of love.

That dory was my office, her forward thwart my desk. She had no name. None of the Lester dories had names; the Lesters were realists, not romantics. They had their dories built in Nova Scotia and shipped down on the deck of one of Perry Duryea's lobster carriers, fast boats with huge live wells that made the run from Montauk to the Provinces once or twice a month to buy lobsters low and bring them back to Montauk, where they could be sold high to scores of restaurants from the Hamptons to Manhattan. Those Novi dories were built by men like the Lesters, built to do hard work in the hands of hardworking fishermen. Those Novi dories made the *Blue Peril* look like a porcelain cream pitcher alongside a milk pail. Every part of Ted's dory was massive. Her oak rails were three inches wide; her knees could support a three-story building; and her mighty planking worked from towering Nova Scotia pines seemed sturdy enough to withstand a cannonball fired from the decks of one of *Captain Kidd*'s corsairs.

Somewhere in Nova Scotia there is a fellow who mixes the dirty mustard-yellow paint that was slapped on those dories just before they were loaded aboard Perry's lobster carriers. Why the color was chosen, I've never known. But I know what it means to me: it means a boat that made me work harder than I've ever worked before or since.

How well I came to know those dories; how well I know them still. Over the five years I rowed those bow oars for Captain Ted, he went through two dories and had a start on a third. Each was the twin of the other, each fashioned from the same woods—primarily yellow pine and oak—built on the same frames and, for all I knew, by the same builder. Had it not been for their immortal design, ancient, tested, and so traditionally inviolate that no dory builder dared dilute its purity, those massive dories could have been ugly, such was the candor of their functional statement. Like a shovel, a hoe, a hammer, a mattock, and like the unadorned, unpainted (for a reason) twelve-foot oak oars that hung so heavy in my hands, those dories were created over the centuries to work the seas of the world, to do a job, day after day, night after night, in whatever waters they were launched, unafraid of wave, wind, cold, or even the breaking seas that crashed on our beach with such tumbling mass that they set the ground atremble a mile inshore.

Ted, impatient, driven, almost reckless, often set his seine in an ocean that challenged a dory's limits. Many dawns, standing there in the half-dark, watching the still-dark seas breaking over the bar a half-mile beyond the beach, the white tumult of rolling surf luminous in the night, I heard Bill tell his crew they could take the rigs back to the yard. "We'll come back and look at it around ten o'clock," Bill would say, "when the sun is up, maybe them seas will lay down. Right now, it ain't fit to haul."

But Ted would wait there on the beach, the hissing, rumbling sea wrapping us in the chill blanket of its song; when Bill and the other crews had left, he would say, "We'll wait here and give it a try. As soon as I can make out those seas coming offshore, we'll find a slatch and get out there." And wait we would until the sun rose on the eastern horizon over a dirty-gray sea dabbed with the whitecaps of a snorting southwest wind. In the spring, because the fish migrated from west to east, headed "up" the coast, we set our seines east to west so the first lengths dropped just behind the breakers would become a fence, blocking those fish from their mission, holding them in confusion long enough to complete our half-circle and thus trap the fish within the net's fluid wall.

Which meant that because the southwest wind prevailed during the early spring when the migration was at its strongest, we had to row into the wind and into the chop it generated. And when that chop was stacked atop surging swells, some of them eight to ten feet tall, the dory became a cross on which its oarsmen were crucified.

With Ted at the stern, his water-blue eyes squinting into the rising sun as he sought to decipher the ocean's inscrutable codes, I would wait at the bow oars—unpainted so the oarsmen could get a better grip on the rough, raw oak—the gunwales of the dory so high-sided that my hands were held chest high. Sometimes on those mornings when the Atlantic pushed us to the limits of our dory's capabilities, we would wait there in the wash for as long as thirty or forty minutes. As stubborn and as implacable as the sea, Ted's search for a launching moment became a battle of wills—his against the Atlantic's.

As we wallowed there in the wash, the dory rising, falling, sliding, yawing, and tugging at the crew's hands and bodies that held and braced it, I would be the only man aboard. There was no small talk; too much depended on being able to hear Ted's orders the second they were given. And I was never to look over my shoulder out at the sea that rolled toward me: that could set my adrenaline rushing on the torrents of anxiety a breaking swell could bring. No, I faced

resolute to the stern, looking down most of the length of the dory
that held my soul in its impeccable design.

I would study my protector, and because there were so many of
those waitings there at the edge of my future, I knew every knot in
every one of the dory's sturdy knees. I could gauge the wear of her
oak rub rails, see the sand and fish slime compacted in every crevice
and joining. I knew how the great seine was hanked into its massive
mound in the dory's high stern, piled there with such weight that it
seemed a miracle that we, just the two of us on those clumsy,
intractable, laborious heavy oars, could ever hope to move such an
ungainly, overweight, and overloaded presence.

It did not happen easily. When, at last, Ted would make his
decision to go, his face contorted with effort as he shoved on the
dory's high stern, up to his crotch in the swirling wash of the waves,
while I and the oarsman amidships took our first stroke, that crucial
exertion, the initial pull against the power of the sea, the stroke that
would set us in motion, give life to the sodden mass that wallowed
there at the edge of doom.

How hard we pulled. Our booted feet jammed against the ridge
of the cross-braces on the dory's bottom, our oars as far forward as
we could get them as we leaned toward the stern, we would dig, in
precise unison, our oar blades into the surf, the leveraged strain
raising both our asses from our seats so we stood, all our strength
and weight transferred to the rough handles of our oars, the oak
wands bending, bowing with the strain.

"Pull, boys, pull!" Ted would shout. It is a cry that has stayed with
me for four decades. And we would pull, and in spite of seas
breaking against her bow, that huge, high-sided, heavy, soggy, beat-
up, work-worn dory would begin to move, to glide actually, into the
open sea—a beached whale come to wonderful, even graceful life as
she feels the waves at her breast.

And in all those years, all those falls and springs, all those many
launchings into all those fierce seas, never once were we forced
back, never once did we fail to make our set. I have watched other

crews swamped at the surf's edge. And I have watched as Captain Frank's sons, Richard and Harry, were hurled from their massive dory as she pitchpoled, upended, her bow screaming toward the clouded sky, her stern buried in the surf as a great wave lifted the dory up and then over, tumbling onto herself, the men yelling there looking down into the sea from their seats at the vortex of the violence, then vanishing in the surf's creamy confusion, trapped there beneath their dory and the swirling folds of their seine. Men rushed from the beach up to their shoulders into the sea, ducking down, reaching under the surging beached whale of a dory still bottom up in the wash. And when it seemed no one could survive there under the weight of that whale, Richard and then Harry were pulled free and stood in the surf in their dripping oilskins, the alarm still in their eyes, their wet hair lying like seaweed over their open-mouthed faces.

Such moments of terror are long remembered. But even though Ted's reputation for recklessness was the stuff of stories among East End fishermen, there were few moments of real danger during the years I pulled those bow oars. He was an instinctive seaman whose three centuries of fishing forebears spoke within him as he pondered the sea, sky, and wind, assessing the risk of its challenge. It was those voices, his commanding presence, and the dory's immortal seaworthiness that combined to become the spine of our design for taking a living from the sea.

We even set seine at night, so pervasive was Ted's desire, at the very same beach where Chick and I dragged the *Emma* across from Georgica to the Atlantic. In late autumn, a small bulldozer from the Village of East Hampton Highway Department would clank and snort its way onto the beach. With its blade shoving sand before it, the 'dozer crawled from pond to beach, carving a shallow ditch in the sand. So full was Georgica from the fall rains of equinoctial storms that it would send a stream flooding the bulldozer's gouge in the sand. Within an hour, that stream became a torrent, washing more sand from the beach, cutting a moving swath four to six feet deep and a hundred feet across. In that brackish river that collided there with the sea, tens of thousands of silversides, herring, mummychogs, and elvers swam, swept to the surf by their home water on the move. Waiting there in the very wash of the breakers were the striped bass, called to this anomaly by sensors we still do not understand.

In Lester parlance, the Georgica Gut set was as close to a sure thing as haul-seiners could get. So fertile was that brackish pond of my boyhood that multitudes of oceanic fish would gather there within hours after the joining of the waters. With six or seven crews on the beach, the strategy for being the first to haul a net around the pond outlet was a mixture of stamina and tradition. For traditionally, no seining crew rolled on to the beach much before dawn; that, at least, was the way it had always been. And the crew that arose earliest and got to Georgica Gut first made the first, virginal set.

Tradition meant nothing to Ted. After losing the set to his brother the previous October, Ted decided to set at night. We parked the trucks and the dory there around ten and watched the moon rise. In its pale light, we could see the breakers on the bar that formed offshore whenever the gut was open. We could hear the rumble and hiss of the breaking surf, the short, quick seas rolling eastward under a moderately brisk southwest wind, still chopping at the Atlantic's surface as it had all afternoon.

"We'll wait for the flood tide," Ted had said when we arrived on the beach. "High water will bring them fish right up in the wash."

So we sat there on the cold sand in our waders, leaning against the truck tires and the trailer, watching the sea in the moonlight, gauging the thrust of the breakers, their sharpness, their frequency, trying there in the dark to decode the mystery of the blurred messages the sea sent us, one after the other as the rollers broke luminous under the moon.

Around midnight, we backed the dory down on her trailer,

poised there in the wash. Then, at last, we slid her off over the roller so she thumped heavily to the wet sand, then stirred as the first wavelets of the rising tide washed under her.

Ted stared off at the horizon, as if he could decipher the confusion of the seas where the pond and the ocean embraced a few hundred feet offshore. The torrent of waters gushing seaward altered the more predictable rhythms of the Atlantic swells. No longer were there wave series, each in its stately order. Instead, the mixing of pond and sea created a confusion of patterns with waters peaking as two sets of thrusts collided from several directions. At night, in the dark, without lights, such conditions were almost beyond the scope of comprehension and planning, even for Ted.

I think he knew it. But he behaved as if he could understand the timing his crew and his dory would have to follow to make a successful set. The moon was high overhead when Ted told me to get in the dory. There, with the pond's current flowing toward the sea, I would have some help getting the dory underway. We rose and fell there in the wash for a few minutes and then Ted called, "Let's go," and we were headed into the dark unknown.

There was nothing for me to do but pull on the oars. Even if I looked over the bow, I could see nothing but white water where the seas broke on the bar—the bar we would skirt—setting our seine as close to its inshore edge as possible.

The dory, that fine, heavy, imperturbable Novi dory, never complained. Jostled in the irregular seas, thumped by short chops from two sides, she kept moving, her high, narrow bow finding its own way in the dark. When we turned the corner at the edge of the bar, there on my right I could see rollers breaking, the white surf of their foaming crests glowing in the moonlight with their own luminous phosphorescence.

Ted had few visible landmarks to tell him how far we had come, how much seine was left to be set. If we went too far, we could not get ashore without abandoning our effort and leaving the net's end swinging free in the sea. But if we did not go far enough, we would have a hundred feet of twine still in the stern when we came ashore: heavy, risky, and a waste.

There were many reasons why none of the other crews would make a midnight haul: not being able to judge the surf or the dimensions of the set were just two of them. And if the dory should swamp there in the darkness out on the bar, there could be no rescue. We would have to strip our waders and swim for it, if we were free of entrapment by our own net.

In the hissing surf as Ted tossed over the bunt—the seine's deep purse at its center—feeling the dory pitch in the slam of the breakers against her sides, I thought about the irony of a mishap in that place, almost the precise spot in the sea where I had struck the shark with that flimsy eel spear, my first ocean adventure. Now, here I was, almost twenty years later, rowing in breaking surf in the darkness of deep night.

At Ted's calling, we turned the corner and headed inshore, the going easier as the seas rumbled at our stern. There was no need to wait for a calm spell; no one could tell what the waves were doing in the dark. We rowed as best we could until the dory rose on a breaking wave just as the net's jack went over the stern and Ted held rope in his hands. We had cut it a bit close, but the entire net was set and we were riding ashore on the bumpy backs of the waves.

When we had winched in our net, we learned we had surrounded about four tons of striped bass, most of them weighing between four and ten pounds—perfect market fish. The bunt was so full, and the shoals so thin alongside the gut, Ted stripped the gears in his huge truck—a World War II relic of the desert campaign—trying to pull the bunt from the sea. We had to wade in, cut holes through the heavy twine with knives, and wrestle the fish free by hand, tossing them to high ground where they were soon covered with dry sand and looked more like driftwood than striped bass. It was dawn by the time we finished; and as the sun rose, Bill Lester arrived with his crew, looked at the great mound of fish, and said, "Well, got a

bunch, did you. Good for you. Come on, boys, we'll head east."
There was no rancor in his words, but he shook his head a bit as he
looked over at his brother Ted still trying to repair the shattered
transmission, lying under the truck with black oil dripping in his
face.

The day did not end until the evening when, so weary we began
laughing at almost anything anyone said, we finished washing the
fish clean of their beach-sand skins, weighing them, and boxing
them in wooden boxes about the size of orange crates, but much
sturdier. We shoveled ice over the bent carcasses, took a hammer
and six nails, and nailed down the wooden tops, then tacked on a tag
with the name of the Fulton broker who would sell our fish before
the sun came up the next morning. When the last box was packed,
we counted eighty-two. At about 120 pounds in each, we had
caught, loaded, washed, weighed, packed, iced, boxed, and labeled
about ten thousand pounds of prime market fish. At the going
Fulton price of thirty-five to forty cents a pound, less the broker's
commission, Ted would get checks that added up to about $3,000.
With five of us on the crew, and an extra share for the rig, each of us
would be due close to $500—a long night's work, and risky, but
worth it, especially to those of us who owed rent money.

The dory had done her work at Georgica. She had performed in
the wild dark and brought us ashore with our net around a big
bunch of fish. If that had happened every fishing day, or even once a
week, I'd probably still be fishing for a living, somewhere, some-
place.

Fishing for a living, however, is not that reliable. There were
weeks when the wind blew from the northeast and made the sea
intractable, even for our giant dory. Other days we would haul six
times and fail to pack two boxes when night at last arrived. And then
there were the fish: striped bass, bluefish, weakfish, tuna, swordfish,
flounder, sea bass, eels, whitebait, porgies, blowfish, fluke, and
more—we chased them all. Each of them moved within a secret
world, and although there were patterns to their mystery, the

unknown sustained. We were never certain of our meetings. One
moment we would find fish, but as quickly as they had arrived they
would be gone. It seemed that no sooner were we properly
equipped and prepared, the fish we sought were no longer about.
Waters that had teemed became deserts overnight.

For an incurable, and seriously impaired, romantic optimist like
myself, fishing as business was a trap that caught and held me in a
chain of great expectations. I would predicate my family's future
and mine on a graph of results like that night at the Georgica Gut.
Our best haul was the base of my projections because I loved fishing
so much I would never tell myself its realities. Like so many lovers, I
was blind.

But for five years, ten falls and ten long springs, I fished the beach
with Ted and his haul-seine crew. I clambered clumsily over the
worn rails of those giant dories hundreds and hundreds of times,
always welcoming the surge of the sea beneath me, lifting me and
our dory closer to the heavens above.

And I rowed. How I rowed. "Pull, boys, pull!" Shoulders, back,
thighs, calves, down to very soles of my feet I strained, holding the
dory's bow into the southwest chop like a man holding the nose ring
of a bull, linked each to the other in a contest of skills versus brute
strength. I came away from those years as lean as an oak post, as
sinewed as fence wire.

Soon after I left Ted's crew, the beaches, and that ocean of my
boyhood, inventive seiners learned how to outfit their dories with
outboard motors. Building a well almost amidships so there would
still be room for their nets in the stern, the seiners created a rig that
could still be carried on a trailer because they could tip up their
outboards so the shaft and propellor were flush with the dory's
bottom. They would back their trailers fitted with long tongues deep
into the wash, so deep water covered the tops of the trailer tires.

When the right moment arrived and the waves behaved, the
truck lurched shoreward and the dory slid sharply off its trailer as
the man on the bow oars pulled for water deep enough to tip the

motor down. The stern man hit a battery starter or pulled a starting rope, the outboard roared, the oars were shipped, and the dory moved under horsepower instead of manpower. With such a gain in energy and thrust, longer seines could be used. Some were more than a mile. It was the end of rowing.

I suppose, as long as it meant fishing, I would have adapted to the outboards. But I'm glad I never had to try. I am pleased to be able to say, "I rowed bow oars for Captain Ted Lester," and I have been grateful throughout the years for the rowing I learned, the seamanship I acquired, the sinew that has sustained me now for my seventy years, and for the knowledge of dories that their rowing allowed me. Rowing a dory, I think, is being intimate with the boat you love. Motoring is a meeting, but the partners don't touch.

Rowing them is one reason I so loved dories, and do still.

Of each of the work boats that helped sustain me, and made my fishing life possible, I worked hardest in a dory. There can be no question about that.

But the quality of work on the water is merely a matter of a very few degrees. It is all hard work. The proper boat, however, can make that work more productive. A boat that fails its function makes a fisherman's life excruciating. In a stroke of sublime good fortune, I never had to force myself on an ill-suited boat during those fishing years.

My good luck was due primarily to Peter Matthiessen, my Fishers Island friend who helped save the day from ignominy when we took the new country club launch on its erratic cruise down Long Island Sound. Peter and his wife, Patsy, became our neighbors in The Springs; he joined Ted's crew, and he and I became partners in a most informal way, using Peter's boats and my optimism during the months when the striper migration was on hold, and on the days when the ocean was too inhospitable to set a seine.

One of those boats—she began life as the *Maudite*—was true to her name ("cursed one") for the first year of her life in the United States. She got off to a good start when Peter acquired her on a trip

to the Gaspé and began an epic voyage southwest along the coast of
the Maritimes, alone and uncertain of his craft and his location.
With good reason.

A rudely built, nineteen-foot, double-ended cod-fishing smack
with a lapstrake double hull of yellow pine planks fresh from the
forests of the Gaspé, the deep-drafted, very broad-beamed, stubby,
almost plump pod of a work boat had decks nearly flush with her
low gunwales—as usual, for a reason. She was built as an inshore
cod-fishing boat, inshore definitely not signifying sheltered in those
North Atlantic waters. With her deep hull loaded with rock ballast
from the Gaspé beaches, the *Maudite* could waddle out to the
fishing grounds, pushed by a slow-turning wheel powered by a one-
cylinder Acadia engine, its huge, heavy flywheel spinning with
enough gyroscopic momentum to hold a Boeing 747 on course.
Codfish trawls were set from the small cockpit in the boat's V-
shaped stern, and then hauled back across the *Maudite*'s low, flush
decks. As fish came over the rail, they would be shaken off their
hooks above one of the several deck hatches opened to receive
them. And as the weight of the cod, if the fisherman's luck was with
him, increased in the hold, the rocks there were hoisted on deck and
rolled into the sea. It was a system that made sense for a Gaspé cod
fisherman whose survival depended on the efficiency of his efforts.
Gaff-rigged with a small, heavy, canvas sail on a stubby mast bumpy
with unplaned pine knots, the *Maudite* could be sailed before the
wind if her pop-popping one-lunger quit. But there was little hope
that she could reach across the wind, and no hope at all that she
could tack.

But Peter had not purchased the boat from her fisherman owner
to take her cod fishing. Indeed, he hardly had fishing of any sort in
mind. What he had wanted was an adventure, a diversion from the
rough spots his ongoing negotiations with his affianced (and then
un-affianced) lady had left on his otherwise happy road through life.
His idea of such an outing was to take this stranger of a boat into the
North Atlantic for the hazardous solo cruise to Fishers Island.

After three days of rough cruising in heavy seas off the Gaspé coast in his wallowing, underpowered boat, Peter had traveled fewer than sixty miles. And those were long, lonely days, starting at dawn and ending at sunset. As he steered into the outer harbor of Port-Daniel in Quebec on the evening of the third day, he sought the relative serenity of the inner harbor and an anchorage that would allow him to go ashore where he could find a hot meal, a drink, and a bed to sleep in.

A bridge crossed the two fingers of land that separated the outer harbor from its more sheltered counterpart, and as Peter powered the *Maudite* beneath it, he got his first evidence of how the boat got her name. The boat's mast, as Peter discovered in a moment of mayhem, was too long by about three inches to clear the bridge. As Quebec fishermen watched from above, mast and bridge collided and the mast broke flush at the deck, slamming back toward the cockpit where Peter stood, paralyzed, his hand on the tiller steering a straight course to disaster. With her rigging down around her helmsman's shoulders and the severed mast rolling on deck, the *Maudite* emerged on the other side of the bridge, steamed steadily onward until she ran aground on a tidal mudflat, heeled over on her stem, and rested there like a dozing hippo at a Serengeti water hole.

After tossing an anchor onto the flat to hold his craft when the ten-foot tide returned, Captain Peter dropped off the *Maudite*'s tilted deck up to his thighs in black mud and stomped toward the beach. Once ashore, he found a bar and in the bar he found a drinking companion, one "Logger" Journeaux whose substantial timber truck was parked at the watering hole's door. By the end of a liquid evening, Monsieur Journeaux had pledged to load the *Maudite* aboard that truck and to haul it to a Massachusetts boatyard of Peter's acquaintance. Thus did the work boat that became a key element in my life-support system complete the first crucial stage of the long voyage that brought her from the Gaspé to eastern Long Island's Three Mile Harbor, a fine, sheltered anchorage at the western end of Abrahams Path, the road that ran from close by my home to the *Maudite*'s new berth at the East Hampton Town Dock just a few feet from Emerson Tabor's lobster pound and his lovely converted dragger, the *Rey Del*.

Peter did marry the girl who said she did not want to marry him after he left his engagement party for the Gaspé, and within the first year of their lives as husband and wife they moved to The Springs, and Peter and I began our association as commercial fishing partners—a partnership definitely unbalanced in my favor. Peter provided the boats that enabled us to sustain our fishing careers; I provided companionship, and on some days, I was not all that companionable.

But then there were those times when the *Maudite* was our magic carpet that would take us to the never-never land of workdays on the water that were the days we had dreamed about when we first departed the world of conventional employment for our lives as fishermen. The best of those days came when the *Maudite* first arrived at her new berth in Three Mile Harbor.

That was September, and the bay scallop season opened on the sixteenth, and instead of the narrow deck of the *Emma* I had the broad decks of the *Maudite* to work from. She was much too heavy for hand hauling, but superb for the system of scalloping known as "picking up." Peter and I would sit on those low gunwales, our booted feet sometimes touching the water. Each of us held a long-handled scoop net with a hoop about the diameter of a softball at its business end. That hoop held a net pouch about as long as a kneesock.

On a good day for picking up, the tide would be low, the sun high and bright, and there would be just enough of a breeze to keep the drifting *Maudite* moving at a steady glide. If the breeze became vigorous, we could drag a scallop dredge off the windward rail to slow us down. Ideal conditions would allow us time to spot scallops on the harbor bottom (most often because their partly open shells revealed their pale mantles), swing our nets into position, and then pry the scallop into the net by pushing gently on the rim of its curved shell. That was enough to tip the scallops on edge, and their specific gravity so approximated the sea they lived in that they would almost float upward and glide, end over end, into the net. When a dozen or so were trapped in the net's toe, we'd whip the twine out of the water and dump our catch like a pile of china saucers onto the *Maudite*'s broad deck. It was about the most pleasant way that was ever created to earn $50 on a September day.

And it was a function for which the *Maudite* was ideally suited. With her deep-V double hull of green lumber, she weighed more than she should have. And with her exceptionally broad beam amidships, she was as stable as most battleships. With both Peter and myself perched at the very edge of her gunwales, she listed hardly at all. But I don't intend to portray her as some dough ball of a dowager who could hardly take a turn around the ballroom floor. The Gaspé artists who built her had mastered the skills of bending wood to their purpose. The *Maudite*, for all her bulk, had a fine grace about her, especially below the waterline, where her hull curved like a wineglass, tapered at both ends. There was not a flat plane on her body; all was curved to allow her to slip through the sea like a watermelon seed pops through your clenched fingertips. But because she was so heavy, her grace was often overlooked. Most observers saw only the wide, flat deck with its crude hatches and lack of brightwork, the knotty, stubby mast, and the defiantly un-painted, weathered hull. She was very much an individual, unlike any boat Three Mile Harbor, or most Long Island harbors, had ever seen.

If every day had been like that September sixteenth I recall so clearly, the *Maudite* would have carried me to fiscal stability. But there is no stability to autumn weather in the northeast; indeed, it is a season certain to provide storms, squalls, terrible winds from every quarter, and a relentless procession toward the brutalities of winter, often previewed as early as October, and certain to arrive by mid-November. By the end of the first week of the three-month scallop season, it was painfully clear to both of us that Peter and I would

have to take the *Maudite* to other waters if she were to produce the
scallop catches we both needed to keep our growing families (now
two children apiece) properly nourished.

On a bright, breezy mid-October morning, we went prospecting
along the edge of the shallows at the northwest point of Gardiners
Island; I had seen scallop shells on the beach there during my days as
skipper of the *Captain Kidd*, and knew they weren't left there by
pirates. They had to wash up from nearby waters.

We found the beds, long ridges of scallops, their pink shells oddly
peppered with quarterdecks. But their meats were large, pure white,
and full of the freshness of the open bay. Miles from the other
scallopers, we were also miles from the bay constables who policed
the ten-bushel limit and the prohibitions against towing scallop
dredges under power. We hoisted the *Maudite*'s coarse and mil-
dewed gaff-rig sail, but we also fired up the four-cylinder Gray
Marine engine that had replaced the boat's original one-lunger.
With the throttle set at idle speed, we towed three dredges, hauling
them back one after another, steadily, each time finding them half-
full, or better. It was steady, hard work, but we would be certain to
get our limit before the day ended.

Tired, we quit for the single-sandwich lunch we had brought,
shutting down the Gray and tossing over our anchor so we wouldn't
drift off our discovery. We lolled back against the bulging burlap
sacks of scallops, feeling the October sun warm on our oilskins even
though a freshening breeze from the northwest told us an autumnal
cold front was on its way, and that the next day would present us
with a whitecapped chop, ill-mannered winds, and equally rude
chilly temperatures. But that was the next day; this day belonged to
the warmth of success as well as the deceptively benign presence of
an Indian summer.

When we had finished lunch, Peter said, "Time to get back to
work," and reached an arm toward the *Maudite*'s simple instrument
panel where he pushed the small, chrome starter button. Nothing
happened. I could hear the *click-click* of the solenoid on the engine's

starting motor and the sound was a bad-news message. I knew it well. My Model A Ford had sent the same message many times: "Your battery is failing." The solenoid clicks meant the *Maudite*'s battery did not have enough juice left to turn over the four-cylinder Gray. Something had gone wrong with the generator that charged our battery; there could be a short somewhere in the boat's rudimentary wiring, which was unlikely, or the carbon brushes on the generator could be worn out, unable to transfer electrical energy from the copper armature to the battery.

Diagnosis of the problem was, however, not our primary concern. We were, both of us, instantly preoccupied with a solution. Peter pushed the starter button several more times, hoping for a kinetic miracle that would touch the Gray with life, get it rumbling and pushing us toward home. The afternoon seemed to grow very short very quickly. The nor'wester acquired increasing authority: violet-gray cumulus, bulging with wind, built on the horizon across the Sound. And, most of all, our aloneness became palpable. There were no boats in sight, and it was unlikely at that time of the year that any would be. The Gardiners Island shore was rocky and hostile; Charley Raynor was no one's idea of a savior; we had no radio, and we had told very few others where we were bound.

But we did have a sail, the very same, original, rude Nova Scotia canvas that had been there when Peter bought the *Maudite* four years before. To my knowledge, it had never been unfurled.

"Let's sail back," I said, upbeat, confident. "We can ride before the wind and we'll make Promised Land," which was a splendid misnomer for the cove on the south side of Gardiners Bay, where the Smith Meal Company operated a rendering plant that extracted oil from the tons of menhaden caught by its fleet of oceanic purse-seiners. The plant, a structure of unadorned efficiency, cooked the mashed menhaden carcasses in huge vats, and on some humid days when the wind blew from the southeast, the airborne effluent was pungent enough to turn the stomachs of well-to-do diners on the Devon Yacht Club's great porch just across the cove.

But on that October afternoon, the yacht club was closed for the season, its porch swept bare by the winds, its doors and windows nailed shut and boarded over. The factory at Promised Land was equally defunct; menhaden are migratory, and the same black "Gullah" crews, whose work chants could sometimes be heard across calm water, were back in their native Carolinas. But the Edwards Brothers Store was still open at the Promised Land dock where, in the fall and winter, Kenneth and Sam Edwards docked the draggers they skippered throughout the winter months. If we could reach Promised Land, we would find help and a reasonably protected spot to dock the powerless *Maudite*.

Hoisting the sail took some doing. The tarred halyards were stiff; the wooden hoops that went around the mast and held the canvas in place resisted any easy sliding over the lumpy mast, the very same one that had broken at the Port-Daniel bridge, about two feet shorter.

But hoist sail we did. In the brisk to husky northwest breeze, the *Maudite* responded immediately. Like a farm wagon on a hillside when its brakes are released, she began acquiring momentum, her dowager bow rising and falling in the chop, the spray hitting both our faces as we perched on the edge of the aft cockpit, looking at each other with tentative smiles. We could, at least, get home. And a good thing, too, because the sun had lowered in the southwestern sky, its light already dimmed by gathering cumulus. In less than an hour, it would be gone.

We sailed away from Gardiners Island on a broad reach that would get us more in the middle of the bay where the wind could do the rest. But as we eased out of the lee of the island, we discovered the chop had built quickly. The short seas packed a heavyweight punch. As she discovered the contest, the *Maudite* began fighting back, slamming into the chop as she came down off the previous wave.

One moment we were sailing, the next we were in shock. As she slammed into a sea, the *Maudite* lost her mast. With the crack of rifle fire, the pine stub snapped flush with the deck. Sail, mast, and rigging, along with our rising hopes, crashed down with it. In moments, our boat lost headway, swung broadside, and wallowed in rough water. We had neither power nor sail. We were adrift on a lonely bay under a darkening sky, pushed around by a wind that had winter in its teeth.

In minutes it became clear that the ebbing tide would be no help. Instead, it would sweep toward Montauk Point and the harsh bad manners of an October ocean. Wrestling our anchor from its stowage belowdecks, we chucked it over the bow, gave it as much line as we had, and then waited until it fetched up and the *Maudite*'s bow swung into the wind on the anchorage she would hold for one of the longest nights of my boating life.

We took stock. We both thought we had told our wives we might prospect for scallops in Gardiners Bay, but we were not certain. We knew we had not told them just where in Gardiners Bay we would be headed because when we left Three Mile Harbor, we didn't know ourselves. The bay is a big place for one small boat, and as the cloudy night took over the sky above us, we knew we would spend it aboard the *Maudite*.

She was an inhospitable hostess. Her flat, broad deck, so welcome as a stable work platform, provided no shelter, none. And the mess left in the wake of the ruptured mast, collapsed gaff, and fallen sail made moving about a clumsy process. Without the sun, and on the wings of that merciless nor'wester, the temperature headed for the low fifties. We had our oilskins, but that was all.

Hunched there in the cockpit, we opened a few scallops and swallowed those sweet, cold meats seasoned with the bay's own brine. I have always loved Long Island bay scallops above all other sustenance from the sea, and even on that tossing, friendless, anxious night I relished that uniquely sweet and tender taste. "This could be worse," I said to Peter, "we could be like Captain Bligh in his drifting longboat with nothing to eat and almost nothing to drink." We had cans of beer, a bottle of fresh water, and a couple of cans of ginger ale.

But as the night shed its baby teeth, there was no more talking. We lay there on the pitching deck in the small shelter of the fallen mast and sail, trying to find sleep, but failing. I watched the clouds scud, flying past hard stars that showed steady in the heavens. I thought of how deliberately time makes its moves when discomforts prevail, how quickly it zips past enjoyments. And always I watched the eastern sky where I knew the first signals of the new day would be raised.

When the day did come, it came with a roar. Both of us had fallen asleep, and the sun was rising over the bay's whitecaps when a quite unexpected sound slammed us from our slumber. It was the roar of twin aircraft engines as a plane soared low just above us. It was a Coast Guard PBY patrol plane, one of those wonderful designs of World War II that survived for decades after. An amphibian with a large, single pontoon hull with retractable wheels, the PBY had a single wing mounted on the hull's topside. This allowed its crew superb visibility from the bulging, Plexiglas cockpit that filled the plane's entire nose section.

Cold and stiff on the *Maudite*'s deck, I could see very clearly the figures of the pilot and copilot as the plane circled and made another pass. I knew they were looking for us. By the third pass, both Peter and I were on our feet. Swinging very close, the PBY roared past at almost eye level. From an opening in the nose section an object was tossed our way. It was a chrome and yellow cylinder about the size of a one-pint milk bottle and it trailed a Day-Glo pink ribbon about six feet long. There was no way we could miss seeing it.

Whoever made the drop did a splendid job. The watertight container landed about two feet from us, where it floated our way, its ribbon writhing in its wake like an oversize, pink eel. I leaned over the gunwale, scooped my hand under the ribbon, and pulled the contraption aboard.

The top of the container had a cap with small arrows that pointed in the direction it should be turned. Unscrewing it, I looked inside and saw a note scrawled on white paper. It read: "Are you the *Maudite* and are you in trouble? If so, stand up and wave your arms."

We were already standing and within seconds after I read the note aloud, both of us were waving our arms like high school cheerleaders at the year's biggest game.

The plane circled one more time. I saw the copilot wave, and as the PBY headed west toward its home field in New Jersey, the pilot wagged its wings in the international airborne signal of friendly acknowledgment.

"They'll probably radio the station at Montauk Lake," I said, "and give them our position. It will take the launch over an hour to get here. We'll just have to wait."

I said it as if we had a choice, but we both knew we didn't. The *Maudite* was just as immobile as she had been the day before and there was nothing we could do about it.

But as it turned out, we did not have to wait more than fifteen minutes for help to arrive from a quite unexpected quarter.

As I sipped on a breakfast beer, thinking of its anesthetic potential, I heard the sound of a boat motor. Looking west toward Three Mile Harbor, I saw a black seine boat headed our way. The double-ended seine boats carried on the decks of the large mother ships in the Smith Meal fleet were popular with East End commercial fishermen. Seaworthy, spacious, and economical to operate, the seine boats were regularly replaced by Smith Meal, much as a taxicab fleet owner might replace his cabs whether they needed it or not. But there was only one black seine boat, and I knew who that belonged to.

It was Fanny Gardiner's boat, and I knew it well because, like me, Fanny liked to troll for bluefish in the bay that bore her family's name. A first cousin of the branch that had owned Gardiners Island for some three centuries, Fanny was very much her own person.

When she and I were growing up, she taught me how to swim and she taught me well. My grandmother called Fanny a "tomboy" because she wore blue jeans and raised and trained horses. Fanny kept to herself, but always gave me a wave when she saw me fishing. I was happy that it was she who had come to our rescue because I knew she understood boats and the ways they could break down. Of course, our misfortune could have been prevented with a regular reading of the ampere meter on the instrument panel, but there was no need to explain that to Fanny.

Lean, tanned, and wearing a beat-up officer's cap, she coasted alongside in her thirty-footer, bantered a bit, told us she'd heard the Coast Guard talking on the radio, and threw us a line. She said she'd called Montauk to tell them she was taking us in and they were, she said, delighted not to have to make the trip. The Coast Guard launch and its crew, Fanny told us, had been out on that rough bay all night long looking for us. I felt guilty when I heard that; we hadn't even had regulation lights aboard—lights that could have helped them find us.

Those seine boats had large, deep-pitched, slow-turning propellors designed for pulling, and although our progress in the chop was slow, it was steady and without strain. The *Maudite* may have looked clumsy, but she slid through the seas with an ease that was an everlasting tribute to her traditional lines.

Fanny dropped us at Three Mile's town dock with a wave, and we tied up in the same spot we had left more than twenty-four hours earlier. Weary, we clambered around in our restrictive oilskins, hoisting the bags of scallops onto the wharf, cleaning up the litter on the *Maudite*'s deck as best we could, and, at last, clambering into my beat-up GMC pickup that I'd bought for a hundred dollars. Until we sat there in the cab, neither of us had realized how close we were to total exhaustion. We had worked a great deal, rested little, and spent hours pondering our uncertain future as passengers on a boat adrift. It was those hours that had drained us.

We took the scallops over to openers in one of the fishermen's

places on the Cross Highway near Ted Lester's and then we each
went home to our wives and infant children. The wives had called
the Coast Guard, but judging from our receptions, neither one was
overly concerned over the whereabouts and welfare of their husband and provider.

I wrote Fanny and the Coast Guard letters of thanks, and I added
several resolutions to my growing list of "things to check" before I
left the harbor on any boat of any kind.

- Make certain you tell someone as precisely as you can
  where you plan to be during your time on the water. And,
  if you can, tell them when you can be expected to return.

- Make a ship-to-shore radio part of your standard on-
  board equipment. These days, many guides I know have
  cellular phones on their boats. All they need to do if
  problems arise is call home. If such devices had been
  invented then, Peter and I might well have had one
  aboard the *Maudite*, although I have my doubts about
  how our spouses would have responded to a call from
  Gardiners Bay. They might have said, "Well, have a nice
  evening," and returned to their suppers.

- Check your ammeter. Make certain your battery is being
  charged. When we returned a day or so later to repair the
  Maudite we discovered that her generator brushes had
  been worn down to their metal holders.

- If you know there is a chance you'll be out after dark,
  make sure you have a couple of flashlights and, if possible,
  a searchlight. Running lights, of course, are required by
  the Coast Guard, but we ignored that sensible regulation.

- Be sure you carry an anchor aboard and plenty of anchor
  warp in good condition. Peter and I had a tough night,
  but it could have been much worse on us and the *Maudite*

if we'd had no anchor and wallowed in the wind and tide.
We could easily have been carried to the open ocean, and
then even Fanny Gardiner might not have found and
rescued us.

Experiences like that October night have a way of sticking with
you. Four decades later, whenever I shut down a boat engine at sea,
there is a voice inside me that wonders, "Will she start again?"
Suddenly I'm back on board the *Maudite* after that fine lunch under
the warm October sun. Most times, these days, I have a small but
serviceable radio on board, a working flashlight, and a couple of
flares. I haven't yet had to go through another night on a powerless
boat, but after the *Maudite* experience, I know it can happen anytime.

From that night on, however, the *Maudite* and I became better
and better friends. As Peter became less able to justify his career on
the water (editors and publishers were successfully persuading him
to concentrate on his writing), the boat he had so impulsively
purchased on Bonaventure Island off the Gaspé somehow sailed
farther and farther into the harbor of my possession. Peter never
sought to sell his *Maudite*, but he generously allowed me to use her
as my own work boat. I was her skipper, with complete autonomy,
and in the way that rationalizers and wishful thinkers do, I had no
problem persuading myself that she was my boat.

One of my first moves in that direction was the abolition of
Maudite as the boat's name. I rechristened her the *Vop Vop* in loving
memory of her original one-lunger engine, which, whenever it could
be persuaded to function, propelled the boat with a merry and
steady "vop . . . vop . . . vop . . . vop . . ." that could be heard almost
a mile off if the weather was fair and the winds calm.

I cut her a new mast from a straight white pine in someone's
woods, shaved it, sanded it, and gave it about three or four coats of
spar varnish. I renewed the stays that held the mast in place, separated the original, rotting canvas from the wooden hoops that went

around the mast, and cut a new, crude but effective sail from stiff, heavy, virginal canvas.

That sail fit the boat's original gaff-rigged arrangement, but within a week after her new canvas was tested, I scrapped that sail for another. That modification was revolutionary enough to win the *Vop Vop* a reputation from Montauk Lake to Shelter Island.

There were many waters of the open bays off Long Island's East End where sail power was a legal method for towing scallop dredges. The regulations that prohibited motor-powered towing were designed to govern the efficiency with which the annual bay scallop crop was harvested. In sheltered harbors like Three Mile, Napeague, and Montauk Lake, manpower was the only legal energy, which is why the hand-over-hand haul-back along the long anchor line was the only permitted system. But on the open waters of Peconic Bay, Gardiners Bay, and others, sailing was allowed.

And because it was, there were many lovely, old sloops at work that might otherwise have spent their days rotting at some forgotten wharf or being stripped of their masts and rigging and converted to motor power. But during scallop season, they would be there resplendent on the bay, under full sail on a broad reach, their windward rail festooned with as many as six or eight quivering tow lines, each fast to a scallop dredge being tugged across the bay bottom.

The problem, as I saw it, was that sailing on a reach meant the dredges were being towed on an angle. The forward progress of those sloops could not be eliminated, no matter how deftly the helmsman tried to get his boat to drift broadside. The immutable physics of sailing a sloop with a standard Marconi rig would not permit any other course. Which meant that each dredge lost efficiency because it was being towed at an angle that shut off a portion of the dredge mouth.

In a stroke of what even all these years later I might safely call genius, I realized that the *Vop Vop* was uniquely designed to sail before the wind. The notion took hold because her hull was shaped and built so much like the hulls of those Viking ships I had read

about on rainy, boyhood afternoons—the ships that carried Erik the
Red and Thor and Odin into the imaginations of all of us who
remembered those N. C. Wyeth illustrations. That's how, years later,
I suddenly saw the *Vop Vop*: she was my Viking ship.

I cut her a new sail, this one almost square, hung between two
spars top and bottom. I wanted to paint a Viking shield or a knight's
cross on the canvas, but I was too anxious to try the new rig to spend
time on needless decoration. The key to the system was a set of
heavy steel outriggers, which I had custom made at Sid Cullum's
machine shop. Sid was an artist in his own right; his medium was
metal and his welding torch his brush. Sooner or later every commercial fisherman on the East End found his way to Sid's in search
of repair to a critical metal fitting or the creation of a new, and
equally critical, part. Over the many years of his career, Sid acquired
as much information about boats and fishing as he did about cutting
and welding.

So he listened patiently as I explained what I needed: two steel
outriggers with their inboard ends hinged to a plate I could bolt to
the deck. The outboard arms would be drilled with two holes each,
with a steel ring through each of the holes. The assembly looked
awkward on the floor of Sid's shop, but once aboard the *Vop Vop*, it
assumed a new identity. Bolted in place amidships, port and starboard, the outriggers could be folded back on their hinges so they
did not stick out over the rail. But once I found my sailing course
over the scallop beds, I could swing the outriggers over the rail,
make a dredge line fast to each of the rings, hoist my square Viking
canvas, and sail before the wind as efficiently as any racing sloop.
Tossing my dredges overboard, one after the other, and adding a
fifth directly off the stern, I made the *Vop Vop* a scalloping machine.

With the equalized drag of the dredges being towed straight
downwind, there was no need for me to steer. I could go forward,
stand on the deck, and tend my dredges. No sooner had I hauled
one back and dumped it on that blessedly broad deck, but the next
dredge was full and waiting to be dumped. I was kept working every

minute, but the pile of scallops that mounted at my feet was nothing short of extraordinary. I had, at long last, and perhaps for the only time during my years of commercial fishing, improved a system developed by generations of scallopers. It was the *Vop Vop*'s unique Gaspé configuration that made the system possible, and within a week she had attracted the attention of fishermen who previously had little or no reason to talk boats with me. After all, the *Emma* might have been odd, but she was still a sharpie and nothing more.

As skipper of the *Vop Vop* during that glorious scallop season, I acquired a new identity, a scalloping identity, a set of commercial fishing credentials I had not had before. Men I did not know strolled by the boat at her berth in Three Mile and asked, "Where would a fella find a boat like that?" Or, even better, "Who was it come up with them outriggers?"

For a few weeks that fall I began to believe that I could, at long last, make it as a fisherman. With my limit of scallops almost every day, I was beginning to make a small dent in the hillside of bills that sloped from the table I used as a desk. At night as I lay dreaming, I would compute the number of bushels of scallops I could land before the season ended, multiply by the number of gallons of scallop meats they would yield, and then multiply that by the market price. And before you know it, there in the dark, I would be out of debt.

Of course, it was not to be. I wonder if silly optimists are the only men who become commercial fishermen. Or do the generational fishermen, the Lesters and the Edwardses, understand dimensions I was never able to perceive? As they are every season, the scallop beds were depleted long before the season's end. With the kind of money those shellfish brought, no scalloper allowed himself to rest until he had taken his limit each and every day, and no scallop bed, no matter how fertile, could hold up under pressures that intense.

But the weeks I did have as the *Vop*'s skipper that final scalloping fall are still some of my most resplendent memories. I was, after all, aboard a boat, an exceptional, affectionate, able, softhearted, beamy wonder of a wooden boat, as a working fisherman every day of the week for about six weeks. I cruised from Three Mile Harbor to Peconic Bay, around Shelter Island and then east through Gardiners Bay to Napeague and on the Montauk Lake.

It was early November when I made the passage from Sag Harbor to Montauk Lake, a cruise of about twenty miles. My friend Peter Scott gave me a ride to Sag Harbor at sunup and said he would meet me at the town dock in Montauk that afternoon. I brought a sandwich for lunch and an extra can of gas, and the *Vop*'s tank was full.

The day was vintage East End autumn, charged by a brisk breeze from the southwest, clear skies, and a sharpness in the air that told everyone winter waited in the wings. Mine was the only boat I saw on the trip past Cedar Point, around the bend until I reached Lion's Head Rock, then south past the Devon Yacht Club and remembered visions of my boyhood sailing lessons there, past Promised Land and the Smith Meal Company factory where I worked for one long, hot desperate summer month mending the huge purse seines and loading boxcars with one-hundred-pound sacks of steamy fish meal fresh from the cookers. Then past Lazy Point and Napeague Harbor where, the previous winter, I had broken through salt ice to tong huge chowder clams that struck the *Emma*'s deck like falling boulders. On good days I could harvest two bushels by early afternoon. Then I'd take them back to our rented house on the Springs-Fireplace Road and open them on a workbench in the garage. I'd measure the meats into paper quart containers and the next morning I'd make my rounds in East Hampton, selling the quarts door-to-door to people who knew what good chowder could be made from my guaranteed fresh shellfish. That way my bushels of quahogs became about twenty times more valuable than they would have been if I had shipped them unopened to the Fulton Fish Market. Except for a bite I got from a startled Chesapeake Bay retriever (he was asleep under the stoop when I knocked on the back door), there were no untoward incidents to mar those days when I made dependable—but not significant—money, although it meant that more of my time was spent processing and marketing than on the water, a drawback that could be justified in midwinter but one I could not long live with when March winds blew soft and salty and red-winged blackbirds called from greening cattails.

Once past Napeague and headed east "down Montauk," I hoisted the *Vop*'s sail so it caught the southwest wind and added a knot or two to the steady eight knots the Gray was able to generate. Like the wide-hipped lady she was, the *Vop Vop* was not about to be rushed. But soon the cliffs of Hither Hills showed up to our starboard, and beyond them the trap stakes that marked Culloden Point.

We, the *Vop* and I, were going to make it, easily. I knew that and wondered why I ever worried. But the memory of our breakdown was too fresh to totally ignore and my years as a boatman too few to allow me to think of a late fall day alone on the water as nothing more than a trip to Dan Miller's General Store in my pickup. Being alone in a small boat on open salt water with the vastness of an ocean on the horizon is one of the most certain ways I know to acquire a sense of humankind's fragility. There is no natural motion that articulates the forces of the elements as eloquently as a husky wave. The seas that rolled behind me, pushed by the southwest wind and sharpened by an incoming tide from the east, posed no real danger to the *Vop Vop*. With her narrow stern and ample, rounded bottom, she was ideally designed to cope with following seas. Nevertheless, as I sat there in her tiny stern cockpit, my hand gripping the tiller and my eyes watching the progress of the curling, foam-capped seas that looked as if they might ride right over the rails, exhilaration flushed my cheeks. I was in love with my freedom and the risks that were its price.

That afternoon glide from Hither Hills to the Montauk Lake breakwaters was one of the most memorable of all my thousands of voyages, long and short. There with the lowering sun directly in my wake, with autumn on the wind and no other boats on the bay, it seemed as if all my false starts and clumsy failures as a commercial

fisherman were being washed away by the hissing seas that helped
shove me gently toward my safe harbor. For that blessed memory
which holds firm still, I must thank the wondrous *Vop Vop*, née
Maudite, and Peter, the man who allowed me the pleasures of his
boat.

And it was another Matthiessen boat that added an offshore
volume to my work-boat history. She was a thirty-two-footer built in
Rockport, Massachusetts. Peter first saw her there riding at anchor,
learned she was for sale, and with her then-owner took her for a test
cruise around Cape Ann.

"She had the most beautiful lines for a powerboat I had ever
seen," he later wrote in his book, *Men's Lives*.

> Her designer, a local sailmaker, had her built as a tuna
> harpoon boat; she was the only one of her kind. . . . With
> her high bow and deep hull forward, her long, low cockpit
> and flat stern, she looked like a trim and elegant Maine
> lobster boat, and she handled well in any kind of sea.
> Powered by a 120-horsepower converted Buick engine, she
> came equipped with a spotting tower, outriggers, harpoon
> stand (pulpit), harpoons and line, a heavy tuna rod and reel
> and fighting chair, boat rods, shark hooks, and miscella-
> neous gear of all descriptions.
>
> Within a few days of our arrival at Montauk Lake, I
> rechristened her the *Merlin*—after the small, swift falcon of
> that name as well as the celebrated magician—and began
> sailing her as a charter boat out of a berth at the town dock.
>
> The season was well under way and there was just one
> slip left, next to Captain John Messbauer, one of Montauk's
> pioneer charter skippers. And from the first, the *Merlin* did
> pretty well. We made up in eagerness and love of fishing
> what we lacked in experience at our new trade. We worked
> hard to find fish for our clients . . . and we welcomed any
> who came along.

And so we did, for two summers from the July Fourth weekend until a few weeks after Labor Day, when the main body of migrating bluefish felt October's first chilly nor'easters and began their migration south. When Peter first put his *Merlin* to work, he had not yet acquired his license to "carry passengers for hire," the very same bit of paper that I had successfully won from the U.S. Coast Guard a few weeks before that commencement I missed so I could go to work for Peter's father as captain of the Fishers Island Country Club's new launch. That bit of paper was good for life if it was properly renewed every five years along with some evidence that its owner had spent some time around boats and on the water in the interim. I had duly renewed my authorization, even though at the time I had no anticipation that I would acquire a boat fit to carry anyone, much less passengers for hire.

But the *Merlin* was an exquisite craft, lovingly fashioned, and I was delighted to be able to contribute whatever was needed to give me an opportunity to fish almost every day of the one season that was, for most commercial fishermen, the slowest of the year. Once we left the dock, there was no question that Peter was the captain and I his trusty mate, as he once called me. But if we were boarded by the Coast Guard, which checked from time to time to make certain both charter boats and private yachts conformed to regulations and carried proper safety gear, then I would be at the wheel, looking as much like a skipper as a mate could look. I've always thought it was a double benefit of my initial acquisition that once took me to that sublime job on Fishers, and then six years later got me on the *Merlin*'s deck yanking hooked bluefish from the turbulent tides under Montauk Light.

We fished inshore most of the time, concentrating on finding striped bass and bluefish. We prayed for bluefish, the ten- to twenty-pound slammers that fought hard, especially on light tackle, struck almost any lure, and traveled in large schools that guaranteed multiple strikes if we trolled in the right places. Then two or three of our charter passengers would have fish on at the same time, yelling, laughing, and, in some cases, complaining that the fish were fighting too hard. Those days when we found fish were the happiest days for us and our passengers. We'd get back to the town dock and I'd toss the fish up on the tarred planks, sometimes as many as fifteen or twenty. Then the bystanders would gather, beckoning others, "Over here. Over here." And I would clamber up from the *Merlin* with my knife in my hand and begin gutting and washing the fish so our clients could take them back to Queens or Stamford or Manhasset, or wherever they had come from so charged with anticipation about their "deep-sea fishing adventure," as the charters were advertised by the Montauk Chamber of Commerce.

Such high hopes, such raised expectations. We saw so much anticipation when we left the dock, and so often such depression when we returned six hours later with no fish. That got to us, that act of taking money from folks who had arrived expecting to catch fish and then had to leave without ever realizing their dreams. Peter and I were equally depressed and we would often stay on the water well past our schedules, trying desperately to break the drought. There were times, I thought, when our desire to find and catch fish for our charters was more intense than any longing on their part.

There were other times when neither captain, mate, nor passengers had fish foremost in their minds. This odd situation unfolded on those few occasions when our clients revealed themselves as bullies, malcontents, and ill-mannered slobs. Because we were new to the business and had no backlog of clients who returned year after year, we would accept any person who strolled down the town dock ready to bargain for a day on the water. Some mornings as we waited, woefully alone there because each of our fellow charter-boat crews was already at sea, a trio or quartet of hard-nosed anglers who had analyzed our willingness to salvage something of the day would begin a conversation aimed at discovering just how far we would drop our standard fees.

Generally, a discount materialized. In minutes the *Merlin* would be gliding past the breakwater on her way to join the rest of the charter fleet crisscrossing Shagwong or trolling umbrella rigs off Caswell's. At that late hour, the best of the early morning fishing had been realized. Often, what fish had been there were "drummed down" by the constant throbbing of the motors of fifty or more charter boats, each after the same trophies in the same small undersea arena.

We would arrive jauntily, however, gliding arrogantly in that superb boat, and I would get the lines out, often set to troll as close to the rocky bottom as possible in an effort to persuade the uneasy fish taking shelter there that this was a lure they could not resist.

With her classic lines, deep bow, and finely curved, shallow-draft stern, the *Merlin* was ideally suited to the perpetual chop that stirred the waters off Montauk Point. With the tides of all of Long Island Sound meeting the currents of the Atlantic there at those rocky and relatively shoal straits, the water never relaxed. Even when there was no wind, not a breath, the tide rips under the light surged and collided, creating waves and whirlpools of their own. And if a breeze did pick up, it only added to the confusion. There were many days in those rips when I watched waves coming from three different quarters, each colliding with the other. Some of the larger, V-bottom charter boats that appealed to Montauk skippers wallowed mercilessly in such conditions. Their high, slim outriggers would arc one hundred degrees one way and then jerk back the other in their own silent signals of instability.

Meanwhile, the *Merlin* with her marvelously slippery hull would pick her dainty way through the mess like a bridesmaid avoiding littered grounds at a wedding reception. I often marveled at the wonders a gifted boat designer can create when love, and not utility, is the prime energizer of his effort. For the most part, our clients were the benficiaries of the *Merlin*'s sea-friendly lines. Even on rough days, they returned to the dock feeling drier and less bruised than their counterparts who had been fishing aboard boats that may have been roomier but were less seaworthy.

Which is not to say the *Merlin* had no wiles. She could be most cooperative when Peter and I decided that we had taken enough shit from those few clients who turned out to be mean-spirited, arrogant, and abusive. When their complaints, whines, and curses at our inability to find fish went beyond the pale of even unreasonable abuse, we would show the *Merlin*'s bitchy side, a process she seemed to enjoy as much as we did.

After trolling deep for a fishless hour or two, and after changing locations several times, trying different lures and different weight lines, we might suggest bottom fishing for sea bass, or traveling to the east side of Gardiners Island where small bluefish might be schooling . . . something to break the monotony and growing tension of being skunked under the light. And, most often, the clients would agree, accepting with good humor the reality that even though the chamber of commerce might promise otherwise, fish do not bite all the time, especially during the middle hours of a warm, windless midsummer day.

But there were those few coarse, bullheaded types who swore first at us, then at the boat, and then began talk of not paying for the charter unless we produced some fishing. Then we would suggest drifting the rip, a technique which could indeed result in a hooked bluefish or striper, but seldom did because it involved a degree of skill which most clients did not have. The process involved attaching a one-pound drail to the terminal end of a stout line. The jig was a lump of lead, sometimes chrome plated, that looked something like a mid-size herring. It had a hook at its business end and a swivel at the other, which was made fast to a stout leader and then the end of the angler's line.

When the heavy weight dropped, the angler's reel was on free spool until the jig fetched up on the bottom. In some of the holes off Montauk, that could be more than one hundred feet down. Once the impact was felt, the angler began retrieving line as fast as possible, trying to make the jig rise quickly enough from the dark bottom so it looked like a small fish trying to escape the jaws it knew might be lurking below.

Jigging, as it is called, is a laborious method and not a very efficient one. Most anglers who pay for the thrills of "deep-sea fishing" never for a moment anticipate jigging's exertions. Which is one reason we put our most obstreperous passengers to work on the process. But there were other, more significant reasons. When the *Merlin* took her clients jigging, she would motor to the up-tide side of the point. Then her engine would shut down and she would drift with the tide across a jigging ground about a half-mile wide. Without her engine, and with her hull broadside to the swells, even the graceful *Merlin* would roll.

To add the proper heat and fumes to the rolling, either the skipper or his trusty mate would open the engine hatch under some pretense of checking the points or adjusting the throttle. On a rolling boat whose partly enclosed deck is steadily filling with hot engine fumes and exhaust leftovers, under a blazing summer sun, even the most stoic stomach can soon lose stability. Landlubbers from the city who had already pumped down several warm beers and a mayonnaise-soaked sandwich soon found themselves wishing they hadn't.

As their distress became more visible—blanched, pale faces, sweat-slicked brows, and a distinct lack of enthusiasm for more drifting—one of the party would, at last, suggest an early return to the dock. "Really?" I would ask, as if I was suprised that anyone would want to abandon an opportunity to catch fish. But I would signal the captain the moment the suggestion was made, and within the half-hour our uncouth clients were delighted to abandon our ship.

Such episodes were the exception. Most often, there were pleasant days aboard the *Merlin*, albeit days when I worked from seven in the morning until nine in the evening, days when we would run two six-hour trips. We'd return around one with our morning charter, scramble to clean the catch, scrub down the boat, and bolt down some lunch so we would be ready by two for the second shift. Those afternoon trips were my favorite. I loved the sunsets and the dusk when the day's brisk breezes dropped out and schools of bluefish that had been invisible since dawn would surface, scattering schools of baitfish like silver coins across the tide. I could hear the hiss of panic, the sound of a cotton sheet torn asunder as predator and prey ripped the twilight waters. And I could smell the fish oil, slick on the water where it marked the rending of a thousand menhaden in the jaws of a thousand Godzilla blues.

The knob on the edge of my hand where my little finger meets the knuckle would be cut and bleeding gently from the slices made by monofilament leaders that I wrapped around my hand when I leaned far down over the *Merlin*'s stern to jerk a hooked bluefish from the foam of our wake and slam it into the open fish box on the deck. Often two or three big blues would need to be boated one after the other, and I would miss the box with one or two and they'd be flopping across the deck, their jaws snapping and dripping blood from a hook in their gills. Soon the deck would be slippery with fish slime, blood, and regurgitated herring, silversides, and menhaden, our anglers yelling, laughing, pumped up with the adrenaline of the moment there in the rich dusk at the end of a late-summer day.

What a great way to make a living. When we had those days aboard the *Merlin* our anglers would be so charged with the excitement of the carnage under the light, so certain they had witnessed a rare natural act, that they would be overly generous with their tips and I would drive the pickup home along the narrow, dark Montauk Highway with an extra $20 or $25 in my pocket, certain once again that I could make a living in boats on the waters that surrounded that fragile and lovely spit of sand that is Long Island's East End. It never occurred to me that arriving home at 10:30 wearing jeans stiff with bluefish slime and so weary that I wanted only a bed where I could rest until six the next morning was not a productive way to nourish a marriage. It took years for that painful bill to come due.

Every now and then a stroller on the town dock would turn out to be an angler who wanted to go offshore after what they always called "the big fish . . . really big." As Frank Mundus was the first to discover, the species mattered little as long as the bulk was there. So Frank converted a huge, old party-fishing boat to a shark-catching machine and made a fortune "monster fishing." Aboard the *Merlin*, there was no wish to chum for sharks. We were, after all, inshore specialists. But on those days when we had no choice, we took that graceful boat ten or twenty miles southeast of the light into the awesome world of the open ocean at the edge of the Gulf Stream's blue-green waters.

We made no promises to our charters, but said we would probably find some school tuna, small bluefins weighing about sixty to one hundred pounds. We could not, in good conscience, talk seriously about marlin and swordfish. Not only were their numbers shrinking, even in those early days of commercial long-lining for billfish, but we had neither the equipment nor the experience that could give substance to any such promise.

But we did know how to hook up with school tuna, and the *Merlin* had, after all, been designed as a tuna catcher. On a few days, we lucked out. Our feathered lures would be bouncing along on the first wave of our wake and then *Wham!* a reel would begin screaming and we would be fast to a school tuna. They are tough, stubborn, strong fighters, and after one or two, even the most eager angler might wonder why he had been so set on hooking a "big fish."

Once we found a school, we could keep them in the neighborhood for a while. When that happened we knew our charter would be a successful day in our angler's memory. And when we got back to the dock, there would be a few hundred pounds of tuna to toss on the tarred planks while onlookers gathered and one or two began negotiating with Peter for a charter the next morning.

But more often our trips offshore were dry cruises alone on a vast ocean. There were many days when the tuna were not on top; others when we could hear skippers chattering on their radios about "picking a few," but of course they wouldn't say where. I never minded those days. I was mesmerized by the constant throb of our engine at trolling speed, the rise and fall of the deep ocean swells as they rolled under the *Merlin*'s rounded hull. And I was thrilled and gratified whenever that ocean revealed one of its wild secrets: a sulphur-bottomed whale surfacing within a few feet of where I stood on the deck, the mist and spray of its spouting caught on my cheek as the wind wafted seawater that had come from a whale's innards; sharks finning past and before us—makos, hammerheads, blues, and threshers—some holding position off our stern, waiting for a fish to be hooked or (I often thought) for me to slip and fall overboard out there in the awesome eternity of that wild, pure, watery world where a man overboard and alone was no more than a single pod of sargassum weed adrift to nowhere.

On more than a few of those summer afternoons when the air warmed above a colder Atlantic, fog materialized and we would have to use our compass and dead reckoning to find our way home. Currents flowed like rivers near the Gulf Stream, and we seldom knew just how far we might have been carried one way or the other. But we had a general idea, and we would head north, edging a bit west so we wouldn't miss Long Island altogether. And after a long hour or so, we'd slow, shut down the engine, and drift there in the mist, listening, listening for that horn at Montauk Light. How fine it was when that sonorous, drawn-out bellow reached out and welcomed us with reassurance and an end to the tension that fog always brought in those days before affordable radar and loran.

And there were just enough mishaps out there on the Gulf Stream's edge to remind us that fishing boats were not invulnerable or fail-safe, as we so studiously tried to believe. One charter boat quickly burned to its waterline when gasoline fumes gathered belowdecks and exploded when the engine was started after it had been shut down for lunch. Another boat heard the radioed distress call and was close enough to reach the crew and passengers and pull them from the sea before darkness made such a rescue most improbable. Another skipper, alone on his boat, smelled smoke, went below, and found the cabin in flames too intense to be quelled. He abandoned ship and drifted two days holding on to a Styrofoam ice chest before he was found and rescued.

Those stories and others like them took hold like lichen in the back of my mind. Even though I made a point of keeping them well covered with positive thinking, they were there always, reminding me that being on a small boat in a vast ocean is an experience guaranteed to keep a person quite aware of just where he is and how uncertain it is that the position can be indefinitely maintained, especially if there is worn equipment and/or carelessness on deck.

On a still August day offshore, I stood at the end of the *Merlin*'s pulpit, the finely fashioned harpoon stand designed by that Rockport sailmaker. A narrow plank extended about eight feet beyond the *Merlin*'s bow, held there by braces from her hull. At its end, the plank broadened into a circle just large enough to stand on with both feet. A rail of thin steel cable held in place by a few chromed braces was all that kept the harpooner from going overboard; even so, it was balance more than any built-in restraints that held accidents at bay. Even on a relatively calm sea, a man had to be alert and poised to maintain stability at the pulpit's outermost end.

But it was a temptation I could not resist. Out there, looking straight ahead, I had wings. All evidence of the boat was behind me; I was her figurehead, her leading edge. Beneath me was the blue Atlantic, ahead the bare horizon's sweep. Rising and falling with the great swells that rolled from the ocean's fathomless heart, leaning into the cable strand that braced me, I could have been a porpoise leaping alongside the *Merlin*'s bow, an entity of the sea, not from the land that still soiled the soles of my tattered canvas shoes.

On that August forenoon with the high sun at my back, the sea acknowledged me with my shadow. Looking down into the clear, depthless ocean, I saw the dark shade of myself skimming the surface as the sun made a star of my head, its rays rocketing from my center, streaming a diadem of light and dark coupled to me as both of us soared across the windless Atlantic.

One moment, it was an empty desert of an ocean; the next, a shark materialized, a looming, slumbering torpedo of a shape as still as a drifting log, dark on the slick surface, its dorsal and tail fin probing the air. Ten feet (well, at least eight); a big mako— wonderful sharks, clean lines. Peter could not see it from inside the cabin where he steered the *Merlin* on a course due west at half-speed to save fuel while we searched for school tuna. Our harpoon was not ready, there was no need for me to call out and reveal the shark's location.

Instead, I was silent, mesmerized by that creature of such restrained violence. A predator, dozing; a lion asleep in the sea's open tundra. How close would we get, I wondered as the mako flashed no alarm. The *Merlin* slipped along the sea as easily as an eel, and there was the shark at my feet, directly below the pulpit, his eye as large as a black apple, shining black in the blue water. Looking directly at me, I thought, there wearing my crown, the sun.

The tail moved ever so slightly from side to side, an indolent fan stirring the still water. The shark eased away from the bow, but stayed directly on our course a few feet in front. As it glided there, it began to sink, at first so imperceptibly that I failed to recognize the mako's intent. Then, as the tail and dorsal slipped beneath the surface, I understood that this shark was moving to the depths, the unknown below the *Merlin*'s fragile skin of its hull, the canyons beneath, some of them almost a thousand feet down.

The shark descended as implacably as a setting sun. I watched from the pulpit, staring. Never before had I witnessed such a departure by such a large, unhurried fish in such a deep sea. Down and down and down it went, a shadow descending.

Then it was gone. Only the sun and I remained, our reflections skimming the surface as before. But all had changed. I knew the shark had been there, was still there, even though it had departed my witness. Its going had given me a dimension of eternity. I sensed the infinite so strongly I was frightened. For this was the vanishing of each of us. This was how we could depart the earth and disappear in depths that had no name, no boundaries, no histories that men can comprehend.

It is almost forty years later and still, when I contemplate death, I see that shark. None of us who have been aboard small boats on vast seas knows what images will abide for the rest of our lives. But those images will survive, outlasting boats and the men at their helms. The shark I saw swims still in the oceans of my soul.

The *Merlin* gave me that. She and the *Vop Vop* were my last work boats. But not the sum of each of the work boats I knew. There were others.

Two of them were berthed with us at the town dock. And like a man greeting his ex-wives on the way to his current boudoir, I nodded to them each morning of those *Merlin* summers. One was Jimmy Reutershan's twenty-three-foot Jersey boat, the *Peasant* (from Shakespeare's *Hamlet*: "O! what a rogue and peasant slave am I"). After I left the *Blue Peril* and joined Ted's haul-seining crew,

Jim became a solo fisherman with gill netting and hand lining his
top priorities. He learned how to launch the *Peril* single-handedly
and set his gill nets off the ocean beach in fall and spring and on the
Sound side in the summer.

In the fall, when the bluefish and striped bass migration peaked,
he worked sixteen hours a day, hauling back and resetting his gill
nets in the morning, bringing the fish to the packing house, and then
taking the *Peasant* to the Shagwong rips or off the point to troll hand
lines. With outriggers on both sides and a line directly over the
stern, the *Peasant* could handle five lines—each about sixty feet of
heavily tarred, stiff line used most often for codfish trawls. When the
fishing was good, two or three fish could hit the trolled lures simul-
taneously. And if the fishing was that good, boat traffic over the
schools was heavy. That meant Jim had to pay attention to the wheel,
making certain the *Peasant* didn't collide with another boat or cross
another angler's lines.

Which meant he needed a mate, and most often I was the mate he
chose. With Jim at the helm, I would tend the lines, hauling blues
and stripers hand-over-hand, unhooking them quickly, and dropping them into the iced fish boxes on the *Peasant*'s deck. On a good
day, we'd fill two or three boxes, which meant close to a hundred
dollars, of which my share was a third. I'd gut the fish on the way
back to the dock, clean up the boat, and ice and box the fish for
market at Gosman's when we made port at the town dock. That was
usually around nine at night, and I'd be back the next morning at
five while most of the stars were still sparkling.

Jersey boats were named after the place they were built: the
state's Atlantic coast. The original, lapstraked, high-bowed, broad
wooden boat with its rounded bottom and high stern was designed
to be launched through the surf that broke on New Jersey's long,
very flat, broad beaches. Like the dory, the first Jersey boats were
rowed with two sets of oars. But with the post–World War II surge
in boating and recreational fishing, the classic Jersey boat design was
used as the master pattern by a number of boatbuilders who gave

the boats a small trunk cabin forward, an inboard marine engine amidships, and plenty of work space on the afterdeck. They were, from the start, designed to be work boats, at home in the choppy waters of the East Coast's many bays and inshore waters, and it's doubtful if there have been many wooden boat designs better suited to their purpose.

But Jimmy Reutershan was, and had always been, an adventurer. A fighter pilot during the war's early days, he flew his P-40 over the Sahara in the Allied campaign against Rommel and was a decorated hero back in the states before many of my generation had seen combat. The first summer he owned the *Peasant*, he took her twenty-five miles offshore into the Atlantic, where he harpooned and landed a swordfish of about two hundred pounds. As he was most often, Jim was alone. The big fish fought hard, and it was after dark before Jim could start heading home with the swordfish lashed to one side of his small boat.

It was a page out of *The Old Man and the Sea,* except that Jim was young, strong, and bold. His feat was the talk of Montauk for the next year or so, and the *Peasant* became a rather famous boat. Most of the other charter-boat skippers gave us a wave if they passed us on the water, something they didn't generally do to hand liners. After all, they made their living trying to catch the same fish in the same places. But they respected and liked Jim; most of them knew he was part of a large family that had been involved with East End commerce and history for several generations. He and I were good, close friends, but when we were aboard the *Peasant* there was no uncertainty about status: he was definitely the captain and I was very much the mate. Among other things, I learned the full roster of a mate's duties and responsibilities working with Captain Reutershan.

Understanding those parameters of work-boat relationships made me a better mate to the other skippers I worked with, although none was a bit like Jim. He was the most organized, most stubborn, most indefatigable, hardest-working skipper I ever met. I realized just how virtuous he was as a skipper when I mated for

Captain Dick Hamilton aboard another Jersey boat that was almost
a twin of the *Peasant*. A twin, that is, in dimension and basic
construction techniques. But where the *Peasant* was tidy, Hamilton's
boat (she was nameless) was sloppy; where Jim's boat was well
maintained, Hamilton's teetered on the brink of collapse. And when
Captain Reutershan said we would go there and do that, we did
precisely as he had said. When Captain Hamilton said we might go
there and we might do this or that, it was a toss-up as to whether we
would even set the net once during our fishing nights.

Dick Hamilton was a loner, a Florida fisherman who brought his
boat to the East End every summer to use the same fishing systems
in Long Island Sound and Gardiners Bay that he used in the Everglades and along Florida's coast, where he set run-around nets for
mullet and bluefish. In the summer, bluefish were his primary target,
but he also set on weakfish and porgies.

He fished at night and if you mated for Dick, you could say good-
bye to whatever might be left of your life at home as husband and
father. We would leave Three Mile Harbor about six in the evening,
which meant I had to have my dinner at five, not a convenient hour
at our house. Depending on the tide, wind, weather, and personal
demons that gnawed at Hamilton's confidence like mice at a blanket, we could go to Montauk, off Gardiners Island, or west to
Shelter Island and Peconic Bay.

The darker the night, the more reluctant the moon and the
cloudier the sky, the better Hamilton's mood on our way to the
fishing grounds. For he fished on the fire: the phosphorescent trail
every fish made moving through the warm, plankton soup of those
summer waters. Sharks left sinuous, pale green snakes in their wake;
schools of menhaden flashed like lights on a Christmas tree; bluefish
went off like Fourth of July rockets, trailing a shower of sparks.

"Got to watch for them rockets, Jawn," Hamilton would say.
"Watch for them rockets." The notion that I could find fish in the
blackest waters of midnight was a revelation to me. And being able
to identify species by the confirmation of the wondrous, fiery trail

they left in their wake was a discovery as dramatic as it was useful. Until Hamilton, I believed night waters kept their secrets.

There were times when it might have been better for both of us if they had. Hamilton's boat—his year-round life support system—was rigged for run-around netting and nothing else. He had built himself a control perch in the boat's very bow: a round hole just big enough for his small frame, where he sat on a one-board seat and operated the throttle and shift levers. On the bow's point was a searchlight with a handle, and once we had set the long nylon net off the boat's stern in a full circle and at top speed (hence a "run-around"), Hamilton would power the boat inside the circle, flash the searchlight back and forth across the surface, and roar around at full throttle. The noise and flashing light would panic any fish inside the net's circle and in their efforts to escape they would slam into the suspended twine, gilling and tangling there.

After five minutes of "drumming" his fish into the net, Hamilton would ease up to the buoy that marked the end of the net that had

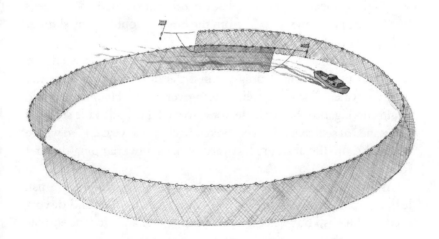

gone overboard last, and with him on one side and myself on the other, we would retrieve the twine, hand over hand. If the lead line and cork line pulled hard, we had fish. Frequently, however, they were not the bluefish we sought. For more often than not, Hamilton misread the night water's fiery omens. His eagerness to find bluefish overrode his judgment, and often we would discover our net sagged with worthless menhaden and not the money fish we sought. Many of those unhappy times—for it took us long hours to pick hundreds of menhaden out of the tangled twine—I had seen the same fires Hamilton had seen, and I had thought they were definitely not bluefish. But I'd learned that a mate does not second-guess his captain, and I would commiserate properly as we endured the wasteful, time-consuming, energy-sapping retrieval process.

One evening as we left the Three Mile Harbor breakwater and turned east toward Gardiners Island, we saw fish breaking water as we passed Hog Creek, a small tidal pond between the breakwater and Lion's Head Rock. Hamilton slowed, watched the action for a while, and decided we had come upon a large school of bluefish in a most unlikely location.

"Jawn," he called back from his bow perch, "get ready to make a set." Which meant I was to pick up the bucket tied to the net's bridle. The next time I heard from the bow, it would be my skipper yelling, "Jawn, let her go!"

Which is when I would toss the bucket over the transom and watch for problems as it dragged first the bridle and then the net into the water. Then I'd yell, "Net's over!" and Hamilton would begin curving into the circle he knew so well. He had made so many thousands of sets that he never looked back, yet always ended where he had begun, the absolute last yard of his net overlapping the first foot.

After an especially enthusiastic drumming, for there were fish leaping inside the net's circle, we began our haul-back and discovered not bluefish but weakfish had been responsible for the surface commotion that had initially gotten our attention.

"We got a charge of weakfish here," Hamilton said, telling me something I already knew. *Charge*, a fisherman's term for a massive bunch of fish, seemed an understatement. We were overwhelmed with fish. They appeared to be gilled in every mesh. The net was so heavily laden we could hardly move it. Yet each foot that we retrieved was so alive with the silver-backed, yellow-bellied fish that we soon had the deck covered with their flopping bodies, even though we had 90 percent of the net yet to haul.

"We'll have to rope in the twine," my captain said, "and pick 'em out ashore." Which meant we would haul back the entire net with its fish still gilled, return to the dock, and then reverse the process from the wharf, pulling the fish from the net as we stood there under the overhead lights.

We had been smitten by excess, and there was no way we could make sense of it. It was a typical Hamilton tragedy: no matter how he tried, he couldn't achieve moderation.

It took us more than an hour to rope in the twine. And after we docked, it took the rest of the night and on into the dawn for us to pick every fish from the net. Most of the smaller ones had been crushed by the weight of their fellows as we motored back to the harbor with the net's great mass piled on itself. It was a warm, midsummer night and a warmer morning. By the time we had a mountain of weakfish piled in the back of my truck and headed for Ted's packing plant, the fish had lost their luster. They were "going soft" as the Fulton Fish Market termed it when a delicately fleshed fish like weakfish had been left too long off the ice. Our big haul lost more than half its market value just because it was too big for us to handle. But there was nothing for us to do but to keep trying.

Twenty-two straight hours of work after we made that fateful Hog Creek set, we had the last of the weakfish washed, weighed, iced, and packed—thousands and thousands of pounds. But instead of thirty-five cents for each of those pounds, we eventually got ten. If ever there was a story that epitomized my work-boat years, that was it.

But there were also those midsummer nights on Gardiners Bay, drifting, the engine shut down, Captain Hamilton in his far-forward perch, half dozing, sipping on a quarter-hour schedule from his pint bottle of rye—Old Hunter . . . "first over the bars"—as we waited for the tide to turn or another natural miracle that would surround that Jersey boat with schools of market-size bluefish dancing as they waited to be netted. At my post in the stern on those nights so windless, so still, so expectant, I could hear Hamilton's Adam's apple bob as the rye washed over his gullet. Far down the Sound, over Stamford, perhaps, thunderheads towered against the stars, Thor's awesome cumulus temple where lightning struck down unrepentant sinners. And as the tides shifted, pulled by an invisible moon, the thunderheads followed, tugged by the ebb beneath. Closer and closer they would march, near enough to chill me with the imminence of their violence. And then as I wondered if it was possible for a boat as small and sloppy as ours to be targeted by a bolt from the black, the clouds would retreat, often returning to their origins, inflicting a rumbling sequel on those hapless Connecticut suburbanites.

They are trying to sleep so they can get up, catch the train, and go to work, I told myself, while I am trying to stay awake so I can live my dreams.

Often those nights would vanish before we found fish of any kind and we would be there alone on the bay, weary from our waiting; Hamilton would push the starter button he had there in the bow cockpit, the engine would rumble, and we would cruise gently back to Three Mile as dawn colored the east. "Well, Jawn," Hamilton would call back over the engine's drone, "not too thick out there, were they?" and I would not answer because if I had spoken I would have said something sharp, like "We didn't spend much time looking," or, as I once did, much to my regret, "Maybe we could find more fish if you were sober." Like many drinkers, Hamilton ravaged himself with guilt; he needed no carping from me. He was so alone, vulnerable, and tragic that I knew he must have come from one of

Ireland's surf-swept fishing villages where men like him put to sea in small boats every day of the year to find fish and absolution in the North Atlantic's merciless scourge.

At summer's end, I quit Hamilton, said good-bye. He said he would see me again next June when he came back from his fishing in Florida. I said sure, but I knew I could not spend another summer working on his boat in the reversed world of fishing on the fire, a world where nights became working days and days became a sweltering search for sleep while the rest of our home was alive and running through the open doors of August.

So I returned to mating on Montauk's charter boats, the job that had begun with Jim on his *Peasant* and would end with Peter on his *Merlin*. In between, there was Captain Al Ceslow and his boat, the

Skip Too, an aging, wooden sports fisher, complete with flying bridge, two fighting chairs, great sweeping outriggers whipping across the sky as the *Skip Too* rolled on her modified-V hull that acknowledged every choppy sea as we trolled back and forth, back and forth across the Shagwong rips, Al sitting high on his flat board seat atop the flying bridge, turning every now then to look down at me in the cockpit, making certain the wire lines were trolling properly and that I was on my toes, raising our clients' pulse rates with talk of big fish about to strike. Al needed a new engine before he could feel comfortable about going offshore, so he specialized in bluefish and stripers, the inshore fish that sustained Montauk's charter-boat industry.

He was a fair, determined, and melancholy skipper who could have been operating a drill press or laying carpet; running a charter boat was how he made his living, not how he dreamed of his life. But I learned something about operating a thirty-five-foot charter boat with a single screw and an engine that would have been sitting in a rest-home lawn chair if it had been a person. Al was straightforward and prompt about paying me; he never once lost his temper or humiliated me the way some Montauk skippers humbled their mates, showing off for their clients. And on the days we had a cancellation and stayed at the dock, I wandered to Duryea's to talk with the dragger skippers and lobstermen.

The draggers intrigued me. They were boats built exclusively for work, and a highly specialized kind of work at that. One or two in the Montauk fleet were steel boats; all the rest were wooden, fashioned from the sturdiest sort of timbers. The stems that rose from their bows and ran the length of their bottoms were as hefty as barn beams—great oak timbers from mature trees selected to become the spines of boats that would take more of a beating from the sea in a year than any charter boat would take in a decade. With their masts, high wheelhouses, winches, and the welded steel yokes that trailed the cables that kept the trawl net in place—that open funnel of heavy twine towed across the sea bottom—the small draggers of those days epitomized the classic work boat, the apex of the work-boat hierarchy. And on those decks were mates who lifted more, tugged more, shoveled more, chopped more, and struggled more than any other crewmen in any other job at sea.

It was a trade of legends, filled with heroic giants. There was Captain Dick Halliday aboard his red-and-white *Undine*. He was a skipper of such reckless reputation and such monumental bouts with the bottle that he could no longer recruit a crew. So he sailed alone, doing the work of the one or two men who should have sailed with him. And in spite of the predictions on the town dock that one day his boat would be found adrift after Dick had been washed overboard, he succeeded at fishing alone.

He even survived hurricanes alone. In August 1954 as hurricane Carol, the most destructive of that hurricane decade, made its way toward eastern Long Island, all the dragger fleet except the *Undine* were in port, their crews busy running extra lines to pilings, to other draggers, and to extra anchors. But Captain Halliday, anxious to fill his hold before his return to Duryea's dock, had waited for Carol to announce herself in person before he headed home along the ocean beach from the fishing grounds off East Hampton.

I was one of hundreds of men and women and children who stood on the wind-battered dunes, the blown sand stinging our faces, to watch Dick Halliday battle the sea. With the wind blowing sixty miles an hour, and gusting to seventy or more, the in-shore Atlantic was an endless tumult of breaking, rolling, towering waves sweeping from the northeast. The *Undine* quartered into them, whitewater often hiding her decks. Up and down she pitched, her progress achingly slow. No more than three-quarters of a mile off the beach, she was there in plain view, a disaster about to happen.

But through the forenoon and afternoon, she inched ever closer to Montauk Point, where the sternest of all tests awaited her. "She may make it down the beach," a draggerman standing next to me said. "But she'll never make it around the point."

I was there at the point as the *Undine* came around, the chaos of tide and breaking seas so confused, so unpredictable that no helmsman could pick his way through. Whenever there seemed to be a pattern to the tumult, a wave would roll from a bizarre direction, impossible to avoid or counter. The *Undine* was pitched on her gunwales by seas that struck her broadside, picked up and slewed by following seas that broke over her stern, and shoved backward by angry waves striking her head-on with mountainous, foaming fists. There were times when the *Undine* was literally within inches of capsizing or swamping. If her engine had faltered, even for a moment, or her steering had failed to respond properly, she would have been gone, capsized, sunk, and rolled ashore on the great rocks that littered the point's shore.

The scores of men and women, many of them fishermen and their wives, who watched Dick Halliday's struggle were quiet, awed, waiting like witnesses to a tragedy whose awful ending could not be changed. But Dick Halliday acknowledged no inevitables. Just as the storm became too violent, even for the spectators, he and the *Undine* had come far enough around the point to reach the relative lee of Montauk's cliffs on the Sound side. The seas there were dangerous, but after what Halliday had endured, they were manageable. A half-hour later, the *Undine* steamed between the breakwaters at Montauk Lake and anchored far up the harbor to ride out whatever winds Carol had left to inflict.

What I remember most about that memorable contest between man and nature is the *Undine*. She was not an exceptional dragger; she was standard, built of traditional materials on traditional dragger lines. She was the quintessential work boat. But because those lines had evolved over decades of Yankee commercial fishing in the roughest and most unpredictable fishing waters on the globe, the *Undine* was superbly ready for Carol's challenge. And she was superbly handled by her tall, melancholy loner of a skipper. Watching them survive together taught me that well-designed boats built from proper materials can endure conditions far beyond what most of us can imagine—provided there is a captain at the wheel who knows his boat and how to handle her.

Dick Halliday must have been frightened when he realized how much too late he had stayed offshore. But he did not panic and he did precisely what he had to do to get his beloved *Undine* safely into port. Both he and his boat had to be in excellent condition, and both he and his boat had to be fully prepared for that ultimate challenge. And when it came, Dick Halliday and every boatman who watched him beat the sea learned that a good boat well-handled can endure more punishment from that sea than most skippers think possible. Ever since, when I have been caught in rough weather, I remember Dick Halliday and he helps keep my head clear and my confidence within reach. However, during those times I have been quite aware that the boat I steer is not the *Undine*, for these days there are few boats built as lovingly, carefully, and from such sturdy materials as those wooden draggers that came out of New England boatyards during the first half of the twentieth century.

And the men who skippered them were often just as tough. Dick Halliday was one; Chris Finney was another. By the time I met him, he had also become a loner. But unlike Captain Halliday, whose solitude was his choice, Chris Finney sailed without a mate because there were none who would sail with him. His long commercial fishing career was nearing its close when he took a job as guardian of the Gardiners Bay oyster beds. Until the bay suffered massive algae blooms (which many researchers believe are caused by pollutants) in the 1960s, some of the world's finest oysters were grown and fattened in its rich, cold waters.

Marked by stakes flying the stiff canvas flags that identified the bed's lessee, the vast underwater acres were paved with oysters that bore no trademarks and could, if they were plucked from their home, be sold for premium prices. To prevent such piracy, the oyster companies hired Chris Finney as the bed's protector.

They hired a man with a reputation for toughness earned over the years and still talked about. One of the stories was often told at Duryea's to young would-be mates like myself.

"Well," one of the booted draggermen would say, "you could always stop by and see Chris Finney. They tell me he's looking for a mate." And there would be smiles all around. Then later one of the men would pull me aside and say, "I wouldn't want you to sail with Chris without you learned something about him." And they would tell me this story:

"Chris was dragging for yellowtail off Block Island and it was blowing pretty good from the southwest, choppy don't you know.

"When they'd haul back and dump the trawl, there would be fish bouncing all over the deck. Chris kept after his mate to get them iced and boxed before the next tow come aboard. It was hard working there 'mongst all them fish with the boat rolling. When he was chopping ice, that mate slipped or something and put his icepick right through his boot top, on through his foot and kept right on going through the boot sole until the pick stuck hard into the deck.

"When he looked at what he done, the mate started to yelling and Chris come down from the wheelhouse wondering what was the matter.

" 'Captain, we got to go in,' the mate yelled, 'look what I done to my foot.'

"Chris didn't say nothing. He reached down and yanked that icepick out of his deck and out of that boy's foot. Then he handed it back to him and said, 'Keep choppin. Nobody's going ashore till we're done fishing.'

"I heard that when they come back to the dock that evening that boy had a bootful of blood."

I never asked Chris Finney if that story was true. I didn't have the nerve to bring it up. When I fished with Hamilton on those long nights, Chris would slide alongside in his watchman's launch once in a while for some of my coffee and a chat. He had to spend every night out there alone with not too much to do. Once the oyster pirates learned who was watching those beds, they never spent much time in Gardiners Bay.

Men like Dick Halliday, Chris Finney, Dick Hamilton, and other lifelong commercial fishermen had been, in my fanciful images of a life on the water, the kind of men I wanted to emulate. For in the abstract, they were wondrous seamen, splendid boat handlers, resourceful individuals with a unique comprehension of the sea and its creatures—a bred-in-the-bone ability to sense where the fish would be and when they would get there. For them, and the Lesters and the Edwards and the Millers and the Havens and each of the other generational fishing families on the East End, their boats were more important than their homes. What they needed from their homes was a dry place where they could keep warm in winter and—when they weren't on the water—take their meals sitting down.

What they needed from their boats was nothing less than their lives. Their boats were their sustainers, their workplace, their fish catchers, clammers, and scallopers. From their boats they tended gill nets, raised traps, trolled for bluefish and striped bass, harpooned swordfish, lifted eel pots, set run-arounds, dragged trawls, and set haul-seines in the heart of the breaking surf. It was the boats that made commercial fishing happen, and the men who piloted them were like men everywhere: many of them fine, some bitter, some angry, some alone, but none who could not work harder than most Americans ever imagined a man could work.

I worked hard too, but not well or wisely enough.

Next year, I kept telling myself, next year I will arrive at an understanding of this compelling business of making a living on the water. I told myself that, but I never told myself the truth. I eased myself around the reality of the debts I had amassed, the trusts I had abused, the relationships I had strained. Nothing in life was as important to me as the water around me, the creatures, the wondrous creatures, who made that water their home, and the men who sought them from the boats that had captivated me since I was a boy building a burlap sail for the *Emma*.

But not even my selfish romanticism, or my capacity for self-deception, could sustain forever. After six years of commercial fishing, six years aboard a fine variety of work boats, I surrendered to reality. Shoved by my exasperated parents, pushed by my tardy recognition that I could no longer abuse my good-hearted creditors, and energized by my awareness that our marriage had suffered a compound fracture, I was offered, and accepted, a "regular job" as a corporate copywriter for the Fyr-Fyter Company at its main office and manufacturing center in Dayton, Ohio.

Dayton, Ohio. About as far from wooden boats and salt water as Pike's Peak. Like an addict quitting cold turkey, I moved both physically and metaphysically as far as I could get from my fishing friends, Duryea's dock, the town dock, Montauk Lake, Three Mile Harbor, Napeague, Gardiners Bay, Cartwright Shoals, Gin Beach, Georgica, and Lion's Head Rock. I left my truck parked by the village green in The Springs. I took the battered but unbowed *Emma* back to the family house at Georgica, where she had first blessed me with her charms. And the *Vop Vop*, my pride and joy, my one successful innovation with her square-rigged sail and Sid Cullum outriggers, was left at the town dock in Three Mile Harbor with the understanding that she would soon be given to Tony Duke's Boys Harbor, a summer camp for inner-city youths. I never saw her again after that early spring day when I got behind the wheel of our beat-up, slime-green Studebaker and began my nonstop drive from The Springs to Dayton. A few years later I heard that she had done yeoman service at the camp. That boat had been built hundreds of miles away on Bonaventure for a few years' service as a codfish hand liner, yet she lasted for decades in her unlikely new life as a waterborne classroom for boys who needed to learn about the miracles a simple wooden boat can achieve.

My life as a commercial fisherman, my seven-day-a-week job as a prospecter of the depths, my years on the decks of a dozen or more different boats, my nights of fishing on the fire, and my dawns of clambering over a dory's rail as it rode the surf's white water had all come to an end, a full stop as sudden and complete as a guillotine's fall.

Except for knowledge. For I had learned something, albeit slowly. And what I had learned best had to do with boats. I knew something about traditional and nontraditional design. I understood much (but not all) of what it takes to keep a marine engine running. I had acquired, often the hard way, a sense of what's needed to operate a boat safely, and what maintenance is essential to that operation. I could row, I could sail, I could steer a compass course. And, best of all, I had locked within my consciousness that image of Dick Halliday's *Undine* battling her way around the point in a hurricane. That taught me everything important about how much of the sea's passionate embrace a good boat can absorb. After that, I was still wary of the sea's impersonal and intemperate power, but I was no longer afraid.

I could not make a living as a commercial fisherman, but those years I shared with fishermen, boats, and the water gave me the materials I needed to build a life.

More Dories

Dayton lasted about a year. In early March 1958, I stepped from a Greyhound bus into a swirling snowstorm in Kennebunk, Maine. The bus had left Boston around eleven and had lumbered through the night for more than three hours as snow cascaded over its windshield and hurried past the headlights. It was nearly three when the driver opened the door in front of the Kennebunk Inn on Main Street (also U.S. Route One). With one small suitcase in my hand, I stepped out into a drift almost two feet deep. The hotel looked closed.

As I stood there, cold and growing colder, wondering how the fates had conspired to bring me to this place I had never before seen, a police car pulled up, its tire chains clanking in the street's packed snow. A broad-shouldered, hearty—even at that hour—policeman got out and asked me if I had a place to stay. It was Frank Stevens, who later became chief. His family had lived in the Kennebunks for generations; he could have been a lobsterman, would have been if he hadn't joined the force.

I told him I had come to work for Sandy Brook, who had just purchased the local weekly newspaper, *The Kennebunk Star*. I had known Sandy's father, the painter, Alexander Brook, during my East End fishing years. He owned a fine old house in Sag Harbor and liked to dine on fresh skate wings, *raie au beurre noir*, every now and then. There was scarcely a haul-seine set made on the beach that failed to scrape up a dozen or more skates. I'd slice off their "wings" there on the beach, wash and ice them when we got back to the packing house, and take them over to Alex the same evening, or the next day. He reveled in their delicacy, and I did too, once I tasted his skate-wing cooking.

Alex gave me two sketches of a clam digger whose portrait he planned to paint, and I have them still. I like to think that if I had not left my background, my natal city, and abandoned the plans my parents had for me and gone fishing, I might never have met Alex and certainly would not have contributed so richly to his table. And it was those times shared with him that led to my contacts with Sandy and my pre-dawn arrival in Kennebunk. And that turned out to be the first hour of the first day of what was to become a thirty-year love affair with the state of Maine.

I rode the bus because the car that carried me from Dayton had broken down in Buffalo. It was my sister Jane's old but still fetching dark blue Oldsmobile convertible—one of the great cars to emerge from the forties. I had to leave it, filled with the rest of my luggage and household goods, so I could get to Kennebunk in time to help Sandy get out his first issue of the *Star*.

My fishing days helped my escape from Dayton in many other ways. But most crucial was the money that made the breakaway possible. That money was the amount I was paid for a painting Jackson Pollock had given me when we lived as neighbors in The

Springs. That was long before his works commanded some of the
highest amounts ever paid for contemporary art. And, of course, if I
had held on to the painting for a few more years, the sale would have
brought in enough cash to corrupt me. Jackson liked fresh fish too,
and after I dropped some by his house for him and Lee, I used to
stay and talk. Over the years, we became good friends. He was an
impulsive and generous, as well as a difficult, friend who gave me the
painting just before I left our home in The Springs for the last and
final time. It was while we were in Dayton that Jackson was killed in
an automobile accident. I never got the chance to tell him his
painting gave me the new life that began that early morning in
Kennebunk.

Frank Stevens knew Sandy was staying in a cottage on an estate
that was one of the finest in Kennebunk, and he took me there in
the patrol car, sliding and skidding on the snowy streets. After he
dropped me there in the dark, his car got stuck at the bottom of the
long driveway in front of the carriage house that had been converted
to a cottage. I had to push to help get the car under way, and by the
time I banged on the cottage door and awakened Sandy, my feet and
legs were soaked and I was sweating. It was not an auspicious arrival.

But the next day during our short lunch hour, life improved.
Sandy drove me to Kennebunk Beach, where the Atlantic's storm-
surge swells rose sharp in the northwest wind and crashed on a
beach half snow, half foam, under a bright blue sky swept by a sun
climbing toward spring. Once I could see breaking waves and feel
their rumble under my feet as I stood on the beach, my faith in the
future was restored. Like Lazarus, I had been released from the
tomb that Dayton had become, a dark place without the illumina-
tion of any sea.

The *Star* offices were just off Kennebunk's Main Street, in the
shadow of what had been a textile mill on the banks of the Mousam
River. On warm days when we kept our office door open, I could
hear the river falling from the dam that had once generated the
energy that powered the mill's shuttles and looms. Within a few days

I followed the river to its meeting with the sea at a wandering salt marsh whose intricate tapestry of water and marsh spread for miles across the land.

It was near there that I wanted our family to live, and within a year we moved from our rented house in Kennebunk to another in Kennebunkport. The new place was just a block from the Kennebunk River, the waterway which divided the two towns and gave both of them a harbor. On the Kennebunk side, just across from Kennebunkport's Dock Square, a working boatyard built handsome wooden boats; across the river, a few lobster boats nestled against the Kennebunkport side at berths that were about a half-mile from the breakwater and the open ocean.

A few miles to the east, the harbor at Cape Porpoise was one of the busiest commercial fishing ports on the southern Maine coast. Scores of lobster boats, herring seiners, and a few draggers were moored there; and the place was in constant motion as lobstermen unloaded their catch, lobster buyers tended their floating holding tanks (wooden boxes called lobster cars), and bait dealers filled barrels with ocean perch carcasses covered with rock salt. Cape Porpoise looked and smelled like a fishing town, and it was there on the docks that I spent much of my time away from the newspaper— which wasn't all that many hours because Sandy and I worked seven days a week most of that first year, many of those hours at back-shop jobs that neither of us had ever done before.

We were also the *Star*'s circulation and advertising department. Taking classified ads was one of my chores. They arrived in the mail and had to be processed for the typesetter and recorded in what I claimed was a ledger. Or the ads were called in over the phone and sometimes they were composed at our front counter, a marble headstone (engraved side down) set on top of our formidable office safe. Shortly after our move to Kennebunkport, a young man stood at the counter with pen in hand, brow furrowed as he thought about the shortest, most effective ways to communicate with our readers.

"Can I help you?" Writing copy was part of my job as editor and circulation and advertising manager. The young man was Brad Sterl; he had driven up from Ogunquit where he worked as a regional marine biologist for the Maine Department of Sea and Shore Fisheries—since renamed the Department of Marine Fisheries. Brad had come to compose a "For Sale" ad. He wanted to sell a dory.

I knew as soon as I came to the counter and read his first draft that this was one ad that the *Star* would never publish. At first, Brad might have thought my questions were asked because I wanted to take a shot at writing the ad. But he soon understood that the newspaperman on the other side of the counter was one of the surest bets a fellow with a dory to sell was ever likely to encounter.

Bargaining has never been one of my talents. I've never been a price negotiater. I ask, "How much?" and if I have the money (and sometimes even if I don't), I buy. The dory deal with Brad was done in less than two minutes. It took much longer to decide how my first Maine boat could be delivered, and eventually Brad agreed to borrow a boat trailer and a pickup truck that could haul the dory from Ogunquit to our house in Kennebunkport.

She arrived and was unloaded in our driveway. I worked a couple of planks under her bow and stern and began walking around her, inspecting, estimating, touching, and rejoicing. I was happier that day than any since I had left The Springs two years before. I had a dory in the yard and she was mine. I owned a boat that had come to symbolize each of those fishing years; I could touch the best days of my life. For me, that day marked my true arrival in Maine.

The dory needed work. I don't believe a second- or third-hand boat has ever been sold that didn't need repairs. No one, well almost no one, sells a boat in top condition, unless they're dealers with new boats in the showroom. Boat owners, especially working fishermen as Brad had been before he got his job with the state, wouldn't give up a boat if she was 100 percent healthy. What would be the point? If she had some life left in her, then keep her. But if her planks are sprung, her rails rubbed raw, her seams open, dried out, and

shrunken after too many days under a backyard sun, then she's
ready to be sold.

As the days lengthened that late spring and we got our newspaper
under some control, I had time to work on my dory in the evenings.
All her original caulking had to be pried from her seams; it was
desiccated beyond any recovery. Once that job was done, I caulked
those seams, first with tarred cotton caulk, then a covering of below-
the-waterline caulking compound for the three planks that were the
dory's bottom. The same process was repeated for the overlapping
planks of the dory's hull, but there I used above-the-waterline
compound. I was in no hurry. Every moment that I spent with that
dory was a moment for reliving my first meeting with the *Blue Peril*. I
was back on the Main Beach sunporch with Jimmy Reutershan and
Gene Winberg, each of us wondering if we had the skill and the
knowledge to raise the *Peril* from the dead, but saying not a word
about our doubts.

I never named that dory I bought from Brad, but she had many of
the same characteristics as the *Peril*: she was smaller than the huge
work dories moored in Cape Porpoise Harbor, sunk almost to their
gunwales by the weight of the herring seines they carried; and she
was almost as neglected as the *Peril* had been when she first arrived
in our lives. But that first Maine dory had one critical difference that
was an integral part of her design: she had a well about two feet
forward of her stern, kind of a box about ten inches square that
ended at a hole in the dory's bottom and came up even with her
gunwales. That well, that added structure, allowed the dory to be
fitted with a small outboard motor. I'd never handled a dory under
power.

After about six weeks of working whenever I could take a few
minutes from the newspaper and our family, the dory was ready to
be launched. She had been scraped, caulked, painted, sanded, and
painted again: black on the outside, green on her inside. Those were
the colors she had arrived wearing, and somewhere I'd heard it

encouraged bad luck if you changed a boat's colors. I was having mostly good luck (except for our marriage) in my life, and I was reluctant to run any unnecessary risks.

I moored the dory at Cape Porpoise and rowed her around a time or two, mostly out to one of the several small islands just outside the harbor. There are so many islands off the Maine coast, some of them scores of square miles large, others no bigger than a good-size boulder, that it's said they have never been accurately counted. They are a gift to people with small boats because even though some of them are less than a half-mile offshore, most are deserted places, scoured clean by winter storms so that when a boatman rows ashore he can believe he is setting foot on a beach that has never known a human's boot.

Often, after that first step, I would find empty shotgun shells, beer cans, and plastic refuse that told me the place had known many visitors. But I never met anyone on those islands except birds, seals, and small crabs scuttling in the tide pools. As dories had so many times in my past, that Kennebunkport dory gave me an escape to my illusions. She allowed me to find room to live with my fishing memories and space to fantasize about a fishing future.

One October dawn I rowed the dory a half-mile or so offshore and anchored there in the chop of a brisk southwest breeze. The morning was disgruntled, cloudy, chilly, as if it knew winter would soon arrive to make these waters quite untenable for casual visitors like myself. I had a string of silhouette scoter decoys: six oversize sea-duck profiles sawed from a sheet of plywood, painted black, and mounted on a single section of pine one-by-two. Tethered to the dory by a length of tarred twine, the silhouettes were intended to attract passing white-winged scoters. The scoter clan has never been praised for its collective intelligence. Large, big-breasted sea ducks that feed on mussels and other bivalves, the jet-black waterfowl with white masks on their faces and white patches on their wings were also never considered a gourmet's choice. But the dark, rich, and tough meat of their breasts has a pungent, unique flavor that I had learned to like on Long Island after I had brought home a half-dozen scoters shot down from the *Emma* after she was towed to Cartwright Shoals by Captain Sam Edwards and his dragger, the *Capt. Sam*. Once or twice a year he organized a couple dozen coot shooters who brought their own sharpies to Promised Land and anchored across the shoals about a gunshot apart.

When the scoters and other sea ducks like oldsquaw and eider flew from the bay toward the open ocean, most of them chose to follow the waterway between Cartwright and Gardiners. Habitual close-to-the-water fliers, they could accelerate to speeds that topped fifty to sixty miles an hour about ten feet above the bay. Some were even lower, hugging the surface. There was much gunfire when the flights crossed the strung-out line of boats with their gunners lying flat on the cold, wet decks. When the scoters were in range, or even before, the gunners would sit up, jam their shotguns against their shoulders, and begin swinging down on the birds, firing as they passed.

It was a risky system. Number-4 birdshot pellets whistled around each boat, sometimes striking its gunner, most often pinging against the planks. Men cursed, laughed, and yelled insults at their neighbor gunners. One morning Charlie Lord got so stiff lying in the bottom

of his skiff that when a lone coot at last flew within range, Charlie sat up and fired before he had his shotgun properly positioned. Instead of the coot, he shot his own boat, putting a sizable hole right through her bottom at exceedingly close range. He stood up and started waving and yelling, and finally Captain Sam had to go get the big boat and hoist Charlie's sharpie on deck, which made so much commotion along the line of sharpies that even the scoters took heed and changed course long before they flew in range. Charlie was not a popular member of the shooting party that morning.

For a long time after those annual shoots at Cartwright, I would think about hunting scoters in the fall. But until I got to the Maine coast, I had no chance. Maine was where the sea-duck population spent its summers; and, if anything, there were more scoters along Maine's incredibly convoluted shores than there ever were in Gardiners Bay. When I set out rowing that October morning, I was on a pilgrimage to my past. I was thinking of Charlie Lord and grinning.

As I reminisced internally, the day became more surly. What had been a brisk breeze gained weight each quarter-hour until the dory jumped and yanked on her anchor warp and the seas slapped her around, switching her stern from side to side. No scoters had flown within range; only a pair of oldsquaws, the male bright in his black-and-white tailored feathers, had whistled past. They had come downwind and were two dots wavering over the whitecaps before I could think of raising my gun.

I told myself at ten minutes of eight that I would leave on the hour and I knew I would have a tough row. As I waited, the waters parted within twenty-five feet of the dory and I was looking a humpback whale right in its huge, black, obsidian globe of an eye. I could see each barnacle growing in white coruscations on its chin, follow the odd line of its mouth, and smell the sea-stuff of its sour breath when it exhaled with a long, sibilant sigh.

Its back kept rising from the water, like one of those platforms that ascends from the stage during a play, coming from nowhere until it is a presence before you, adding new dimensions to the scene and new significance to the drama. That whale's back was so vast, so impersonal, so alive with a force beyond my ken that I became frightened. It could capsize this dory, I thought. But there was nothing I could do except wait and watch. The dory and I were both at anchor.

Then, at last, the whale's flukes appeared, raised like a forked black flag from the gray sea. They hung there for a moment against the clouds and were gone. The entire mass of the creature had vanished, the waters closed, disturbed only by the wind. But I knew the whale was close. It could, I thought, be underneath my dory. With its rancid breath, obsidian eye, and barnacled jaw, it had projected no friendliness; it was not a creature I wanted to know better.

I waited a few minutes, pitching and yawing there in the nervous dory, and then pulled in the scoter silhouettes, hauled up the anchor, and rowed back to the harbor. That was the last time in my life I went sea-duck shooting.

Before the following spring, I had quit the *Star* for a job as the editor of the *Brunswick Record*, a much larger weekly in Brunswick, about fifty miles east of Kennebunk. Brunswick, the home of Bowdoin College and the Brunswick Naval Air Station, was built between the banks of the Androscoggin River to the north and Casco Bay to the south. There was plenty of water, fresh and salt, to sustain a water person like myself.

Yet our first home was in Bowdoinham, a small (population 900) farming community about twelve miles inland from Brunswick. But Bowdoinham was on the shores of Merrymeeting Bay, one of the world's unique bodies of water, a place where six rivers meet and where salt water and fresh collide but do not combine. As the tide pushes in from the coast, rushing up the river every day and night, those rivers cease tumbling toward the sea and back up into Merrymeeting, a broad, shallow saucer of a bay surrounded by marshes of bulrushes, wild rice, and duckweed.

We bought our small farmhouse, a barn and five acres of

meadow, from Linwood Rideout and his wife. Linwood had lived his life on the bay as had his wife's father, Earl Browne. For both men and their families, Merrymeeting Bay was the focus of their lives, especially its waterfowl. As the northeast's only freshwater tidal basin with a plentiful stand of wild rice, the bay has long been one of the nation's major gathering grounds for ducks, geese, and shorebirds.

Our new home was on Browne's Point Road, and we could see the point off to the east of the cove that lapped at our waterfront. Earl Browne's place there had once been the finest duck-hunting lodge on the bay, and the lives of its people and the guides Earl hired during the gunning season pivoted around the migratory schedules of blue- and green-winged teal, black duck, Canada geese, brant, bluebill, mallard, pintail, and a dozen other waterfowl species that came to the bay in whirling, whistling flocks, circling in feathered masses like curtains blowing in the wind, back and forth over the sedge—brown, ripe rice and dark green duckweed—settling at last in wavering rafts in the shallow water, gabbling through the still nights as they filled their crops with Merrymeeting's sweet sustenance.

It was August when we arrived, and I first walked to the bay across the field in back of that house and barn. The teal had already arrived, always the first. As I sat there in the high grass on the bay bank as still as stone, the small, vibrant, swift ducks with their brilliantly painted wing patches would fly a few feet above the tops of the swaying bulrushes, their wings curved to catch the air. I could see their eyes' dark pupils and the tips of their webbed feet tucked under their feathered rumps. And I would watch them fall like maple leaves into one of the silver-dollar puddles of the marsh, where they would chatter to each other like marketplace wives as they paddled here and there searching for grains of ripe rice.

And when I stood, stiff, having to get back to the house, the teal would see me for the first time and rise like a fountain that never falls to earth.

I'd left the dory in Kennebunk with a friend who would try to sell her, so I had no boat on Merrymeeting. But Linwood, one of the bay's best-known and most-respected gunning guides, like each of the good ones had a couple of Merrymeeting Bay gunning floats. A lovely, highly specialized wooden boat, the floats were about four-teen feet long, narrow, a bit like a kayak with two small spaces for two people, one behind the other. The sport would sit forward, almost lying down, his legs and torso well up under the long-decked bow, his shoulders resting against a slanted lattice so only the top of his head showed above the boat's profile. In the stern, the guide would sit the same way, but he would have both hands gripped around the handle of a long sculling oar that rested in a deep, curved socket carved for it in the float's low stern. Lying half on his side, half on his back, the guide had just enough room to move his hands and arms back and forth in a curious, twisting motion that turned and swept the oar's gracefully cupped and curved blade a few inches under the water, creating a strong thrust that propelled the boat at a surprising and quite silent speed.

Fashioned from one-inch square strips of white pine glued and intricately curved on frames kept away from prying eyes, Mer-rymeeting Bay gunning floats had a national reputation for grace and easy sculling. They were quite different from Chesapeake gun-ning skiffs, more complex in their design, looking as if they were built as much for beauty as efficiency.

Linwood was generous with his time that first autumn, and he sculled me around the bay on early mornings before the short gunning season opened. Gliding soundlessly on windless, silken water we would ease around a bulrush hummock where startled teal and black duck would spring to the sky, the sound of their beating wings a small thunder on the air. I tried sculling, but could not learn well enough to move the boat with any sense of direction. Whenever I was alone in the float, which Linwood left for me at his old place, I sat up straight and used a canoe paddle.

As the waterfowl populations declined year after year, while the birds were overhunted and were denied their nesting grounds by increasing drainage to make room for development, the guides had to travel farther up the bay and back into its rivers to find quarry for the sports who hired them. Instead of sculling such distances, some guides put small outboards on their floats and the silences that allowed us to hear ducks gabbling a half-mile away were no longer possible during the day. Only at night when the motors shut down could we hear the raucous name-calling of black duck hens, the same wild sound I had heard every now and then at that boyhood house on Georgica on the last September nights before we had to leave our summers for school.

In Bowdoinham, the bay was our only water, but it was full of mystery and needed to be no larger to nourish me. We had friends, however, who lived in a striking home on Harpswell Neck. Built on the edge of a thirty-foot sheer granite cliff that rose like a stone iceberg from Harpswell Sound, the house overlooked most of Casco Bay, and when we were invited there with the children on a sultry late-August day and they swam in the cove that reached around the point where the house stood spreading its shingled wings, I knew I wanted to live closer to the limitless spirits of salt water.

The next summer we sold the Bowdoinham place and moved to another old house in Brunswick. It was not on the water, but it was less than a mile from Middle Bay, one of the thousands of fingers reaching northeast from the Casco Bay bowl that stretched from Cape Elizabeth on the west to Boothbay Harbor down east. Scooped from the Atlantic by massive Ice Age glaciers that scoured the northeast ten thousand years ago, Casco Bay was shallow enough and protected enough to hold a great saucer of solar-heated water that maintained temperatures a few critical degrees higher than the chill seas off most of Maine's convoluted coast. Those few degrees' difference are enough to create a richly textured marine environment, one that exists as a wonderful anomaly, bringing creatures and life cycles to a place that might never be expected to sustain them. Such was the richness that would sustain me for the nearly three decades I lived by the bay and discovered some of its secrets.

Those discoveries began a year and then some after we moved from Bowdoinham. During those difficult months, Cynthia and I divorced and she moved to Cambridge, Massachusetts, with our children, Marshall and Darrah. A few months later, I married Jean, a widow with four children and a house in Pennellville close by Casco Bay. More than twenty-five years have rolled by and Jean and I are happily married still, as are five sons and a daughter. We are grandparents three times over, but neither of us admits to considering ourselves "old." I'll have to wait until I can't row a boat or ride a bike before I'll accept that definition.

Pennellville was then and still is a splendid place for a boat person to live. Its nine elegant homes were built by the same ship's carpenters who built nineteenth-century sailing vessels for the Pennells and Skolfields. Those graceful schooners, launched on the ways at the end of the Pennellville Road into Middle Bay, sailed from there to China and on around the world. When they returned, they brought to the southern Maine coast a wealth of fine silks, porcelain, jade, silver, teak, condiments, and wines that allowed the ship captains of Bath, Brunswick, Portland, and Freeport to bless their finely constructed homes with appointments equal to Boston's finest.

By the time I moved to Pennellville, just one direct descendant of the family kept a homestead there. But at the end of the road, the skeletal timbers of the ways that had once led seaward from the original shipyard could still be seen at low tide, the great, dark bones of an era when Yankee wooden ships were the envy of the world.

I found another dory the same way I had found the one I had in Kennebunk: through a classified in the newspaper I was editing. This dory was waiting on blocks at a small boatyard on the Kennebec River, a mile or two downriver from the Bath Iron Works. Once a shipyard known for its craftmanship, the Iron Works became a major national shipbuilder during the Second World War when Maine men and women built destroyers for the navy, and built them faster and better than any shipyard on the continent. During the 1960s and 1970s, the Cold War kept the yard busy building missile-launching cruisers, and by the time I arrived, the Iron Works was Maine's largest industrial employer, paying the best wages. Its cranes rose like prehistoric creatures come to drink at the river, and the gray hulls of unfinished cruisers lay side by side at the Iron Works' docks—huge steel whales towed in from the hunt, waiting to be processed.

As I looked over the dory there on a set of blocks in the boatyard, I could see the cranes upriver. They were, I was told, the tallest structures north of Portland. I never got used to their brooding presence there on the Kennebec, that rich and historic river whose banks had provided landfall for the first of the nation's settlers and whose flood tides of salmon, herring, sturgeon, and striped bass had nourished men and their crops since the earliest days of the Red Paint people, whose men and women looked to the Kennebec for sustenance thousands of years ago.

I bought the dory, of course. I wanted her so deeply I would, if I had had the money, paid ten times the modest price her owner sought. She was almost a twin of the one I had left in Kennebunk, about the same dimensions and fitted with a well near her stern. She was in better shape than any other dory I had owned or shared. Unlike the *Peril*, her planks and ribs were solid, her seams reasonably tight; even her paint held fast, with just a few chips and blisters here and there. Compared to the dories in my history, this one needed just a few accessories to be ready to launch. And when I'd found a pair of oars, oarlocks, a bailer, some anchor line, and a grappling hook that could serve as an anchor, she was ready to go.

I brought her over from Bath on a borrowed trailer and launched her at high tide at the end of the Pennellville Road, there where the timbers of the old ways snaked dark beneath the flood and weather-vanes watched from the roof peaks of the Pennell homes, white sails rising above the swaying grasses of the Pennell hayfields.

Because the tides of Maine are more strenuous than any elsewhere along the nation's coast, the dory needed a haul-off if I was to be able to reach her at high tide. Which meant I had to wait for a minus low tide before I could plant a proper stake. The first notable ebb came early on a still, summer morning, the sun not yet above the ridge of scrub oak and pine that topped Harpswell Neck's granite peninsula a mile to the east across Middle Bay.

Like most of the tidal fingers that reached northeast from Casco Bay, fingers of water probing, wanting to grasp the fingers of rock and sandy soil that pointed southwest to mark the place where glaciers had at last reached their mother sea, and, sighing, had drifted into the salt ocean and surrendered their lives to their creator, the tributaries were shallow sweeps with scarcely any change in profile for mile after mile after mile. At high tide, perhaps no more than three feet of invading sea covered the primordial mud of those long, broad, black bottoms. And when the tides ebbed, children who had strayed too far rushing back to their mother sea, great plains of mudflats were exposed, the remains of pure Penobscot clay pushed and pressured by the glaciers grinding massively against the land. Left to mourn the glaciers on their way to the sea, the clay sat there on the plains of its own making, as if laid by a huge trowel swept level over the granite beneath. After a millennium of washings under the moon, the clay became black mud, rich with the sea's detritus, pungent with the life and death of countless organisms and the tiny skeletons of ten billion copepods.

It was mud that easily swallowed a man's legs if he stood too long in one place, mud that sucked and tugged at a man's boots, unwilling to surrender its invader. And when it did, the stench was the stink of centuries, a noxious whiff of sulfides distilled from the mute, airless decay that is the perpetual companion of the bay's unquenchable fertility.

Holding a small sledgehammer in one hand and in the other, steadying it on my shoulder, the oak stake I had cut from the third-growth woods across the road from our home—a stake peeled of its bark, heavy with sap—I walked along a granite whaleback, then across cobbled rocks, pebbles, and the white crescents of soft-clam shells and the blue rubble of crushed mussel shells until I reached the beginning of the mud plain and stepped off another twenty-five feet, my booted feet sucking as I stepped. I had pointed one end of the stake with a hachet before I brought it from the barn, and now I pushed that end into the mud, twisting and swinging the stake from side to side to make it penetrate. Black flies and mosquitoes found me before I really got started, and in that airless morning on the stinking mud they probed my nostrils and ears, their high-pitched humming echoing in my skull.

Once started into the mud, the stake kept its place as I reached awkwardly to tap it with the sledge. Slow going, and my boots were vanishing in the mud. But the stake seemed firmly enough in place to stay through the rising tide, when I could take the dory on the top of the flood and pull alongside it with purchase enough then to swing the sledge hard enough to drive the stake deep into the mud. Then I could attach a simple pulley and run a haul-off line through it in an endless loop through another pulley fast to a tree limb on the bank. From that looping line I could run a painter from the dory's bow. When I came to the bay at high tide, the dory riding safe well offshore, I could pull her in by tugging the long line through two pulleys, much as a city housewife tugs at her clothesline from a tenement window. After a row around the bay, I could come ashore, make the dory fast to the haul-off, and pull her out to the stake beyond the rocks that might do her harm. At the low ebb when there were only flats where the bay had been, she would be sitting there on the mud like a turtle taking the sun.

That first Pennellville summer, that wonderfully happy summer, the dory was without a motor. I often rowed her across the bay to a small cove where, at high tide, the water was clear as any Pacific lagoon, deep even against the sheer granite banks where half the roots of the oaks and pines were bare, prehensile fingers gripping the granite, splitting the hard rock in their effort to survive, to hang

on there at the edge of land where their reflections greeted them on
every flood tide.

I would drift there in the dory, standing so I could peer down to
where starfish and anemone waved. Up against the granite the scent
of salt and pine combined, and although I knew there were roads
and houses and barns and schools within a short walk, because I
could see and hear and smell only the woods and the bay I could
believe I was the only man in that world, there alone with the fish
that swam beneath me and the great blue herons that spread their
broad wings and squawked so hoarsely as they protested my inter-
ruption of their fishing.

Often in the evening I would walk down the dirt road from our
home to the bay and check on the dory's welfare. If the tide was
high, she would be swinging there in the wind, alive with the motion
of the bay, a living creature of the sea moving at her tether, a sea
horse champing to be ridden.

Often when I had no time for rowing, I would walk from the
house to the shore and sit there for a few minutes on a granite
boulder worn smooth by the eons and warmed by the sun. Watching
the dory alive there on the bay and knowing that beyond the oaks
that hung over the clay banks there were houses of classic symmetry
crafted by genius builders of wooden ships, I would comprehend
the great good fortune that had brought me to that place, those
rolling meadows, green forests, and barns rising like clipper ships,
their white clapboard sails filling with wind, and all of it peopled
with men and women and children whom I loved, and who loved me
back. The dory became the icon of the fulfillment I had, at last,
discovered.

The land there by the bay where a high point pushed southwest
was once owned by Robert P. Tristram Coffin, Maine's unofficial
poet laureate and Pulitzer Prize winner. Atop the point's outermost
end we found the collapsing walls of the cabin he had built as his
writing place, a one-room space of log walls and a door opening on

the southwest front so Coffin could look down the reach of Middle
Bay as he worked. His will was complex, his relatives scattered,
making a clear title to the land all but impossible. Perhaps he
wanted that, because those legal thickets guaranteed the point
would stay uncivilized, undeveloped.

The ruins of that cabin were our favorite ending place for our
walks. We would stand there and look over the bay's long run to the
sea, and across the small cove to the northwest where an almost
perfect circular curve of marsh grass embraced about an acre of
clear bottom that was waterless at low tide and not quite three feet
deep at the top of the flood.

One early September evening I stood there on the poet's doorstep, impressed by the sun's gathering colors in the west. The
equinoctial stillness of that early autumn had settled like a cat in
the cove. The flood tide stood stock still, a silver cloak dropped from
the sky. As I watched, a circle the size of a dinner plate blossomed
on the surface, its ring widening as a gentle turbulence boiled at its
center. In seconds, another bloomed, this one with a water sound I
knew well.

There were fish feeding fifteen feet below where I stood. What
kind of fish I did not know, but in my incurable optimism and my
longing for the creature of my past, I hoped they were striped bass.
And as I ran back up that dirt road to the house where I kept a
spinning rod and reel, I convinced myself they were stripers and my
heart pounded more from my wish than my running.

When I returned to the cove, my breath booming in my chest,
and cast a small plug toward one of the rings still blossoming, a fish
took the lure seconds after it touched the water. It was a fair-sized,
strong fish, but until I had it there at my feet where I stood in a foot
or so of salt water, I could not be positive of my catch. But then
when I saw the pearly, striped side flashing silver, I knew it as I
would know my brother. It was a striped bass, a fine, healthy,
gleaming striped bass who had followed me to Maine to bring me
my days on the beach, my world of sand and sea and surf and

gladness under the sun, my friends Jim and Peter and Ted and Stuart and Francis, all of them flashing there in the water blazing with sunset at my feet. How far they had traveled, and how welcome they were.

Those stripers changed everything. It had been many years since their migrations had probed beyond the waters off Massachusetts and the tributaries of the Pisquataquis River on the New Hampshire border. And it had been half a century since striped bass had lived in the lower reaches of southern Maine's Kennebec River and Merry-meeting Bay. The Kennebec had been so polluted by the pulp and paper companies along its upstream banks that there was no longer enough oxygen in the water to support any species of fish.

First steps along the long road to cleansing the Kennebec began with the Maine Legislature's passage of a water quality act in 1960. By the spring of 1964, a few long winter months after that September evening, there were, I was told, striped bass in the lower Kennebec, off Popham, Seguin, and Arrowsic, with some fish being taken a few miles upriver above Parker Head.

I powered the dory with a second- or third-hand ten-horsepower Johnson I bought from one of the newspaper's typesetters, put the boat on a trailer, and launched her and her modest outboard motor in a curving tidal creek that flowed into the Kennebec from George-town, a small settlement south of Bath on the river's east side. Access to the creek was granted me by the man who owned the land around it, a gentle artist who was the father of a friend of ours on the Bowdoin College faculty. The artist spent his summers on the Ken-nebec's Back River, a tributary that began its northward push at the very point overlooked by his handsome, white summer house that rose like a heron on the river's high granite banks.

On most days during that spring of 1964, the stripers would arrive on the flood tide, a push of seawater rising from Seguin and mixing with the river as far north as Chopps Point, the narrow entrance to Merrymeeting Bay, about fifteen miles upriver from Seguin. Chasing the small herring, menhaden, and grass shrimp that had returned as soon as the river began its convalesence, the striper schools swept the water like summer squalls, dappling the Kennebec's mobile surface with patches of white foam and the shimmer of turbulent swirls.

Most often, I would shut down the dory's motor when she and I had moved within sight of a school. I would be upriver and we would drift on the current until it took us within casting distance. In those days, there were no other boats. The word had yet to spread. The dory and I shared the river with her creatures: the striped bass, sturgeon, vast schools of menhaden, and flocks of herring gulls and terns which, like us, followed the stripers upriver and down.

This taught me several lessons, some of them more important than others. Among the most relevant to the safety of myself and my boat was a new understanding of river navigation, which the Kennebec was quick to teach me.

Fishing upriver in the coves of Georgetown one early morning, I failed to locate the striper schools I had been so certain would be there. I told myself they must be nearer the river's mouth; perhaps they had discovered shoals of silver sand eels along the beach at Popham. Opening the throttle on the ten-horsepower, I followed the current toward the sea.

When I reached Gilbert Head on the island that guards the river mouth, between Fort Popham and Bay Point, I noticed I was barely maintaining headway. The ebbing tide had joined forces with the Kennebec's considerable flowage to generate a current that moved a bit faster than my old outboard could push the dory. Instead of being in control, I was on the brink of allowing the river to take over.

I had, however, too much confidence in a dory's abilities to consider turning back. But as I neared the river mouth at Pond Island where the Atlantic and the Kennebec meet in what is a perpetually restless embrace, I wished I had been less presumptuous. A southwest breeze shoved the ocean against the ebbing tide and the river's flowage, creating a series of impressive standing waves, some of them six to eight feet tall, their tops hissing white water.

Roughed up by several of those, the dory was a chip in a maelstrom. I began to see quite clearly how she could be swamped by one of those rollers if I allowed her to broach. My underpowered motor was the key to my crisis; it simply could not cope with the combined forces of wind, river, and tide.

There are times in a small boat, times you can never forget, when you recognize the potential for serious trouble. These moments are charged with low-voltage currents of fear, those anxious tendrils that elevate the pulse, amplify the heart's pumping until it echoes off your chest wall, and motivate evasive action, almost any action, that will alter the situation, ease the danger, and bring the scales back to balance.

On that perilous morning, I steered the dory for the shores of Pond Island, easing her bow to port but not allowing her to turn broadside to the seas. She crabbed over until I found myself in an eddy of relatively calm water. Because the current rushed with such force a few feet offshore of where I had found sanctuary, it built an eddy against the Pond Island shore, a fifty-foot strip where the deep water moved against the ebbing tide, just as water on one side of a whirlpool moves in counterpoint to the other.

That unexpected eddy was my great good fortune. It gave me time to reestablish my equanimity, to make something of a practical plan as opposed to desperate move. Because the dory was a relatively shallow-draft boat, I was able to make headway upriver just a few feet off Pond Island's lonely shore, littered with driftwood timbers bleached by sun and salt, wrecked hulls of lobster traps wrenched from their moorings, and the nonbiodegradable shells of plastic containers, white, red, yellow, and blue. Foot by foot the dory pushed back toward where I'd come from and the relative security of less violent tides where the Kennebec broadened off a wide strip of white sand that bordered the outermost Popham dunes.

Once I had cleared the narrow straits off Pond Island and the granite bottleneck that compressed the elemental forces of river, wind, and tide, the dory, her motor at full throttle, could make slow headway and within thirty minutes we reached the stability of the broad waters off Gilbert Head. Looking downriver at the Pond Island beacon, I realized there was no visual warning of the risky turbulence I had just escaped. An unknowing helmsman, new to the Kennebec and its difficult entrance, could be in trouble before he or she fully understood the magnitude of the maverick energies at work.

I never again took that dory downriver any farther than the walls of Fort Popham, almost a mile upriver from the Pond Island chute. And I learned to be wary of all river-mouth navigation, especially where tides as powerful as Maine's are part of the sea's restless rhythms. It was a lesson underscored by the grim data that came my way years later when I edited a news story about a young couple whose boat was capsized and swamped in the very spot where the dory and I began to tremble. The young woman drowned, and I shuddered just a bit as I read what a Coast Guard spokesperson had to say about it: "It's a tragedy," he told the press, "but one which could have been avoided if only boaters took the time to learn just what to expect when they plan a trip through those waters off Pond Island and Seguin. Somebody gets in trouble there every week or so during the summer. And it seems like every year at least one person drowns. That place is no spot for a novice, especially one in a small boat."

Perhaps I hadn't been quite a novice, if you count the number of years I'd been at the helm of a variety of small boats, but in terms of my ignorance of those risky waters, I might as well have been. I was glad I was in a dory. I've always been glad to be in a dory.

Nevertheless, I was about to give her up, to desert her for a different sort of girl—younger, a product of the times, a genuinely new kind of small boat.

Whaler and Pram

One of my friends introduced us. He was Frank Webb, a fellow a few years older than I who ran a small-boat storage facility on his waterfront property on the shores of Maquoit Bay, a duplicate tidal finger that pushed northwest on the west side of Mere Point just as Middle Bay did on the east.

Frank was one of the first boat people in the region to buy a Boston Whaler, a boat that has since become a classic. In the early sixties, however, very few Maine people had laid eyes on one of the triple-V-bottomed, wide, square-bowed boats built of a porous plastic compound sandwiched between layers of tough, slick-surfaced fiberglass. Because of the buoyancy of the inner material— a rigid plastic mass filled with millions of tiny, trapped air bubbles— early Whaler ads showed a hull sliced in two but still afloat, even

though an outboard motor was fast to the transom. *Unsinkable* was
the operative word in all Whaler literature, and indeed, they were.

But that was far from being their only attribute. Because their
outer hull was a seamless, tough, rigid stretch of synthetic material,
quite leakproof and already white, the Whaler was a boat that did
not have to be painted, would not leak, and had no seams that would
shrink if she were hauled out and left on a trailer for a month or
more. Nor would a Whaler hull absorb water, no matter how long
she swung at her mooring. And because of her incredible buoyancy,
a Whaler could be left on a mooring with her stern plug removed.
Rain, and waves that might break over the bow, ran along the
watertight deck and out the drainage hole just above the waterline at
the base of the transom. As far as ease of maintenance and mooring
was concerned, the folks who designed the first Whalers seemed to
have thought of everything.

Frank Webb's early model was a thirteen-footer, at one time the
only model manufactured; now there are dozens, some large enough
to be beyond the "small boat" category. That first Whaler was
square-bowed and square-sterned. She looked something like a
white front door, laid flat on the water like a raft with an outboard
on one end. She had sides, of course, but they were low, probably no

more than eight inches of freeboard. It was what was underwater on those Whalers that counted most. The molded fiberglass hull had three small keels that flowed the length of the curved base. On each side, the secondary keels were just a few inches from the outermost edge, and between each of them and the center keel, the hull curved upward in two slick and graceful concave depressions. Like an aircraft's wing, the twin curves pulled the Whaler up off the water's surface once she attained planing speed. That, in turn, allowed the boat to ride as much on air as on water, which meant she could be very fast for a boat with the profile of a front door. Frank powered her with a thirty-five-horsepower Evinrude—plenty of torque there for a thirteen-foot boat. But the Whaler could have handled a fifty-horse without significant strain.

By the late spring of 1965, when Frank first invited me to spend an afternoon aboard the Whaler fishing the Kennebec for stripers, the fish had made a full-scale comeback along the Maine coast from the Kennebunks to Boothbay Harbor. Some were being taken as far down east as Mount Desert's tidal estuaries and bays. But the Kennebec was their favorite, primarily because it was so rich in the food fish stripers most favor: small eels, bite-size menhaden, grass shrimp, silversides, herring, and alewives—the river was home to them all. Very few stripers negotiated the southern Maine coast without making a stop at the Kennebec.

One June afternoon, fishing from the Whaler with Frank just upriver from the point where the Back River begins, we began to hook stripers with almost every cast. Some of them were large enough to charge off with our plugs, moving like freight trains with the tide, never turning, never stopping until we either had to increase our drag or kiss a couple of hundred yards of line good-bye. Those lunkers probably weighed close to forty or fifty pounds. They simply kept swimming until the line snapped.

We did land a few twenty-pound fish, some better, and a dozen more five- and ten-pounders before we quit. Fishing from the Whaler was almost like fishing from the shore: that broad beam coupled with the hull's configuration and the incredible buoyancy of the flotation material allowed anglers to stand almost on the boat's gunwales without any noticeable effect. That small skiff was so stable, I wondered just how much weight it would take to get her listing badly enough to ship water over her rails. I never did find out.

We released most of the fish, and with more than enough stripers in the boat for our families and our friends, we started for home around 4:30, that time of a Maine summer afternoon when the sun has sufficiently warmed the inland air so it rises at a fairly good rate. That natural process, in turn, creates a vacuum that pulls cool air off the Atlantic. Which means that on most Maine summer afternoons, the southwest breeze picks up by the minute until it's chuffing along at fifteen or twenty knots. Which is what Frank and I and the Whaler met head-on as we cruised from the Back River past the southern tip of Arrowsic and turned upriver. That was when I learned another Whaler lesson.

The boat's hull configuration gave her remarkable stability and, on relatively smooth water, allowed her to plane effortlessly. But in a heavy chop that virtue became a weakness. Because of her relatively flat bottom and her squared-off bow, that thirteen-foot Whaler pounded heavily in oncoming seas and severely in quartering seas. When we first turned the corner off Bald Head, Frank refused to back off on the throttle. *Wham!* And then again. *Wham!* Slapped hard enough by a chop that pushed short seas to at least two feet, the Whaler came down hard. And water, even warm water, can be as unforgiving as cement when it's hit by a flat surface. That small Whaler was plenty tough enough to take the pounding; she was not about to break apart. But her two passengers were not as tough. Resisting the impact had us both tense, hanging on, trying to anticipate and brace for the shocks as spray blew back over the low bow and soaked us to the skin with a few gallons of lower Kennebec.

Long before we got to Goat Island, less than halfway to the Bath launching ramp, Frank had throttled back, slowing enough to get the Whaler off its plane. We were making perhaps six to eight knots, but the Whaler was riding along the chop, rising and falling with it instead pounding across and into the seas. For an impatient man like Frank, who surely represents most skippers with a thirty-five-horsepower motor on a thirteen-foot boat, having to run at less than half speed was an aggravation. In the great American boating tradition, he wanted to run wide open at top speed from the minute he took to the water until the minute he left it. There are boats, I suppose, that can do that. None, however, is a flat-bottomed thirteen-footer, Whaler or not.

When we reached the launching ramp, the salt drying in our hair and sticky on our skin, I realized that not only was the Whaler a fine boat afloat but she also worked well ashore. Having a boat that is easily pulled from the water onto its trailer is a major asset. Finding one that also rides the trailer well without chafing or bouncing or being difficult to center is another quality to be praised. That breezy evening there in Bath, as the southwest wind turned the western sky smoky, was my first as an assistant at the task of pulling a Whaler from the water and stowing it aboard a trailer. As pleasantly tired as I was from our afternoon on the water, I didn't look forward to a struggle there on the ramp. And there was none. Frank backed his boat trailer down the ramp where I waited to ease the Whaler's bow up on the rear roller.

As I held the bow in place, Frank walked back pulling a thin wire cable from its spool at the trailer's front end. Hooking that to the Whaler's bow, he went back and began turning the crank on the spool. The cable tightened, Frank kept cranking, and the boat slid easily from the water, inch by easy inch until she was settled squarely on her trailer, her bow less than a foot from the cable spool. I was much impressed. With a trailer and a vehicle to tow it, a boater's range became almost limitless. If I wanted, and if I had Frank's rig, I could fish from Portsmouth to Boothbay, exploring waters I might otherwise never get to cruise. If I had Frank's rig.

When we got to Pennellville at sunset, Jean and the children came to the front porch as I tossed my share of the striped bass from

the Whaler's fish box. They hadn't been out of the water long
enough to turn dull, and they lay there gleaming pearl and bronze
against the green grass as I exulted in the children's high-pitched
astonishments. It had been a great day, one more of those unantici-
pated and unforgettable times on the water when all seems so right
with the world.

Frank sensed my delight and my infatuation with that Whaler.
About a week after that trip he called and told me he wanted a larger
boat. At the time, the Whaler company had begun to manufacture
two larger models. "I'm going to sell the rig," Frank said, "and I
thought I'd call you before I put an ad in the paper."

I asked how much, and Frank said $1,200, which seemed like a
bargain (and was) for a boat, a motor, and a trailer. I said sold before
another two seconds went by. Unlike those days when I scrambled
for a dollar or two as a commercial fisherman, I was earning regular
paychecks as a newspaper editor. Perhaps I could not afford the
Whaler in terms of our annual budget, but I could pay for her
(which is different) and I did.

The very next thing I had to do was take my old car to Bamforth's
Automotive on Brunswick's Maine Street and have its rear bumper
fitted with a trailer hitch. That evening when I arrived home, the
Whaler was riding behind my car, and the children's squeals were
even more shrill. Jean, on the other hand, was more restrained. She
had, I believe now, already begun to wonder a bit about a man who
brought home a boat, trailer, and motor when he already had
another boat—my dory—and motor swinging on the surface of
Middle Bay at the end of its haul-off just a few steps down the road.

I saw no conflict. The dory was there because ever since I discovered myself in the surf off eastern Long Island, I had kept a dory
close at hand. I believed that without a dory to sustain me as an icon
of that seminal experience, those memories and what they meant to
me might slip away, might begin to vanish in the turmoil of my new
life as a man with a "regular job." Knowing I could take that
wonderful walk to the end of the dirt road, across those rolling fields

and past those Euclidian houses, and then find my dory there, a star in the center of a flowing blue sky, was why that boat was there. And if I had to give up each of the material life-support systems that nourished my days and nights—my car, my radio, my typewriter, even my home—I would let each of them go before I surrendered my dory.

Which possibility, although her demeanor may have implied it, Jean never articulated. And the children were deliriously enthusiastic for the opposite possibilities. The more boats, the merrier; on that they agreed unanimously. Which may have been one of the reasons why I spent the next decade or so trying to keep them happily surprised.

Keeping the Whaler in the same way I kept the dory would not be practical. While a haul-off might serve adequately for a flat-bottomed, wooden boat whose outboard was light enough to be conveniently removed, the system was not secure for a boat as valuable as the Whaler and her relatively cumbersome thirty-five-horsepower Evinrude. And once I realized that, I quickly discovered another fact of life that almost every boat owner must confront: I needed a place to keep the Whaler where she would be relatively secure, quite accessible, and I would be able to buy the fuel that would keep her going. In short, a marina.

In Brunswick, there was only one: Paul's Marina on the Middle Bay side of Mere Point about three miles west of our home. Paul Derocher, the marina's founder, proprietor, administrator, dock master, chief mechanic, and mooring setter was a true master of all things marine. He had lived most of his life on the Maine coast and, in the late 1950s, long before small-boat fever had struck so many Americans, he had dredged a channel from the deep water just offshore his home to a small dock he built in what was his tidal front yard.

Paul had a working relationship with what was then Maine's Department of Sea and Shore Fisheries. As one of those men with an innate comprehension of machinery and how machines are crafted,

Paul worked with the department on a number of experimental improvements on the ancient implements designed to extricate shellfish from the unyielding Penobscot clay that covered so much of the state's shellfish beds. A master welder as well as a fine helmsman and navigator, Paul helped design, build, and perfect Maine's first hydraulic clam dredge, a floating monster of brass, steel, and heavy-duty rubber tubing that forced seed clams from their mud beds with jets of seawater and then pumped them onto the dredge's deck unharmed and ready to be transplanted in what was one of the nation's first successful aquacultural operations.

As a journalist who reported on the pioneering effort to husband and manage some of the sea's rich resources, I had got to know Paul and had even assisted him during some of the more innovative—and perhaps not quite successful—trial runs aboard that clanking, puffing, hissing, gurgling monster of a dredge. If he had wanted, Paul could have made a handsome living as a marine designer and mechanic, working for both the State of Maine and private industry. But he prized his independence and valued his own days alone on the bay in his double-ender launch with its sturdy four-cylinder inboard.

His marina happened more than it was planned. Paul was too independent to ever visualize himself as a person who dealt each day with customers and their endless needs. He dredged his channel and built his first small dock to accommodate his boat, the state boats, and the clam dredge. Then neighbors began asking if they could moor their boats, perhaps a small cabin cruiser, a lobster boat, and, during the summer, a sloop or a catboat. Paul would say yes; he was a yes-saying man. And he would help set their mooring. Often, he would provide the mooring without really thinking about how much it cost him in time and materials.

By 1966, the first full summer I had my Whaler, there were probably twenty boats swinging on their moorings off Paul's dock. He had built and floated a couple of finger piers to make space for the dinghies boaters needed to get back and forth from the moorings, but the place was still small and personal. Paul had time during the week for his work with Sea and Shore Fisheries marine biologists like Dana Wallace, but on weekends he would sit in the doorway of the small dock house he had built at the inshore end of his docks. From there, he could keep track of the comings and goings, and watch his daughter at the tiller of his double-ender as she ferried some of the boat owners to their cabin cruisers and sloops.

I was proud to be one of Paul's people. When I walked down the steep stairs that negotiated the high, clay bank that rose from the water's edge to the bluff where Paul's shingled cottage and garage overlooked the blue bay, I would pick *my* Whaler out of the flock of moored boats that glided here and there in the wind and tide like a flock of white geese paddling in the current. But watching the Whaler while I pumped up my pride was not the same as being at the Whaler's helm, her motor throbbing in my ears as together we set off on our Casco Bay adventures. And I spent a good many collective hours watching and waiting while Paul or his daughter found the time to ferry me from the dock to my mooring. Sometimes, with Paul's standing permission, I would crank up the pull-start outboard on the small, battered aluminum skiff he owned and kept loosely tethered to his dock. But once I reached the Whaler, I had to go through the rather cumbersome process of towing the skiff back to the pier and making it fast.

What I needed, I realized with a decided lack of enthusiasm, was one of the small prams so many boat owners had tied up to Paul's finger piers. A third boat! How could a man with six children—plus a stray who had come to live with us—justify a third boat on a journalist's salary? There was no way I could answer the question honestly. I did what I so often do and obliterated every negative; the positives were clear. If I had a pram of my own, I would be dependent on no one. I could ferry myself and a passenger to and from the Whaler and the dock at any time: before sunup until after sundown. I would, I told myself, at last be free. I would have every boat I needed, and then some.

As I had several times before, I found what I needed in the "For Sale" columns of the classified. A Mere Point pram owner wanted to sell for one hundred dollars. I drove to her home, knowing as I did that I would buy the pram unless it was quite beyond repair. I needn't have worried. The pram was in good shape, a home-built model of half-inch marine plywood some fairly skilled builder had put together in a basement. Flat-bottomed with a nice bit of sheer curving upwards at her bow and stern, the rather high-sided little boat—a bit less than eight feet—was just a hair beyond being a squared-off plywood crate with one side missing. She came with oarlocks and oars and one seat amidships and another in the stern, although I never ferried a passenger small enough to fit on the stern thwart. All of them had to balance on the skinny top of the transom, holding on with both hands to the pram's gunwales.

She was small enough to fit in the back of our old station wagon and twenty minutes after I handed her owner a check, she was in the water at one of Paul's finger piers. There, I thought, now the fleet is complete.

For the rest of that summer and fall, and the next spring, summer, and fall, I spent more than half my time away from my job aboard the Whaler. I made trips to most of the islands within five miles of Mere Point. I fished for striped bass, bluefish, and mackerel. I took

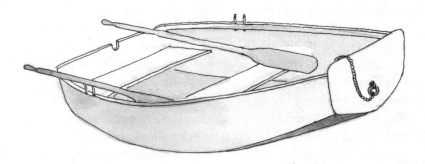

the children and Jean for rides. But mostly I drifted with wind and tide.

For what I learned to love most about the Whaler was her shallow draft and her incredible stability. Whenever I discovered a cove in the lee, out of the wind—and there must have been several hundred quiet coves along that wondrously complex and corrugated coast with its dozens of pristine islands and great humpbacked granite ledges scattered like a schoolboy's marbles by the massive glaciers of one hundred centuries before—I would lift the outboard's prop and the motor would click into place, holding there at an angle on the stern, giving the bay bottom nothing to grab but the Whaler's slick hull, itself able to float cleanly in eight inches of water, maybe less if I stood far forward in the bow to counterbalance the outboard's weight.

Sometimes I would have a fishing rod ready, my fly rod with its blue Lefty's Deceiver on a short wire leader, able to defy those razor bluefish teeth, and more than able to deal with a striped bass. Other times I had nothing but my senses to soak in the majesty of those crystal Maine waters, those rich, but so cold, tidal currents that blessed their environment with a wealth of plankton that, in turn, nourished a multitude of marine organisms that, in turn, supported great fleets of small fish: mummychogs, spearing, herring, elvers, and clouds of grass shrimp. With pastures of living silver to graze, herds of giant bluefish and schools of three- to ten-pound stripers would tumble and splash far up into those Casco Bay fingers that probed meadows where cattle stood near barns shipbuilders had raised one hundred years before.

Drifting in that Whaler, borne so gently by the flooding tide, so quietly that not even the great blue herons took flight as I passed, I joined those flashing schools of oceanic fish far from the depths that could keep them invisible.

On occasion, those joinings were more intimate than I planned or desired. Tracking schools of large bluefish across a platinum bay on a windless, early August morning, I watched as the predators herded thousands of hapless menhaden into dark spheres of panic. Seeking surcease from the razor teeth of twelve-pound blues, the one-pound menhaden bunched so tightly their silver backs broke the surface, creating instant living islands of scales, fins, frantic tails, and blood blossoms that rolled dark in the bright water.

As predators do, others joined the massacre, taking their dividends from the bluefish initiative. Great black-backed and herring gulls wheeled on the morning air, their shrieking calls ripping the quiet. And below all, below the bluefish, below the desperate menhaden, were the harbor seals, circling on the ebb tide's current, riding its underwater tradewinds. When the menhaden mass became condensed to near solidity, a seal or two would rocket mutely from beneath and explode there on the surface, its head straight up, nose toward the sky. And there in its jaws, a silver menhaden about to vanish in what I swear was a smiling mouth.

An instant later, the Whaler ran aground, hard aground in what I was certain was eight feet of water. The jolt flipped the outboard shaft up, clear of the surface, the sound of its racing prop startling me with its shrill whine, out of control. At the same moment, the jolt and the sudden stop tossed me forward, my knees banging on the Whaler's seat as I fell hard on the deck, the palms of my hands stinging as I tried to break my tumble. As I rose, bewildered, I wondered how the hell such a mishap could happen, there in a shallow-draft boat in home waters I had navigated for years.

When I looked behind me, I understood. Chunks of menhaden rose and floated on the surface, turning gently in the waning turbulence of my mishap. Already the gulls circled, swooped down for the rent remains, and flew off trailed by heckling others trying to force the leaders to surrender their menhaden morsels. Although it took longer than it should for me to realize what had happened, even though I was surrounded by the gory evidence, it was difficult for me to believe, and still is. For what the Whaler had done was to run up on a school of surfacing, panicked menhaden at the instant of their maximum terror: the moment the entire school compressed and surged to the surface as if there they could grow wings and escape the murderer below. The fish had, in fact, dried up the sea even as I crossed it. And with such wondrous mass that their compacted presence kicked the outboard from its purchase and stopped the Whaler in its tracks. I was lucky I had nothing more than bruised knees.

When I reasoned through the suprise, I still was slow to believe. But the evidence was there around me, gleaming and bleeding on the bay. I checked the prop and shaft for damage, made sure the motor was less bruised than I, and turned toward my home port, certain to stay alert, especially for schooling blues and terrified menhaden. I may be one of the few skippers who has run aground on a living shoal.

The Whaler was in better shape than I. She was an extremely durable boat, and if each of us could shoulder our increasing years and the weight of our workloads with a Whaler's durability, we would be young at a hundred. For that boat not only gave me the gift of freedom, solitude, discovery, and adventure, she gave each of the children their marine education. She saw them safely through their childhood, adolescence, and teens.

Five years after I acquired the Whaler, Jean and I made a decision to build a new home on a fine, wooded point of land that pushed southwest into Middle Bay. The point ended in a high bluff where old oaks had been stunted by one hundred years of wind off the water, their limbs gnarled, their trunks twisted, and their topmost branches curved inland like a woman's hair caught in a gale. Standing at that point's absolute end, I could see southwest the length of Middle Bay, past each of the islands and whalebacks, past even the far end of Harpswell Neck and beyond to the full sweep of the open Atlantic where giant bluefin tuna schooled off Halfway Rock every summer.

Before we had cleared the land on our home site, before we even had a proper driveway built through the woods over the half-mile from Simpson's Point Road to the spot where our barn would be, before we could comfortably walk through those woods, I had placed moorings for the dory and the Whaler off what I would name—in a spasm of humility—John's Point. On the southeast side of that point a cove scooped inland from the tip of Simpson's Point, a quarter-mile across the water. The cove opened on some fairly deep water; only minus tides would leave the boats aground on exposed mudflats. With Crow Island about a half-mile off that shore to the southwest, and the high banks of Spinney's Point to the west, our anchorage was well protected.

There is a ship's bell that hangs at our current front door, a fine bell of heavy, chiming brass, forged in Maine. On it is engraved: "John's Point—1972." That was the year our new home, which our sons and daughters and their friends helped us to build, was finished and we could move in and join the boats that had waited for us more than a year.

When we staked out the house—one that Jean and I had designed together—I stood in a wheelbarrow where I thought I wanted the corner of our ground-floor bedroom to be. I figured the wheelbarrow was almost as far off the ground as the floor of our eventual bedroom, and that there would be a window about where my head was. I wanted to be sure that after the place was built and I awakened in our new bedroom, the boats would be the first things I looked at each morning. It was from the stake driven at that southwest corner that the rest of the structure was plotted. And when our new home was finished some nine months later, and I rose from the bed we had hauled in the day before, I stood naked at the window and there was the bay and the boats, each of them, the dory and the Whaler, swinging like seabirds at their moorings, dancing with the tide and the wind.

I could also see the float we had built of timbers and Styrofoam slabs. A cumbersome rectangle fourteen feet long and eight feet across, the float was so buoyant less than four inches of its side planking was underwater. It was connected by a long ramp to a granite whaleback on the point's east side, and two long walkways from the ramp's inshore end—also anchored atop two boulders—allowed us to walk to the float dryshod, even on the highest tides. The pram's home was there, atop the float, turned over and securely fastened to keep her dry and in place. I would miss Paul but not the marina, which had become increasingly popular and crowded over the years.

I have never been a material man, as anyone who has known me for more than a month will tell you. But surely the closest I ever came to being assaulted by the pride of possession was during those years at John's Point when I could stand there at the window and contemplate *our* boats, *our* dock, *our* moorings, and what I soon began calling *our* cove. Any person in his or her right mind would have assumed I would not only be grateful for the treasures life had strewn before me, but satisfied as well. So satisfied that I would never look at another boat.

How wrong they would have been.

The Hobie Cat

Sometimes I think that if I had succeeded as a commercial fisherman I would not have acquired so many boats. After all, none of the working fishermen I knew made impulse purchases, not boats, not television sets, not anything. Their lives had been spent making do, getting the most from their equipment and soon discarding any equipment they could not get the most from. When you live close to the edge, there is no room for impractical indulgence.

But by the time I'd begun my second decade in Maine I had become more journalist than fisherman, more deskbound than waterborne. And as the editor and reporter for a small weekly publication, I read just about every word that appeared in its columns, and thousands more that did not. Those thousands more included skimming the full deck of news releases that thumped onto my desk each

morning, a mass of efforts by publicity-seeking folks who tub-
thumped for this product, or that candidate, or merely otherwise
civilized individuals who wanted nothing more than to see their
names in print.

Ninety-nine of a hundred of those news releases were filed in the
large circular file by my desk, a wastebasket that often had to be
emptied twice a day. However, just because they would not fit the
paper's rather restrictive publishing criteria did not mean they escaped my perusal. Often I was fascinated by items I knew would
never be given a headline or forwarded to the typesetter. I liked
learning, for example, about the media personalities who had discovered the prune's amazing therapeutic benefits, and I took heart
when I was told that even my doubtful soul might be saved by the
church of the holy mercenary.

Very few of those rambles through the releases afforded me
significant information, much less revelations that changed my life.
However, on one fateful morning I held in my already ink-smudged
fingers a message from southern California that would not only steer
my boating hours on a radically altered course but would also
elevate the adrenaline levels of each of our several offspring.

The message, properly mimeographed, double-spaced, and
headed "For Immediate Release," informed me that Hobie Alter, a
designer and builder of small, single-sail catamarans, had attained
such success with the boats he built in his own shop near the beach
at Malibu (or some equally distant Pacific shore) that he could, at
least, begin to export Hobie Cats to sailors on the other side of the
nation. The first, the very first Hobie Cats ever to be seen in Maine
were on the way, so the release informed me, to the Falmouth
gentleman who had been awarded the sole right to sell Hobie Cats
in southern Maine.

Along with the release I also read the four-color brochure that
accompanied it, in case ignorant editors needed more information.
And in the same voluminous California envelope were eight-by-ten
photographs of Hobie Alter himself riding one of his incredible

inventions across the frothing, breaking crest of an awesome Pacific wave. The Hobie's windward hull was lifted clear of the sea by what must have been a brisk breeze and white water curved before the leeward hull as it dug into the Pacific and left more white water in its hissing wake. Even if the literature had not told me the Hobie Cat was one of the swiftest, if not the swiftest, sailing craft ever designed, the photographs portrayed a sense of speed so vividly that I was left feeling like Toad in *Wind in the Willows*: I wanted to shout "Faster! Faster!"

What I did was pick up the phone and call the man who would soon receive Maine's first shipment of Hobie Cats. When will they arrive? I asked. How much will they cost? How soon can I have one delivered? And so on. These are obviously not the queries of someone likely to be considered a tough sell. The distributor knew he had me from the moment he heard my voice on his phone.

"You're a lucky man," he told me. "Tomorrow, I'll be getting my first two Hobies. I need to keep one as a demonstrator, but if you buy the other, you'll be the very first person in Maine to sail his own Hobie on Casco Bay."

Well, if I had any hope of hesitation, of time to "think it over" as folks were always advising me to do, those hopes were creamed by the knowledge that I would be the first, the only, the sole skipper at the helm of a sailing revolution. As I skimmed the bay in the Hobie of my dreams, other less fortunate and more timid souls would look up from their plodding sloops as I whistled by and ask their crews, "What the hell was that?"

That evening I was perhaps more animated than usual after a day behind the editor's desk. But I was also more close-mouthed, not daring to inject any conversational catalysts lest they precipitate loose talk from my equally loose lips about the magnitude of my newest acquisition. No, I thought, until the Hobie is delivered to this door, I'll keep mum, a strategy I saw as the only one certain to avoid the disaster of a Hobie prohibition laid down on the spot by the true master of the home, who, on countless previous occasions had stymied my impulsive expenditures on the grounds that ignoring our obligations to feed and clothe our offspring constituted cruel and unusual punishment, negligence, mental illness, and a host of other capital offenses and/or physical failures.

What I did was to retire early that evening, claiming a remarkably bad day ahead. What I did, in fact, with the following day was to move as quickly as possible through the pasture of my editing duties and leave for home some two hours prior to my normal quitting time. I considered it crucial that I arrive before the Hobie was delivered by its ebullient salesperson.

Too late. I arrived about ten minutes after the trailered, disassembled Hobie had been towed into our drive. "No, I'm absolutely certain," I heard the lady of the house say through tightly drawn lips as I disembarked my car. "There must be some mistake," she continued. "John already has three boats. What could he possibly do with another?"

I had two choices, and no time. The Hobie rep was looking straight at me, obviously in need of support and a counterattack. Either I could agree with Jean and say, with much vigor, "Yes, this is an inexcusable mistake." Or I could own up and acknowledge that the check had already been written. What I said was, "Isn't she an incredible boat!" Whereupon the front door slammed and I was left alone with the salesman and the invisible hailstorm of Jean's anger.

Which soon dissipated in the warmth of my enthusiasm. There was, however, the tempering presence of a Hobie Cat dismembered, as opposed to a Hobie under sail. Long after the relieved salesman departed, two of our sons and I were still working at following the assembly instructions, a job burdened not only by my stunted mechanical abilities but also by the reality of a boat designed unlike any we had ever seen before.

Marshall, however, heading for engineering school via auto and motorcycle racing, was already a fine mechanic and, more important, much less likely than I to either ignore or grow impatient with printed instructions. With his attention and even temper as the

critical element in our mix, the Hobie took shape: its twin hulls
joined by aluminum struts; its mast fitted to its step in the forward
strut's center; stays from the mast running abeam to each hull as well
as fore and aft; a stretched canvas deck laced into place; and, finally,

the twin rudders hooked to the stern of each hull and linked by a single crossbar that became the tiller.

She was light enough, mast and all, so four of us could carry her to a grassy bank and slide her toward her new home on Middle Bay.

I had sailed before: dinghies, catboats, and Star-class sloops with their heavy keels and sleek hulls designed for racing. But no sailing I had ever done prepared me for the Hobie Cat. She was, indeed, something new. She announced herself on that first day when I hoisted sail and slid out of the cove. When that sail caught the wind, the Hobie came alive in my hands. She seemed to become part of the air, her receptors tuned to every kinetic thrust the breeze might generate. I could feel the sinews of her speed with one hand on the tiller and the other attempting to rein in the main sheet. I shouted in delight as the Hobie bit into a puff that ruffled the water and then filled the sail. Like a watermelon seed pressed between thumb and forefinger, the Hobie shot forward, one hull lifting, the main sheet tugging like a roped steer.

Yes, she needed headway to come about and without it she often drifted back, helpless, in irons as I sculled her double rudders. But as we began to understand each other, I learned to use her speed and I learned some finer points of jibing, the certain and most exciting way of changing tacks.

And when the wind bunched inside the great gray hummocks of clouds in the northwest and hurled itself across that north-south narrow bay (too protected for seas to build), the Hobie and I would fly before it, one hull singing its sibilant song as it sliced white through green water. I hung my butt over the whitecaps as the Hobie's windward hull lifted beneath me, surging free, a wild horse bucking as I held her on a reach racing toward the open sea beyond the outermost islands, then jibing, hurtling back toward our home cove, the contest for stability jolting every muscle: arms, legs, back, and the taut line across my belly as I leaned, steered, pulled, and, every now and then, gave way as a squally fist of wind threatened to flip us as easily as a leaf tumbles over itself, bewildered by the gale's wild force.

Always, I would be the first to weary; the Hobie could live with the wind as her brother, playing together throughout the long day. Their energies were limitless. Mine were not. After an hour or two under sail in a twenty-knot nor'wester, I'd make for our home cove where I'd jibe one last time, drop the sail with headway to spare, and glide until those twin, curved bows nudged the grassy shore and let me rest there for a while, still lost in the exhilaration of our adventure.

On other days when the wind gentled, the Hobie and I would take a different kind of cruise—more exploratory, more leisurely, more curious and playful. Had I been a proper captain, and had the Hobie had a captain's cabin where I could keep our ship's log dutifully sustained with written records of each voyage, there would have been many entries like this one:

Captain's log: Short cruise, Middle Bay.

Distance: Five nautical miles.

Time: Two hours, seventeen minutes.

Weather: Skies clear; wind, south-southwest, 10 to 15 knots.

We are greeted by several flocks of white-winged scoters, probably nudged our way by the onshore breeze, holding in the same quarter now for the past three days. The young scoters in the flocks are comical; two months out of their nests, they are still children with much to learn before they migrate south and cross Gardiners Bay, where gunners still wait at Cartwright.

But here in Maine waters, these young white-winged are my unwitting playmates. Sailing the Hobie before the wind directly at the scoter flocks, I discover the fledglings have little or no fear of the boat. Because they can take wing only by flying directly into the wind, the birds are in a quandary when they discover how quickly the Hobie is closing the open water left between us. Too late they realize that they can take wing only by flying straight at us. One or two try, nevertheless, their wings beating the surface frantically as they run—slap, slap, slap, slap, slap, slap—taking long steps with their clownish webbed feet pushing at the water. Airborne at last, they find themselves within inches of the Hobie's twin bows; I can see their startled eyes, sense their discomfort, their embarrassment at their predicament. One youngster flies over us, so close I could reach and pluck him from the air. They are the sponsors of my laughter, a splendid comic relief. I tack upwind several times, replaying the same game, but after a time or two, the teenage scoters learn our tricks. Instead of flying, now they dive and swim, submerged, to safety.

Seeking surcease from the breeze, we glide into a cove on an island's leeward shore. This, I know, is a wild island. And yet some natural whim has created a small grassy meadow at the water's edge, a circular open green, shelving gently to the bay and ringed with high pines. It is an inviting spot for a small-boat sailor to catch his breath, out of the wind and under the sun.

As I glide toward the cove (and the Hobie is a superb glider) a pair of mergansers—the birds I knew as sheldrake when I was growing up on Georgica—slip from the shore and paddle across our bows. These, I know, are normally open-water ducks; if they are here alone as a pair, it is because they are nesting. In a moment, the drake certifies my assumption as he begins his crippled-wing act, fluttering and splashing awkwardly just in front of the boat, all the while making certain there is the same margin of distance between us. This drake is so obviously alarmed and yet so distinctly courageous that we test him no further. Pushing the tiller hard over, I steer the Hobie out of the cove and back into the bay. There I discover the sheldrake hen, paddling nonchalantly, confident, I'm sure, that father drake is doing right by their hatchlings.

Off the point of the island across the channel from the sheldrake's cove is a single, large rock rising like a whale from the bay. This rock belongs to the Middle Bay harbor seals. The bay embraces scores of similar rocks, but this one is owned by the seals. It is their chosen meeting place and they can be found here almost every day, sunning and surfing, slipping into the water every now and then to chase herring, menhaden, and mackerel. This day, about a dozen are there, taking the sun. I can tell they have been relaxing for several hours; their fur is quite dry and they appear to be sound asleep. There are some adolescents among them, and they don't notice us until we are within a few yards. Then the group becomes a shuffling, surging mass of brown and pale gray bodies, heads in the air, flippers scrabbling for purchase, the heavyweights sliding, slipping, and finally splashing one after the other until the rock is deserted and still.

In the clear, shoal water I can see seal torsos curving and flashing beneath me. One bull is curious and surfaces just off the port bow, his round, pitch-black eyes staring directly at me as he snorts his irritation with us for disturbing his nap under the sun.

Then the water wrinkles with a breeze. We are underway in a hurry, gone before other seals can surface. We head home, the only boat on the bay. I suppose someone seeing us from shore might think it a lonely pastime to be sailing solo, but then, they could not have seen all our company.

Captain's log closed.

There were many such cruises in the Hobie, just as there were many other days when she flew across the whitecaps as I pulled hard to keep her under control. One windy morning on a long reach we overtook and passed a lobster boat underway on our same course. I will long remember that lobsterman's look as we sailed by. Like so many watermen, he had just seen his first Hobie Cat.

She was as kind to the children as she was to me and taught each of them to sail. Trial and error was her technique, and as I recall, not one of her students avoided being capsized when they pushed her past her limits. Yes, Mr. Alter, you did yourself proud when you created that gem.

And most straight-thinking folks would have concluded that with a sailboat, a pram, a rowing dory, and a motorboat as able as the Whaler, even a family as large and as rambunctious as ours would consider ourselves sufficiently boated. In retrospect, we were. But that's looking back; in those days I could hardly see beyond my nose.

One Inflatable,
Two Strays,
and a Swampscott Dory

With three boats swinging at their moorings and just one pram on the floating dock, our sons and daughters were after me to get another pram. They had each developed a fine affection for boats and the places boats could take them. Some were addicted, others more reasonable, but each chafed whenever he or she had to swim from the dock to the moorings to arrange their days and evenings and often nights on the water.

Looking over a Sears flyer that was stuffed into every Bath and Brunswick mailbox, I discovered the regional store was going out of the inflatable boat business and had put their two or three models up for grabs at rather remarkable sell-out prices. Well, they seemed remarkable to me. So I motored across town to Sears and purchased my first boat in a box I could carry unassisted.

She turned out to be no Jacques Cousteau Zodiac. She was able enough, however, on first inflation to do her job of transporting a single body across the short stretch of open water between the dock and the moorings, although she was not noted for her dryness. Even a moderate chop, we learned, would slop over her inner-tube rails. But there was a more significant problem. The inflatable's thin skin was not manufactured to withstand a typical Maine bay bottom with its barnacles, mussel shells, clam shells, and unfriendly rocks. Nor was the inflatable designed to withstand the ungoverned exuberance of young men and young women filled with the stimulus of a Maine summer's freedoms. After two weeks, our "new" inflatable could wrinkle before your eyes as air seeped from a dozen poorly patched ruptures in her fabric. Anyone wanting to use her for transport had to pump hard and paddle fast.

Even as that poor boat, if indeed that's what she was, struggled to maintain her shape, two strays drifted our way within a week of each other. That increased the size of our fleet to seven, and there was increasing concern at the breakfast table for my mental health, especially from Jean, who, she argued, had little choice. After all, what other person who worked in an office six days a week had saddled himself with responsibility for seven small boats? That was the central question she sought to answer.

I had no explanations except the obvious. What was I to do, I asked, when two boats literally washed up on our shores? The first was a great wedge of a sharpie, a cumbersome, flat-bottomed,

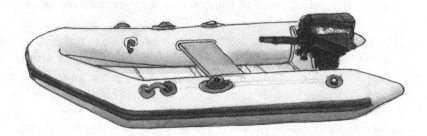

twenty-six-foot clamming skiff with all the grace of a hog trough.
Built in some digger's backyard from yellow-pine planks and common nails, she had the stolid heaviness a work boat should, but lent
herself to no purpose we could readily determine. In spite of their
excellent physical condition, not one of our sons evidenced the
slightest inclination to launch a new career as a clam digger. The
skiff had arrived without oars or oarlocks and even if she had them,
she would have been a bitch to row. But I did what I could for her
several leaks, cleaned her up so she could face the world with some
dignity, and gave her a home on the grassy slope below our point. To
my knowledge, she was never the boat of choice for any of our
offspring or their friends.

Our second gift from the sea was a narrow aluminum scow, a boat
called a "johnboat" (of which, more later) by the freshwater
largemouth-bass anglers who favor the model for its trailer por-
tability and its shallow draft. Both functions are essential for this
most popular angling sport. Being easy to haul from lake to lake
gives the bass hunter a much greater range, while the shallow draft
allows him to fish the strange swamps and backwaters so favored by
trophy largemouths. *Lunker* is the word most often used by bassin'
writers. What this was doing in a Maine coastal bay I can't imagine.
Perhaps a basser had struck hard times and was forced to take up
clam digging.

She was sufficiently battered to give credence to that theory. But
unlike wooden and fiberglass boats, an aluminum craft does not
lend herself to patching. The best tool we could find was a ballpeen
hammer that jolted some of the worst dents back into shape, but
could do little for the boat's overall decrepitude. Like her wedge-
shaped sister, the johnboat was not readily employed to fulfill any of
our marine functions. She, too, rested on the bank like a senior
citizen taking the sun and making a career of it. On one or two
occasions, she was loaded with supplies, tents, sleeping bags, and a
couple cases of beer and towed by the Whaler, which, in turn, was
overloaded with young people off on an overnight camping expedi-

tion to one of Casco Bay's scores of lovely and conveniently uninhabited islands. In that role, the johnboat performed well.

But if she had never drifted our way, she never would have been
missed. And it was after her arrival that I told myself that seven
boats was certainly enough for one family and that it was quite likely
to be too many. There were times during that summer when I
wondered if I should be the first to organize a chapter of Boats
Anonymous.

If I had, and if others similarly afflicted had joined me, they
would have understood what happened next. Like the wedge-
shaped skiff and the johnboat, my next marine acquisition sought
and found me. I never went looking for her.

I did look up from my desk one morning and there in my office
door, which was generally open to all visitors, was a comely young
woman asking if I could help. I'm not sure, I said. What is it you
need help with?

She had a friend, she told me, an older man who had begun a late-
in-life career as a boatbuilder. Once a ship's carpenter, he had lived
his way through tragedies never revealed to me. But now, with his
former skills regrouped, he was building the pilot model of a small
wooden boat that he hoped to use to acquire orders for more. This
first was a demonstrator, proof of care and craftsmanship.

Would I, my charming visitor wanted to know, "put something in
the paper" that might help her friend, that would tell our readers
about this exceptional boat-buying opportunity?

I said it was a possibility, but before I could decide, I would have
to see the boat.

That, of course, was my undoing. I knew it the moment my escort
arrived at her destination and slid back the door to the builder's
shed and sunlight spilled over a Swampscott dory suspended there
in its builder's frames. There was no way, my heart told me, I could
leave that shed uncommitted.

She was small, probably ten feet along her keel from stem to
stern, maybe fourteen from the tip of her curving bow to the top of

her angled transom. Already painted, her lapstraked cedar sides gleamed white and smooth as marble. Her rails and thwarts were bright with varnish, her fittings polished brass, and her transom flourishes hand-carved with whorls and curves taken from the details of an ancient admiral's gig pictured in some naval history. Her lines, her form, her proportions, her details were breathtaking, clearly a work of genius, a result of the same singular concentration Michelangelo had sacrificed to the Sistine Chapel ceiling. That boat was a poem, wrested from the soul of a tormented poet—a once-in-a-lifetime creation that could never be duplicated, in spite of resolutions written or self-binding promises made.

In less than a week, she was trailered to Simpson's Point and

launched. She was finished, complete in every detail, including brass oarlocks, a pair of feather-light white cedar oars, and a rudder that slipped into place on two brass tongues fast to her stern. Once in the water, she was so perfect, so light and so lovely, she took my breath away.

I set her mooring so she could be watched from every window. When I awakened, I could study her as I dressed and gauge the wind and tide from her response to the slightest elemental shifts in the balances of her marine universe. From my seat at our family table, I could look at her over the heads of guests, friends, and sons and daughters.

Oh, that Swampscott dory. She swung on her line like a tern in flight, the water like air beneath her curved and narrow bottom. Her movements were an endless ballet, symphonic testimony to the harmonies possible when design, craft, genius, materials, and heart-break combine to produce a marine mobile, a sculpture as pure as Michelangelo's *David*, a sonnet, a song sung each morning and on through dappled afternoons and moonstruck nights.

I loved her more than any other.

I built and sewed a leg-o-mutton sail and mast that I could carry, and on long summer evenings she and I would glide over Middle Bay, the only dancers on the sunset. She was all things to me. She caught the wind as fairly as the Hobie. She was as able as the larger, heavier Banks dory. And she alone seemed able to embrace me as we sailed before the wind, the entire bay gleaming as it waited for the two of us.

So why, when she and I had found such fulfillment, should I acquire yet another boat?

The Old Town Canoe—
and Subsequent Events

Friendship and sentiment in equal doses compelled me to buy yet another boat.

Richard Barringer had helped me build our home, our life in Maine, and my newspaper. When he told me that Greg, his oldest son, was hoping to earn some tuition money restoring an ancient Old Town sailing canoe discovered in an Aroostook County barn, what was I to do but offer to become her buyer?

And then there was that other, sentimental reason.

During those boyhood summers of mine spent in that great ramble of a house on Georgica Pond, my brother Chick and I ate many of our suppers in a dining room that looked west over Georgica and into the setting sun.

Often, as we ate, an Old Town canoe would sweep into view, its single sail punctuating the sun's bright line across the water. Always at its helm would be our neighbor, Mr. Jewett, his white panama hat and his tanned features about even with the canoe's gunwales as he lay almost prone inside her, adjusting daggerboards, steering with two lines attached to a tiller perched on a crescent stern, trimming the gaff-rigged cotton sail, and, in general, always appearing to be in total and gentle control of his summer evening's solitude. His easy mastery of that Old Town, I often thought as I watched, was a skill I hoped to emulate when I grew up.

I grew for almost sixty years before I got the chance. By then, there was no way I could pass up the opportunity. She arrived almost ready to sail, needing sideboards, a mast, and a sail, each of which I provided over a spell of some four weeks. The sideboards were the greatest challenge. I had to shape them from single, clear twelve-inch white-pine planks, each almost four feet long. I had no patterns to follow except my long-ago memories of those that I'd watched Mr. Jewett raise and lower as he tacked across the sunset. But with the help of a two-handed wood shaver that had come to me from my Uncle Ben's carpenter's chest, power sanders, and many coats of varnish, I was able to produce a reasonably graceful and balanced pair that I mounted on a bracket of my own design. Held in place by two grooved bronze discs slightly larger than a silver dollar, which meshed together when the turn screws that held them were tightened, the boards could be raised and lowered with relative simplicity.

That Old Town was light enough for me to haul from the bay and slide up onto a damp grassy bank with enough mud in its mix so the canoe's bottom was scarcely scratched. It was nearly October by the time I got her in sailing shape, and although I took her on several short cruises when the wind gentled almost to calm, I never spent enough time with her to build a passion that could compete with my love for the Swampscott dory.

Then the first frosts arrived and with them the day of reckoning in my life that I had managed to postpone for so many gloriously extravagant years.

During the almost two decades since I'd first moored the dory in
Middle Bay and then taken her on her Kennebec voyage, a mountain range of debt had built on my fiscal horizons. That October, the
mountains moved closer, their towering shadows made even more
depressing because they fell across so many empty spaces in our
home—spaces left by sons and daughters grown to men and women
laying the keels of their own lives.

When Sam, our youngest, left, the house became a cavern. Even
the Swampscott dory on her mooring behaved like a bird bereft.
Jean and I decided we had to put our home on the market, the home
we had built ten years before with our two hands and the help of our
children and their friends. In November, the place on John's Point
was sold to a California couple and the Whaler and the Old Town
canoe were part of the deal. The Banks dory was left on a Back River
marsh where she continued to rot and return her soul to the sea. The
pram stayed on the dock and the Hobie Cat was given to Sam and

his older brother Bob, who eventually kept her in good repair and took her to Portland where Bob lived. Later in life, there were times when I would be driving into the city along Interstate 295 where it borders Back Cove, and if the wind was brisk from the northwest and the tide high, I could see the Hobie with Bob at her helm, both of them alive with the wind, hissing across whitecaps just as I had done so many years before. For the first Hobie in Maine, she has had a long and fruitful life. A few years later when he became a wind-surfing addict, Bob sold her to a fellow who lives on the Back Cove, so I still see her once or twice a year. She appears to be wearing her years better than I.

The sodden wedge of a clamming scow and the beat-up aluminum johnboat were set adrift, returned to the bay that brought them our way. Somewhere in the rafters of the barn that now belongs to a second generation of new owners, the inflatable sags in perpetual deflation, an experiment failed.

But I could not let go of the Swampscott dory. After November when the house was sold, deeds were signed and recorded, we stayed on through the winter as tenants because the California couple planned to move in the following spring. That worked for us; the small house we had bought just a few steps from the Bowdoin College campus in "downtown" Brunswick was still being put through the renovations Jean and I had planned.

Along the shores of Middle Bay, the first skim ice traces the marshes during mid-October nights. In the early mornings, the brown sedge wears a white halo that surrenders to the noonday sun. But by November, if the wind and tides and temperatures are right, the cove can ice over from bank to bank. No lovely and delicate small boat should be left on her mooring through a Maine November.

But I left the Swampscott dory on hers. I wanted her to be part of my awakenings until the last possible morning. I knew when she came ashore she would be leaving, and she was my last boat, the one I loved most.

In December's second week, the cove froze hard. I had to smash

the ice with a hatchet and an oar to free the dory. I hauled the trailer
around to the landing at Simpon's Point and paddled the dory
across, breaking ice as we went. After she was safe in our yard, I
went to my office at the paper and wrote a "Boat for Sale" notice for
that week's classifieds.

The following Sunday a lean, close-cropped woman drove down
from Camden. She asked me what she thought were tough questions
about the dory, technical nit-picking, making certain I understood
how much she knew about boats. She never once said how lovely
that boat looked, there with all her graceful lines flowing under the
pale December sun. But she bought the dory and the next afternoon
arrived with another woman in a truck to pick her up. I shed some
tears as they drove away.

A few weeks later we moved to our new home, just five miles
north of Middle Bay, but light-years from my small-boat salad days.
For the first time since the *Emma* I could foresee no boats in my
future. What fishing I might do would be from the decks of boats
that belonged to friends kind enough to invite me along, or as a
guest of one of our sons or daughters, several of whom either owned
a boat or were dreaming about the day they could acquire one.

Looking out the windows of our town home, I could see only the
homes of our neighbors and their carefully tended patches of lawn.
The asphalt of our street did not ripple under the wind, and never—
even on the calmest night—would I hear a fish jump. And most
difficult of the new lessons I had to learn, never again would I be
able to indulge myself in the nourishing and healing solitude of a
solo voyage around the bay. The prospect of a life without a boat was
something I tried hard not to think about.

Quite unexpected events, however, came to my rescue in a relatively short time and from a most surprising source.

Key West

On a warm September afternoon while I was carefully tending our own patch of lawn, Jean called to me to tell me I was wanted on the phone. The call was from Key West and the caller was a young man named Pritam Singh.

"John," he told me, his voice full of excitement, "I just bought the Truman Annex."

"The what?"

"The Truman Annex. The biggest parcel of waterfront property in Key West. I got it at auction. I read about the sale in *The New York Times* and flew down here one day and bought the place the next. You'll probably read about it tomorrow."

He was right about that. Not only did the *Times* run a long article, but the Maine dailies put the story on their front pages. After all, it wasn't every day that a hometown boy (and one who had been part of our household) came up with $17.1 million for almost one hundred acres of waterfront property on the nation's southernmost island.

Our friend Gary Merrill read the piece early. He had usually finished with four or five newspapers before Jean and I began to think about breakfast. The phone rang when we were doing just that, and Gary's voice boomed, "Well, I see where one of your boys made good."

Pritam was "one of our boys" in Gary's eyes because Pritam had been living at our home when Gary made his frequent visits. A contemporary of our older sons, Pritam began life as Paul LaBombard—his parents separated when he was an adolescent— and later changed his name after a journey to India and a visit to Amritsar's Golden Temple where he converted to Sikhism and began wearing a turban, growing a beard, letting his hair go untouched by scissors, carrying a small dagger on his belt, and, almost as if his success was the result of his new god, making a great deal of money in real estate, primarily as the builder or renovator of condominium projects in Maine, California, New Mexico, and Massachusetts.

When he said the words *Key West*, he revived a dream of mine that first took shape when I was a boy, a boy who had yet to set foot aboard the *Emma*. City-born in Manhattan, I was also the beneficiary of its remarkable resources, including the Metropolitan Museum, one of the many cultural treasure-houses toured in our mother's wake by each of her offspring, who would have to wait many years before any of us recognized the wisdom of her determination to educate. I'm certain she never knew which of those framed images have stayed with me forever.

It was the Caribbean art of Winslow Homer: those watercolors that catch the Gulf sky's turbulent drama, the sea's emerald dazzle, the countless natural wonders of a world of small islands surrounded by the vast, undulating mystery that is the tropical sea. I would, I promised myself as I stood before Homer's splendid creations, put myself in those paintings.

More than five decades had gone by when Pritam's call arrived, and I had yet to keep that promise to my boyhood self. But hopes and dreams had never died and as soon as Pritam had accurately described his latest real estate buy and told me something about the city it is part of, I told him that I would be down for a visit, and soon.

A week later I was in Key West, smitten by the sultry September softness of its humid and fragrant air. After dinner on that first night I walked out on the Truman Annex pier, the former navy-built mass of concrete and pilings in more than thirty feet of water, a place where World War I submarines docked on the corner of the world where the Gulf and the Atlantic meet in a liquid collision of aquamarine and indigo, a place that gives life to countless fish and sea creatures so exotic some have yet to be discovered.

On that first night the tarpon were there to greet me, their great silver forms gliding in and out of the planes of light that fell from the dock's overhead lamps. They captivated me with the grace of their wildness and I stayed for hours to watch them.

It was those tarpon more than any other incentive that found me in Pritam's office the next day asking about a job with his brand-new Truman Annex Company. I was hired as a writer and public relations person, the sort of nebulous title with generously defined areas of responsibility that allowed me more than considerable freedom to indulge the excitement I knew as I stood on the brink of living a dream.

My office overlooked the pier and the former navy harbor. Because the breakwater-enclosed cove had been dredged to thirty feet or more right up to the bulkhead, and because it lies just off the main channel from the ocean to the Gulf, it was frequented by many varieties of fish, fish I could watch from my office window, fish I could catch on a fly tossed from the bulkhead just below that window.

I did just that on a fine April day when a school of oceanic jack crevalle—big ones, up to thirty pounds—came slashing into the basin, herding a school of mahua up against the bulkhead timbers. I grabbed my fly rod off the wall above my desk and ran down one flight of stairs. Five minutes later I hooked about a twenty-pounder. As adoring secretaries watched from their office windows, I landed and released my fish in about fifteen minutes.

"There aren't many offices where you can spot feeding fish and catch one on a fly," I explained to Pritam, who was mildly peeved at my exhibition. "We should write about this in your brochures. I'll bet you could add an angling premium to your prices."

Fishing from the Annex pier was a once-in-a-great-while diversion, however. Most of the time I would stand in that office building's second-floor hall where a large window looked west past the keys and hammocks that embroidered twenty miles of emerald, aqua, and pearl shallows at the edge of the Gulf. Mule Key, Archer Key, Barracouta Key, Big Mullet and Little Mullet, Woman Key, Man Key, Ballast Key, and Boca Grande: on a clear day I could see them all, wild dark-green outposts lining the edge of the ocean and the beginning of the Gulf from Key West to Boca Grande Channel, and beyond that the Marquesas and Tortugas. The largest water wilderness in the nation, a rare and prime habitat for sea creatures of all kinds: water birds, sea turtles, porpoise, sharks, barracuda, tarpon, and such an infinite variety of game fish and food fish and curious fish that as I daydreamed there on the landing, with office sounds chattering just beyond the walls, I imagined myself out there, out there in my boat, any boat, a boat I did not have.

Being introduced to the wonders of those waters by my friend, Captain Jeffrey Cardenas, who shared his flats skiff with me from time to time, tightened the cables of my boat-owning compulsions. Jeffrey, a superb fishing guide and a gentle and generous friend, opened my eyes to thin-water discoveries I would never have found on my own. But as word of his talents spread and his guiding business grew until he was booked seven days a week, week after week after week, I could no longer reasonably expect to be his guest.

As giving and talented as he is, he could not add an extra day to a seven-day week.

"Don't worry," I told him when he said he missed our fishing together, "I'm going to get my own boat."

That's what I said, but I had no idea how to go about it. Pritam was already encountering the fiscal difficulties that would eventually force him to cut his staff from forty to three, and I could see what was coming. Our two-state lives were expensive; our incomes were modest. Rents in Key West are high during the winter, and Jean and I could afford no such undisciplined indulgence as a boat for John.

Nevertheless, I soon had what amounted to majority control of a johnboat. It was a leftover from one of the high-flying subcontractors who worked on one of the many Truman Annex improvement projects that had to be done to salvage what was left of the property

after twenty years of neglect. This boat, a larger version of the beat-up skiff that the tides had brought to John's Point, was an eighteen-footer, a big, rugged aluminum rectangle squared at bow and stern. She reminded me of a heavyweight boxer who just lost a fifteen-round decision to a hard hitter. She was battered, her sides sprung here and there, her stern gunwale bent. And she was deckless, quite without accessory, or even most of the essentials. She did have an outboard, a sixty-horsepower, oil-injection Suzuki—a motor powerful enough to move her right along once she got up on a plane.

When I first appropriated her, neither boat nor motor worked well, if at all. After a hard year of use by the contractors, who filled her with power tools each day and crossed the channel from the Annex to Tank Island, where they dismantled the navy's large abandoned fuel storage tanks, she had simply been left at the dock the day those contractors finished their job and headed for their upstate homes. They had made enough on the contract to write off one badly bruised johnboat.

With the help of some friends in the Annex maintenance crew and the use of a hoister, we lifted her from the Gulf and deposited her on terra firma just in back of the Harry S Truman Little White House, one of the Annex properties included in Pritam's purchase. I always liked Harry when he was in the big White House, and I knew his spirit would look kindly on the work we were doing.

Roger Gaudette, another of the schoolboys who shared our bed and board in Maine for many years, a boy whose friendship with Pritam helped him get a job at the Annex, was the key to that johnboat's renewal, repair, and conversion to a first-class (well, maybe not quite first-class, but damn close) flats fishing skiff. It was with Roger's essential assistance that we acquired a few sheets of five-eighths marine plywood, some Styrofoam slabs, and the power tools needed to build a full deck, as well as a casting deck forward: a raised deck in the bow that came back about six feet. Free of all cleats and obstructions and almost level with the gunwales, the deck would allow a fly caster plenty of room to strip line and cast from a smooth surface with no hangups. We added some nonskid mix to the dark green paint we used. I built in a bulkhead about eight inches from the stern for gasoline and oil storage, drilled through the gunwales on both sides to install oarlocks, and equipped the johnboat with a pair of twelve-foot oars and a push pole that I could handle from the stern thwart.

Our conversion efforts might have been compared to creating a racing bobsled from a tin washtub, but what we had when we finished was a most workable flats fishing skiff with plenty of casting room and a draft still so shallow that she could fish about anywhere Jeffrey could pole his Maverick. Indeed, no sooner had Roger and I finished our work—which took about about a month's worth of spare time—but everyone, including Pritam, decided they'd like nothing better than to take the johnboat fishing.

None of them, however, was going to leave home before dawn to do it. There were many dark predawns when I'd ride my bike through the Annex gates and out onto the pier where lamplight still touched the water, illuminating nocturnal fish around the coral heads and rubble just off the pier's west end. By first light I'd be off Fleming Key or at the entrance to Jack Channel, watching for a tarpon's roll. And on Sundays Roger and I would anchor at one of the snapper spots Jeffrey had shared with us. With shrimp-tipped feathered jigs, we'd catch enough gray snapper and yellowtail for our table. On the way back to the Annex dock, I'd open up that Suzuki and the "new" johnboat would slam and pound her way across the chop, her flat bottom feeling the full heft of every choppy sea. Both of us would laugh, bouncing there in our aluminum boat, delighted to be on the water, to be free, to be discoverers of the true treasures of the lower Keys: those much abused small islands that provide a land base for so many water people like me and Roger.

One afternoon as I chatted with a young visiting water-quality engineer from Tampa, he told me he loved fishing and all his life had wanted to catch a tarpon. It was a warm day in late May, the air moved languidly under a southerly breeze—ideal tarpon conditions. "At five," I said, "we'll take the johnboat. The tide will be rising. Perhaps we'll find some tarpon in Jack Channel."

He was not a fly caster, but there was plenty of spinning tackle in my office (I could, as one of my coworkers suggested, have opened a tackle shop). We took a light spinning rod and a few Mirrolure silver minnow plugs. On our way to the channel just off Fleming Key I saw a tarpon roll on the silken, windless surface. A good sign.

Just south of the entrance to Jack Channel I shut down the outboard and we began drifting toward the channel entrance, carried there on the rising tide as softly as a gull gliding on tropical thermals. Tarpon rolled around us, their silver backs and shoulders touched with violet by the approaching twilight.

My engineer stood on the johnboat's plywood casting platform, the one Roger and I had built so painstakingly, making certain each brass screw was properly countersunk and sealed with marine putty. He was a fine spin caster; the Mirrolure soared out more than a hundred feet. His retrieves were fast, jerky; I could see the rod wobble. I could tell his adrenaline was pumping as he watched more and more of those gleaming, languid creatures roll on the velvet surface, the sibilance of their motion whispering of their presence.

"Slow down," I said, my voice soft as if I knew the tarpon had ears. "This is deep water. Let the lure sink a while after you cast. Then retrieve it slowly. Stop a second or two every now and then."

"Okay, okay," he said. And he tried, but the excitement of being surrounded by leviathans was almost too much for that angler.

"Slower. Got to be slower," I told him. "Let it sink."

He tried harder the next time. I counted for him: "One . . . two . . . three . . . four . . . okay, now start reeling." This time, he made certain to slow down.

It must have been his twentieth cast and he had begun to believe, I think, that I had overstated the chances that a tarpon would eat that Mirrolure. His adrenaline had subsided; he was close to being relaxed. That, more than my instruction, accounted for the slowdown of his retrieve.

He had recovered most of his line. Not so many tarpon rolled. His disappointment reached me.

Ten feet from the boat, a silver torpedo shot from beneath. More than six feet of giant tarpon leapt more than its length, the sunset glowing between its great tail and the rustling foam that marked its exit.

"Jesus Christ!" The engineer stood as motionless as a barber pole. "Look at that!"

Tilting toward us, the tarpon began its fall. For a moment, I panicked, thinking it would fall across our gunwale. A fish that large could capsize us.

It tumbled mightily, splashing us, the gobs of warm Gulf water slapping audibly against the johnboat's aluminum sides.

That engineer didn't realize that the tarpon he watched with such awe was also a tarpon he had hooked. He discovered that just after the waters folded over the submerging fish, when the rod was almost torn from his hands and line began ripping from the reel.

"Jesus Christ!" he said again, holding the rod tightly as it bucked in his hands.

"That's your fish there," I said. "He ate your plug." Before I had finished the sentence, my angler was quite convinced he had, indeed, hooked the tarpon he had wanted so much, and for so long. The fish ran off almost two hundred yards of line and appeared to be able to polish off the remaining hundred on the reel. I started the outboard and idled in the tarpon's direction, allowing the angler to regain some line.

The tarpon jumped, then jumped again. Each time we could hear its gill plates rattle as it shook its bucket-size head trying to rid itself of the tiny plug fast to its bony jaw.

"Wow! Did you see that?"

"Yes," I said. "I saw it."

Forty-five minutes later and deeper into the gathering dusk, I assumed the fish and the angler had reached a standoff; each time the angler regained a few feet of line, the tarpon would yank it back.

"It's getting dark fast," I said. "You might as well break that fish off and we'll head home."

I might as well have suggested that he gaff himself through the foot. "Hey, no way," he shouted from the bow. "This is the first tarpon of my life, and I'm going to land him."

I had my doubts. The line on the reel was fifteen-pound test, and there is only so much any line can take from a fish well over one hundred pounds. But I knew I would never persuade that angler to let go voluntarily, so I used the motor to try to get the battle turned a bit more in our direction.

We gained line, the angler, the boat, and her motor working against a single, tough, large, strong, and stubborn fish. Within twenty minutes, the tarpon was alongside, parallel to our starboard gunwale, dark in the water, seeming to be almost as long as the boat. I sensed the fish was weary, but not exhausted. It could, as I have seen so many tarpon do, rest a moment or two and then blast off, rocketing across the channel as if it had just felt the hook.

"Reach down and touch it," I said. "Then it will be a caught fish. I'll hold the rod."

Handing me the rod, the engineer slumped to his knees, stretched an arm far over the gunwale, looped it down toward the water until it brushed the tarpon's slippery shoulders. As it felt the contact, the great fish lunged and the short, frayed bit of line that held it snapped with a cap-gun crack and the tarpon was free. The engineer groaned.

"It's okay," I said. "You caught it. We would have released it anyway. That's the law."

"But I wanted you to take a picture."

"Pretty dark for that. But," I said, "you know my phone number. If anyone doubts that you caught a tarpon over a hundred pounds, tell them to give me a call."

As I opened the throttle a bit to get us underway and headed toward the Annex dock, the engineer bent over the rail, heaving, literally sick from the excitement and strain. I waited until the heaves ended and the angler stood up. As he did, I pushed hard on the throttle, anxious to be home before pitch-dark. The big Suzuki had plenty of torque; the johnboat shot forward and the thrust caught my passenger off guard. He fell back hard, cracking his knee on the edge of an aluminum thwart. I slowed, helped him up, and waited while he rubbed his bruised patella.

"Jesus Christ," he said, for the third time that afternoon. "First I almost faint from the excitement, then I toss my cookies, and then I damn near break my leg. There's more to this tarpon fishing than I thought."

As I learned many times after that memorable episode, there is always more to most kinds of fishing than almost anyone thinks. I did many kinds from that johnboat. She was my first Key West craft, and it was with her that I made the solo discoveries and lived the solo adventures that taught me better lessons than any instructor.

But as that year moved along into the sultry summer of the Gulf, the ebb tide of Pritam's fortunes began to gather speed. The large and rather random office staff of some forty folks began to dwindle and then dwindle some more. At last, the trimmers reached my branch and Jean and I headed back to Maine for a brief vacation. By the time we returned to Key West, the ignition locks on the Suzuki had been changed. And very soon after that, the johnboat was beached, dumped from a front end loader into the Annex parking lot, and left there: an asset, I suppose, for the bankers to ponder. Whatever her status, she was no longer my passport to the vast freedoms and splendors of the marvelously complex waters I had just begun to comprehend.

Desolate, I moped. I moped at home, I moped to David Ethridge, the magazine editor and publisher who had given me a new and better job. And I moped at the various social events Jean and I attended as guests.

Among those was a "stop-by-for-a-glass-of-wine" visit with Jill Walters, our friend and neighbor just across Newton Street from our rented house. A hearty, energetic executive who was in charge of sales for the local cable-television provider, Jill was a fine neighbor: friendly, helpful, and welcoming. A great fan of Bette Davis, she was delighted to meet our friend Gary Merrill, Bette's former husband, and even more pleased when Gary gave her a copy of his auto-biography, *Bette, Rita, and the Rest of My Life*, and inscribed it to Jill with some warm words.

That incident, I believe, was the catalyst that helped precipitate Jill's decision to let me become a part-owner of her small boat, the *Booba*. During the course of our conversations, Jill often told me how much she loved fishing, and when I asked where she went and what sort of fishing she did, she would say, "Oh, we just get together and take the *Booba* out in the bay. Nothing real serious, hand lines, hooks baited with shrimp, and a case of cold beer. We have a real good time." I got the feeling that Jill had a real good time at whatever she did.

But a few days later when I asked her how well she had done on her latest fishing trip, she told me she hadn't gone out. Something, she wasn't sure what, was wrong with the *Booba*'s outboard, a thirty-horsepower Mercury. I said perhaps I could try to fix it, and Jill said, well, go right ahead.

The *Booba* was docked in a canal alongside a Geiger Key home owned (and rented out) by Jill and her brother, Stephen. She looked like a friendly, small, but somewhat taken-for-granted boat. Molded from some type of fiberglass compound, obviously Whaler inspired (same flat bottom with three ridges acting as stabilizers and same wide beam), she was one of the several less costly Whaler look-alikes that followed in the wake of that innovative boat's immediate accep-tance and record-setting popularity.

I'd gathered from Jill's description of her fishing that having fun on the water was the top priority, as opposed to serious angling. My first look at the *Booba* told me I'd come close to the mark. A few hand lines were tucked in a corner forward, beer-can openers were lashed here and there, and several sponge rubber holders for glasses and cans indicated that even though she was just fourteen feet long, the *Booba* served most satisfactorily as a recreational vessel. Her outboard, however, looked the way all machines look when they have been missing their maintenance and have been rather carelessly treated. The propellor was no longer in balance; too many trips over too much coral bottom covered by not quite enough water had bent the prop blades and broken off the tip of one of those blades. And those same trips, which in Keys waters stir an abundant supply of sand and silt, had attracted enough sand and silt residue to the cooling system intake to clog the small openings and prevent coolant circulation. When the motor, thus deprived, overheated, its automatic shutdown (a safety device) performed as it should and the outboard quit. It could be started again when it cooled down, but the process takes a great deal of time and it's only temporary.

I pushed some thin, strong wire through the intake holes in the propellor shaft and then tried to clean out the interior passages by hooking the engine up to a hose and running the motor at close to full throttle. The Mercury came away from these crude ministrations much improved. After I invested in a new propellor, changed the plugs, and ran some fresh gasoline through the system, I hoped the engine would be dependable enough to move the *Booba* from that Geiger Key canal to the Garrison Bight Marina in Key West, where I could have the boat forklifted out of the water and put on a rack so I could overhaul the hull while the Mercury man from Murray Marine did the same to the outboard.

The trip from Geiger to the Bight covers about twelve miles, not a long trip for a boat that could get up on a plane (if its motor were working properly) and average about twenty knots, or more in ideal conditions. The *Booba*, however, was not at her best, or anywhere close. Because she had been docked in a canal's warm waters, her bottom had become a hothouse for all sorts of underwater creatures, green, growing algae, and other marine flora. Resisting such invasions is a price every warm-water boat owner must pay. Although a Key West boat may be able to cruise three hundred sixty-five days a year, the convenience of climate makes its own unforgiving demands. Maintenance is a must, and the *Booba* had not been meticulously maintained, to say the least.

Which meant she generated a great deal of drag as she pushed through the water. My twelve-mile cruise would take a while, and it would require attention to my charts. For like waterways everywhere on the Gulf side of the Keys—and many places on the Atlantic side—I would run into miles of thin water, places on the flats where less than a foot of water covered the green turtle grass, coral heads, and marl. Running aground on a shoal, especially on a falling tide, off Key West can mean spending most of a day—or night—stuck fast. And being stuck in the back country means spending time quite alone in a genuine wilderness. For even though you may be no more than two or three miles from the lights of downtown Key West, you are hard aground in the world's largest shallow-water wilderness: hundreds of square miles of uninhabited keys, tangled mangrove hammocks, and vast flats that seem to stretch to the far horizons. Boating in the Keys is not a pastime; it is a skill that requires careful preparation, good equipment, and precise orientation. For if you are uncertain of where you are and where you're going, and if you fail to read the water and heed its signals, your voyage will run into trouble, and quickly.

I know the rules better now, after seven years in the Keys, than I did on that bright, windy January morning when Jill drove me to Geiger Key so I could bring the *Booba* to Garrison Bight.

"I'd go outside, if I were you," she said, meaning that I should take the boat south to the Atlantic and motor west along the coast where I'd find deeper water. But to my way of thinking, the southeast wind was a bit too brisk for a fourteen-foot, shallow-draft boat in the open sea. If I headed north and then cut toward Key West, I'd be protected from the worst of the wind by the back-country keys and hammocks. Good thinking, but one problem: I'd never made the trip before, and the strange waters were dotted with flats so shoal that even the shallow-draft *Booba* would have no problem running aground. But I had checked the tide tables and learned that high tide in Key West coincided with my departure time. Because tides in the Keys average a foot or so, high water would mean a flat that showed up on the charts as a foot deep at mean low water would have two feet of coverage. Two feet was plenty for the *Booba*, so I left the canal with a wave and the confidence the top of the tide had given me.

Within five minutes I'd learned one of the many hard lessons I've been taught by these waters. As I turned north and began my passage through Shark Key channel, I realized the tides were almost the opposite of my predictions. What, I wondered, as the *Booba* bumped over shoals, could be going on? Had I misread the tide tables, gotten them reversed?

I might as well have. As I've since discovered, the tides around Key West are some of the most complex on the globe. For it is here that the Gulf of Mexico and the Atlantic meet, and where two seas collide, the tides are fractured. I could, for example, ride my bike the ten miles from Key West to Big Coppitt, so when I knew my course would take me on Big Coppitt's northeast side, I assumed the tides in Key West would apply. Ten miles on Long Island Sound, for example, would hardly make a minute's difference in tide times. Here in the lower Keys, however, it makes all the difference. The tides off Big Coppitt are almost exactly the opposite from Key West. High tide in Key West Harbor is low tide off Big Coppitt.

Instead of the optimum tide I sought, I had to deal with the minimum: dead low. That was a memorable trip. There were times when I had to get out and push. Other times when I ran the motor in its "up" position so the prop barely bit into the water's surface. And other times when I shut the motor down, stood in the bow as a human sail, and let the wind carry us across flats that allowed us eight inches of water.

Never again would I wing it, I told myself when the *Booba* and I reached the familiar channels off Fleming Key. And I've kept that promise to myself. I don't cruise in unfamiliar waters. I keep good charts on board, and I study the back-country tide tables, because in these waters a few miles of flats can make a critical, and sometimes astounding, difference. Even on short trips, I take my ship-to-shore radio and before I leave the dock I make sure Jean knows where I'm planning to go. The *Booba* taught me these lessons, and I'll always be grateful to her for that.

She also gave me many hours of pleasure and discovery, for although her low freeboard, especially across her stern, made her a boat ill-suited for a husky chop, she was, after all, a splendid alternative to no boat. Even the nearby waters of Calder Channel and Archer Key Basin cannot be reached on foot. For anyone who loves being on the water, any boat is better than no boat.

And a boatless future looked to be my fate when Jill told me she had sold the place on Geiger Key and that the *Booba* was part of the sale. The day came, and she was gone. For two weeks my depression gained momentum. If I had found a wreck, I would have sought to salvage her.

But on the first morning of the third week, I looked up from our breakfast table and saw a trailered boat being backed into our narrow driveway alongside that Newton Street house. The man doing the backing was Roger, our favorite stray who had come to live with us as a boy when he was in junior high school. The boat, a sixteen-foot Grumman aluminum skiff, was the boat he used for clamming and scalloping in Maine, and he had towed it all the way to Key West so he and I could go fishing while he was here. Like me, he worked for Pritam, a boyhood classmate and friend. And, like me and Jean, Roger would also eventually be laid off when the Truman Annex project hit hard times.

But those events were months in our future when Roger arrived, unannounced as always, on that happy day. I was ready for a shake-down cruise even before Roger unpacked. And I made no apologies for suggesting just that. Roger, however, knew better. He explained why as he showed me around the Grumman, which was not quite the boat she first appeared to be.

Her throttle and shifter lever on her side-mounted control panel was missing, broken clean off. Her gunwales were dented here and there, and the entire lower unit on her forty-horsepower Evinrude was bent far out of true. Yet both the boat and her motor looked new.

"What happened?" I asked.

"Well, my brother Gary was towing the boat through town on a trailer when some guy cut him off as he turned into a shopping-center parking lot. Gary got angry and tried to turn the corner into the lot to follow the guy. But he forgot he was towing a boat, and he gave his car too much gas. The acceleration pulled the trailer out from under the boat and the Grumman slammed onto the pavement and rolled over on her side. First the lower unit got creamed. Then the shifter control was snapped off. It's a brand-new boat. There's hardly twelve hours on that engine. That's one reason I brought her down. I didn't want anything else to happen to her."

The details of her damage, especially the loss of the shifter and the wreckage of the lower unit, took the edge off my joy at the Grumman's arrival. Both repairs required skills at the outermost reach of my mechanical abilities. And neither Roger nor I had a budget that would allow us professional help. I began to think I was back to my no-boat status.

But two days later, my brother-in-law, John Graves, arrived for a visit just in time to save me, Roger, and the Grumman. John is a writer, a Texas writer with an international reputation for some of the finest prose in print. But he is also a rancher who, with my sister Jane, built his own home in Glen Rose. They began with the land, and from there they not only built the main ranch house but the barns and stables and outbuildings that they needed for their stock: horses, cattle, goats, chickens, dogs, and more. John did it all, and in the process learned plumbing, wiring, tool making, well drilling, and goat tending. And on that ranch that's hundreds of miles from the nearest salt water, John designed and built a fiberglass flats skiff, complete with special touches that make it a first-class fly-fishing skiff for two.

Over several decades of absolute independence and self-reliance, John Graves learned how to fix things—just about anything and everything. When he ran his knobby, calloused rancher's hands over the Evinrude's crimped lower unit and fractured propellor, and then spent a good twenty minutes contemplating the wrecked control panel, I knew in my heart that the Grumman would fish again, and that when she did, I would be at her helm. It was that image, held close, that sustained me and maintained my good spirits over the next four weeks as John and Roger worked to restore life to the sixteen-foot aluminum corpse in our driveway.

Cast aluminum, John explained to me, cannot be heated and hammered like iron and steel; however, it can be pounded into shape with a rubber mallet as long as the repair is not too drastic. In other words, we could restore the shaft to some semblance of straight if we were lucky and the stress was managed well enough to keep the aluminum from fracturing. John and Roger pounded, carefully and precisely, and bit by bit the angle of the shaft's mis-alignment began to decrease. It never quite returned to plumb (it's still out of line after three years of use), but it did get back to a degree of straightness that allowed the gears and engine to function at close to 100 percent efficiency.

The propellor and the drive gears in the lower unit had to be replaced, creating a cavity in my budget, but not a catastrophe. After a week or so of work, the basic power unit was termed recovered enough to go back to work. Controlling it was another matter. Replacing the entire control panel, installing new cables, and doing a proper job of linking them with the engine was a job that could have been done at the marina. But it would have cost close to four hundred dollars, and that would leave me with a basket-case budget.

When it snapped on impact there in that Brunswick supermarket parking lot, the throttle and shifter lever broke well down near its base. All we had left to work with was the bottom half-circle of metal that had been a disc that rotated a quarter turn forward and back when the lever was moved. Forward engaged the engine's thrust and farther forward its throttle; full forward and the boat would be moving at top speed. Moved back to neutral, the lever allowed the engine to slow and then slip into reverse when the lever was moved backward. There was nothing left of the lever, which had snapped off across the center of the cast aluminum disc that was its base. Movement of the half-circle that was left was the only way the engine could be controlled. This meant the fragment's manipulation had to be managed with a pipe wrench—obviously not a helms-man's best choice.

John studied the problem for two days or so in his deliberate, thoughtful way. Then he said, "Well, this might work." And he tapped five threaded holes in the half-circle disc along its outer rim. The holes were tapped to accept quarter-inch bolts. Then John took a two-inch-wide piece of steel bar stock about a foot long and one-quarter-inch thick. Drilling holes through that to match the five he had drilled in the disc, he bolted the bar to the disc, adding some liquid aluminum to make certain the bolts would not vibrate loose. The result would get no points for grace or beauty, but it scored a perfect ten for function. I wrapped some rubber electrician's tape around the bar stock to minimize its corners and we considered the job complete. The Grumman, which I have since named the *Jolly Roger*, is almost certainly the only outboard skiff in South Florida with a shifter fashioned from bar stock and fastened with five stainless-steel bolts. It reminds me of the Frankenstein monster sometimes, but most often it's there as a monument to John Graves's ingenuity and his make-do ethic.

And he didn't stop there. The *Jolly Roger* was an unadorned, unmodified Grumman, which meant she had come from the factory on Long Island with her outer hull and three thwarts—forward, center, and stern—and that was it. What John and Roger and I added was a marine plywood deck for the stern and midships sections. And forward from the bow thwart, John Graves built and installed a meticulously fitted casting platform of half-inch marine plywood, scribed perfectly to fit flush against the hull and cover the span from the bow to the stern side of the thwart. About six inches lower than the gunwales, the platform gives a fly caster the perfect spot. The angler can stand tall, get fine visibility, and have plenty of deck area for his casting line.

John also designed and built a hatch joined by flush-set stainless-steel hinges that ran the length of one side of the hatch cover so it could be lifted easily and would be sure to close snugly. It was a job a cabinetmaker would have been proud to display, and after a primer coat, plus two finish coats and a cover coat of clear, tough polyurethane, our new casting platform was ready for some hard use.

We launched the new and improved *Jolly Roger* three years ago at the Garrison Bight Marina where she stayed that first year. In the fall of 1990, Jean and I moved into what is now the Key West Anglers Club at 800 Eisenhower Drive. It's a fine old building, originally designed as housing for the families of Methodist missionaries being schooled and prepared for work in tropical and subtropical venues. A long, two-story concrete structure that occupies an entire city block, the place has about ten bedrooms, meeting rooms, and extra kitchens: the perfect layout for a small club that caters to ardent anglers, most of them fly casters who come to Key West for the tarpon, permit, bonefish, mutton snapper, barracuda, sharks, and scores of others that will eat a fly and then fight harder, pound for pound, in one of the loveliest and most exotic shallow-water environments on the globe.

Just across the street is the Anglers Club dock on Garrison Bight, and there at the dock the *Jolly Roger* waits for me each day. Her Evinrude is still functioning perfectly, although it has been extensively overhauled once in the past two years. The boat herself is perfect. John Graves, Bud Trillin, and the Episcopal bishop of the state of New York are among the illustrious visitors who have cast at, and hooked up with, fish from the boat's casting platform.

Every Sunday every week of the year I go snapper fishing with "Big Bird" Tidball and with Roger, if he is in town. Other days when I finish work and the surge within is too passionate to resist, I stroll across the street, step into the *Jolly Roger*, turn the key, push the Frankenstein control lever into gear, and ease out of the bight on a cruise that may take me to Archer Key Basin, Channel Key, Calder Channel, Fleming Key, or up toward Jewfish Basin and the lonely, forever wondrous, breathtaking purity of the back country, a place where a person alone can meet his soul sailing toward him.

If, that is, he has a boat. And thanks to Roger, I do. And thanks to Pritam, I came first to Key West, the one place in this country where a boat, and especially a small boat, can make enchantments come alive, add a fine mystery to life, and, above all, keep an elderly boatman pumped with a zest for life.

That is what small boats have always given me: nothing less than my life and the joy I have found in it.

A person cannot hope for more.

Final Thoughts

Keep a Weather Eye

It's about twenty-six miles over water from Key West to the Marquesas, a circular collection of wilderness keys that embrace a lovely inner lagoon embroidered with channels where tarpon, permit, and bonefish like to gather. The small-boat passage west from Key West is in the lee of keys and hammocks except for the last five miles across Boca Grande Channel, a deep cut between the Marquesas and Boca Grande Key. Here, the Gulf of Mexico collides with the Atlantic and the meeting creates constant turmoil. Even on windless days, clashing tides build choppy seas that can unsettle an inexperienced skipper.

Crossing that open expanse of Boca Grande Channel in outboard-powered skiffs no more than seventeen feet long, at the most, is an adventure I have experienced often. I can, if I check the dates, remember almost every crossing. There are several I will never, ever forget.

Early on a mid-June morning some years ago, Roger, Jeffrey, and I fished inside the Marquesas lagoon. Thunder rumbled in the distance and the air was still, heavy, listless. But scores of permit tailed busily on a flat, happily nudging crabs from their hiding places in the soft bottom. We cast to dozens of fish; none would eat our lures.

But we kept believing that the next cast would be the one, and the permit stayed where they were, the flash of their feeding firing our adrenaline. Fishing, for each of us in that boat, was an all-consuming passion. We paid little heed to anything else except the fish, not even the approaching thunderheads and the increasingly bright flashes of lightning.

But when the sodden, still air around the boat began to crackle, when Roger's shoulder-length hair literally stood on end, lifted toward the sky by the static electricity that gathered, waiting to energize a lightning bolt, and when a ball of blue electric light hissed at the tip of the long graphite rod I held in my hand, then I paid attention.

"Put those rods down," Jeffrey said. "It's time we got the hell out of here." Within minutes after we stowed the rods and started the engine, lightning struck less than a quarter-mile off. Lightning reaches for the highest point when it flashes down from a thunderhead. My graphite rod might well have meant the difference if I had still held it high.

Lightning does strike open boats, especially sailboats with their tall masts. If the mast is properly grounded and the charge is diverted to the water, lives are not generally endangered. The experience is no fun. Most of the time it is a trauma that can be avoided, for thunderheads do not appear in moments; the towering, dark, anvil-shaped clouds gather on the horizon in an unmistakable prelude to their tumult. Small-boat skippers who keep a weather eye out, and who comprehend what they see, can usually steer around a squall or beat it back to shore. And even if they can do neither, they don't stand high in their boat holding aloft a fishing rod made of one of the finest electrical conductors known.

Their common sense tells them it's a bad idea.

Common sense is the key here. When it comes to surviving the collection of nasty occurrences the sea and sky can so swiftly generate, common sense is the best strategy. Yet the ever-increasing number of boating mishaps, disasters, and fatalities indicates that common sense is all too often ignored, or simply not present.

Which I can understand. There have been times—just about the only times I have been in trouble in a small boat—when I ignored the whispers of common sense trying to be heard above the high volume of my exuberance, or the whine of my impatience. The lessons taught at such times can be hard; every now and then, they can also be terminal. I was lucky to be granted clemency, fortunate in each case that the damage was borne by the boat, not inflicted on its skipper and passengers.

Common sense. Keep a weather eye. These days the process is aided by global communication of weather forecasts that are, on the whole, fairly accurate. The U.S. Weather Bureau broadcasts around the clock, and radio receivers designed specifically to stay tuned to the appropriate frequency for your region are available at many stores and at low to moderate costs. They are well worth their price.

Learn to read the sky as well as you must learn to read your charts. The clouds will tell you most of the time where the wind will come from and how it will behave. Your charts will tell you, once you learn their language, where the waters are likely to be rough, where the currents run most rudely, and where the sea bottom allows only the most perilous passage.

Common sense. When in doubt, stay home, even if you've waited a month for the day. And if you do leave the dock, be prepared. Take a radio. Be as certain as you can be that your boat and every bit of its equipment is functioning well and will continue to do so. And don't run so far offshore you may not be able to beat a squall to the harbor.

But most of all, try to minimize risk. Which means understanding and measuring the risks at hand. If they include running out of fuel, carry an extra tank or oars, or if it's a boat you can't row, an extra small outboard in case your motor malfunctions. If you are caught by a squall—and they can pack killer winds—know how your boat can best cope with the challenge. And if you need help, don't be reluctant to use your radio to ask for it.

Common sense. The one lesson I've learned above all others after all my years afloat in small boats is that the sea doesn't give a damn. She is truly implacable; she acknowledges no entreaties and grants no exceptions. She can, and will if you are not aware, prepared, and properly cautious, kill you—and do it without batting an eye.

Brief Survey of Small Boats

Here is an informal compendium of the various types of small boats—from the smallest of forty-footers—that includes basic data, some opinions, and information that should prove useful to anyone contemplating small-boat ownership.

PRAMS AND DINGHIES The seven- to eight-foot pram is the smallest small boat in general circulation. Where the pram stops and the dinghy begins has always been something of a terminological mystery, but in general dinghies tend to have more conventional, pointed bows. They're also larger, up to twelve feet long. Prams, on the other hand, are always small and are almost always squared off at both bow and stern, making them look something like a floating orange crate. Both prams and dinghies are used almost exclusively as waterborne taxis. Small enough to be stored aboard a larger boat, or towed behind one, or hauled up on a dock or float, they travel to and from boat to shore or boat to boat.

But I have seen prams moored in farm ponds just in case the farmer or his wife and children want to go for a short cruise. Prams and dinghies are now made from many different materials: wood, plywood, fiberglass, aluminum, various molded plastic compounds, and resins. There is a pram with an absolutely transparent hull for anyone who wants to be able to see the underwater features of her voyages. Most prams and dinghies are outfitted with oars and oarlocks, but they can also be equipped with sails and outboard motors (very small outboards).

If a pram or dinghy is to be your only boat, then you should acquire a good sailing dinghy. She will always be small, but she'll also be fun. Many prams and dinghies are owner built in basements and garages; others are assembled from kits; and still others are bought "off the floor" at marinas and boatyards, or through the "For Sale" classifieds in local newspapers. Your best bet for a top-quality pram or dinghy is one of the boatbuilding schools, where student-built boats are handcrafted with diligence, care, and excellent materials.

As one of this book's readers, you may recall that I owned two prams, both at the same time. One was made of marine plywood, the other of aluminum. They both suffered greatly from negligence and hard use, but both held up through the years. I could not recommend one over the other; the wooden pram was more quiet, but not as easily hauled up on our float as her aluminum counterpart. As is true of all small-boat decisions, you must be quite careful, honest, and objective about what you want your boat to do for you and with you. Once you have those factors in place, and your budget in mind, your choice of make and model of pram or dinghy will be vastly simplified.

KAYAKS Prams and dinghies and kayaks have almost nothing in common except their size, and size being the criterion for this listing, we come next to kayaks. These are specialized small boats in every sense of the word, designed primarily to carry one person safely across challenging and sometimes dangerous waters. Adapted from the Eskimo kayak fashioned from spruce and sealskin, contemporary kayaks are molded from polymers, resins, and fiberglass; made from laminated wood; or made of waterproofed fabrics stretched over wood and aluminum frames, some of which are designed to be taken apart so the entire small boat can be collapsed and packed into a large duffle bag and carried like a suitcase.

There are few two-person kayaks, but there are some. The kayak, however, seems to work best as a single-person craft, and because few non-Eskimos need to hunt seals, polar bear, and walrus from their kayaks, the boat has become the marine equivalent of a mountain bike or hang glider, used almost exclusively as a fitness device, for adventure, and as a fine solitary experience on everything from placid rivers to white-water rapids and the open sea. When I fished for striped bass off Maine's Popham Beach, a kayaker appeared regularly at sunrise paddling his craft over the Atlantic swells from Parker Head to Seguin and back. He was a summer visitor from Boston or Philadelphia, and I have always considered him the quintessential kayak owner south of the Arctic circle: a man who

used his small boat to make possible a brief, but intense, meeting with the natural world's elemental presence.

Which is a reason why kayaking is more risky than most other small-boat adventures. The kayaker is most often alone, seldom equipped with an alternative to his paddle as a power source (although a few kayaks can be fitted with a small sail), and is often either in a rapid's rough water or far offshore where a rogue wave can easily capsize such a relatively fragile craft. At such times survival depends on keeping a cool, clear head, often difficult in moments of great stress. Anyone considering becoming a kayak owner must be in good physical condition and know the skills (like the Eskimo roll) the small craft requires. These are not boats for Sunday sailors.

CANOES   On the Restigouche River that is the border between the Canadian provinces of Quebec and New Brunswick, anglers (most of them Americans) who cast flies for Atlantic salmon do it from a twenty-six-foot-long canoe powered by a five-horsepower outboard mounted on a squared-off stern. This small boat is a far cry from prams, dinghies, and kayaks, yet is perhaps more traditional than any small boat; its ancestors can be traced directly to the earliest bark canoes built by Native Americans centuries before Columbus, Erik the Red, or any other intrepid sailors set foot on North America.

The large, graceful river canoes of the Canadian provinces are fashioned from wood, steamed strips bent to their graceful arcs, and covered with canvas, soaked with enough coats of paint to make it quite waterproof. These canoes are built during the long Canadian winters in the basements and sheds of the river men and guides who have learned the techniques from their elders, who learned from theirs. Aside from their exceptional length (the Restigouche is a big river), they are some of the last contemporary examples of the wood-and-cloth-covered canoes that until this century were the only sort on the water. However, since World War II, when so many new materials were developed, canoes have appeared in a number of forms, sizes, and materials, including laminated, fiberglass-coated wood, fiberglass, polymers, resins, aluminum, and a few traditional models fashioned with great care from cedar and other hand-selected woods.

The Old Town sailing canoe that I once owned and which is mentioned in this book was built at the company's shop in Old Town, Maine, sometime during the late 1930s. Those famous canoes with their cedar planking, spruce ribs, and special canvas sheathing were some of the largest canoes, each built by skilled craftsmen in the sheds near the Penobscot River. Founded in 1906 by George Alexander Gray (the grandfather of my friend Joseph Sewall, the only four-time president of the Maine Senate), the Old Town Canoe Company stayed in family hands until the early 1980s, when the Grays sold to Johnson Wax. Since then, the plant has been largely converted to the production of molded fiberglass and Kevlar canoes, and Old Town ships some 30,000 each year to canoe owners around the world. But if you would like one of the cedar and spruce originals, the company still has the molds and will make one just for you. While these triumphs of design and craftsmanship are not built for the budget minded, they are still one of the finest small boats available.

There are, of course, dozens of other fine canoe makers, including individual master craftsmen who build one or two splendid wooden canoes a year, and the equivalent of "canoe factories" that turn out tens of thousands. You can buy plans and build your own canoe, or you can purchase kits that give you most of the materials you need to put together a do-it-yourself model. Canoes can be as small as eight-foot, one-person models or as large as the Restigouche giants. They can be sailed, or motor powered, or both. Most, however, are paddled, and there are a score of small companies and a few individuals who do nothing but design and build good canoe paddles.

The canoe is the one small boat that seems to best satisfy the yearnings of small-boat owners around the world. Equally at home in fresh water and salt, on lakes, rivers, streams, bays, and oceans, riding white-water rapids or gliding across a summer sunset on Georgica Pond, the canoe has been fulfilling dreams and generating adventure since its genesis long before North America was on Magellan's charts.

INFLATABLES These small crafts are the only boats sustained by the compressed air within their flexible skins, the ultimate technological derivative of the ancient craft that plied the Tigris and Euphrates, kept afloat by the air trapped in inflated goatskins lashed to crude wooden frames. Air has lost none of its buoyancy over the centuries, and now it is pumped into a variety of plastic-coated, abrasion-resistant fabrics that end up looking like giant inner tubes shaped something like a pram with sausage sides, and a bluntly rounded bow and stern with a thin, flat, fabric bottom protected most often by a plywood deck cut to fit. These are the only boats that can be carried in a laundry bag, removed, pumped full, and launched from wherever the skipper happens to be. Some come with built-in foot pumps; others that are larger need the power of a mechanical air compressor to be properly inflated. Even the smallest inflatable poses a challenge to human lung power; should you get the task of "blowing up" your children's inflatable, you'll find yourself light-headed and short-winded within minutes of your first puff.

But precisely because they are so portable and so affordable, inflatables are enjoying increased popularity, a trend likely to continue as long as Jacques Cousteau and his crew turn up on television darting about the world's distant seas in Zodiacs, France's worthy contribution to the inflatable fleet. Other high-profile users include the U.S. Coast Guard, which has discovered that even large inflatables can be moved at very high speeds with a standard outboard motor. Because so much of the boat sits on top of the surface, there is little or no drag for a motor to overcome. Inflatables are replacing dinghies and prams in the ever-increasing flotilla of small craft towed by sailing yachts or stowed aboard motor yachts. Easily towed behind a yawl or sloop, an inflatable is also gentle to her mother ship's hull when she is pulled alongside to pick up and discharge passengers and freight.

Able to be paddled, rowed, sailed, or powered with small outboards, inflatables range from eight feet to more than twenty-five. They tend to be wet; that sausage bow does little to fend off choppy seas. But they are popular because they are among the most affordable new boats on the market. I bought the inflatable mentioned in this book off the floor at Sears in Brunswick. She was, however, not tough enough to withstand the abuse of Maine's rocky coast and the enthusiasm of six teenage sons and daughters, who quickly learned that being aboard that inflatable was the best position during a water fight.

I have a good friend here in Key West, a Parisian now an American citizen, who is nevertheless loyal to the Zodiac. Jacques fishes the waters off the Keys almost every day, and takes his blow-up boat deep into the mangroves. I have fished with him, and found the boat does most anything and everything a boat should do. And sitting on those inner-tube gunwales is definitely as comfortable as most easy chairs. Nevertheless, and in spite of Jacques' pledge that there is no small boat as good as the Zodiac when it comes to affordability and convenience, I'm quite certain that inflatable I bought from Sears is our first and last. But don't let me dissuade you; what Jacques says is true. It's a matter of personal preference and whether or not you have anxieties about being afloat in a craft that will begin deflating the moment its skin is punctured.

And yet if inflatables weren't fine boats, why would the Coast Guard be using so many of them? The larger blow-up boats are a series of sealed compartments; one puncture will not mean all the air can escape. And besides, inflatables never need to be painted.

WATERBIKES With our progression from prams and dinghies to kayaks, canoes, and inflatables, we have come to the end of the class

of small boats that can be conveniently moved atop the family car.
From here on, a trailer (or more) will be preferable in many cases
and essential in most.

Which brings me to the most popular trailered watercraft in the
world: the waterbike, or the personal watercraft, Jet Ski (now also a
trade name), and a bunch of other names. For in what surely must
be a difficult irony for the growing number of manufacturers of
these one- and two-person powerboats, there is still no agreement
on what they should be called.

This does not mean, however, that there is any confusion about
what they are. These are the metal, fiberglass, and plastic laminate
small boats that look like the offspring of a motorcycle and a
muscovy duck. The motorcycle part is above the waterline, and
includes a powerful engine, handlebars, and a jump seat where every
advertisement specifies a handsome young woman who is apparently overjoyed at being motored over the water at better than thirty
knots. It is the muscovy duck part—the machine's broad-breasted
hull—that makes the speed possible. The engine that roars like a
motorcycle creates a jet of water that propels these ubiquitous
seagoing snowmobiles.

There are more than a million of them registered in Florida alone,
and spokespeople for the state's "personal watercraft" association
tell me that sales projections based on current data indicate there
will be something like ten million by the year 2000. In response to
these projections, regulations are being written and legislated in the
hopes that some control can be imposed on their use and operation.
Florida has already prohibited waterbike riders from zooming along
any waters that are part of a federal or state sanctuary or preserve.
And there are those more traditional small-boat people who would
like to see waterbikes excluded from the entire coast and restricted
to circling abandoned rock quarries and sinkholes.

That, however, is certainly not going to happen, not in Florida
nor in any of the other forty-nine states where waterbikes are still
rocketing upward on the popularity curve. But it is this sudden and

booming demand that is causing some of the waterbike's sociologi-
cal problems. There were many traditionalists, for example, who
sympathized when the owner of an anchored sloop put a rifle shot
through a waterbiker's leg (and his craft's engine) when the noisy
machine disturbed the sailor's early morning meditation.

Noise will always be a problem because these are definitely
powerboats. Many under eight feet are propelled by 70- to 100-
horsepower engines, which is something like mounting your family
car's motor on a bicycle built for two. All of which having been said,
there is no argument with the fact that these machines fill a need
heretofore unaddressed by small boats. They are relatively inexpen-
sive ($3,500 to $7,000), easy to acquire (at least eighteen national
manufacturers), simple to transport, and able to be operated by
anyone who has started the family car.

They cannot, however, be sailed or fished from. They have very
little storage space, and they are designed primarily for recreational
"running around" or picnic trips to islands and other nearby shores.
I have a friend (yes, in spite of his waterbike madness) who takes his
watercraft on long cruises from Fort Lauderdale all the way to the
Marquesas, almost 200 miles. And he somehow packs enough food
and extra fuel to sustain him and his machine while he camps
overnight on one of the offshore keys. His recreational use of the
waterbike is the exception, however. Most often they are employed
as weekend escape mechanisms that will take you in circles on any
bay, lake, river, ocean, or reservoir at speeds close to 50 mph.

That function, as sales prove, is what most personal watercraft
owners want and expect for their money. There are already many
millions of satisfied customers around the globe. Perhaps you'll
join them.

PULLING BOATS On the other side of the small-boat coin, the term
pulling boat is comprehensive enough to include just about any boat
that can be rowed with a pair of oars. However, it is a term that
suffers from its breadth: there is as much difference between some

kinds of pulling boats and others as there is between trees and
flowers. Each may be called a plant, but you wouldn't want to send
your parents a larch for their window box.

In some circles, *pulling boat* strenuously implies a small craft that
is designed specifically for recreational rowing, a mobile fitness
machine that puts water instead of a gym floor beneath its wonderfully curved hull. The purest of these is the rowing shell, or scull, a
variation of the kayak hull with a small cockpit that has room for an
oarsman, a sliding seat, and little more. The disproportionately slim
hull supports a pair of oarlocks and braces, and the rower sits high,
with feet locked against a rear bulkhead to enable him to put all his
power into the stroke of his long oars, their wonderfully graceful
blades curved to catch the most water.

A bit further along on the pulling-boat charts are the sturdier
ocean shells like those made at Martin Marine in Kittery, Maine, a
yard I visited years ago. I was there to write an article for a now-
defunct magazine about the Alden ocean shells, both single and
double, ranging in length from sixteen to nineteen feet. These
fiberglass boats with foam flotation were primarily designed for
skilled rowers who lived along the northeast Atlantic coast.

They are a long way from the *Emma*, my first boat, and the

difference demonstrates just how varied and how specialized the art of building small recreational rowboats has become. Comparing those ocean-going pulling boats to the *Emma* is a bit like putting Leonardo's *Mona Lisa* alongside a drawing of Charlie Brown clipped from the Sunday funnies: they are both portraits, but that's about all they have in common. The specialized, narrow-hulled pulling boats, created and built for rowing and nothing more, are part of the same boat family as the *Emma*, but it is such a large, inclusive, and complex group that it defies easy classification.

Nevertheless, if you want a small, open boat that you can row, start with a single-seat shell and work your way through the peapod, the Swampscott dory, the Whitehall, the Catalina skiff, the Appledore, the wherry, the Durgin livery boat, and something called a Key West smackee, which I've never seen, even though it's named for the place we live. In the process you will come across dories, although few will be as massive and as difficult to row as those ocean-going dories from Nova Scotia used by the haul-seiners I worked with those years I tried so to make a living as a commercial fisherman.

You will, doubtless, also meet up with small, open boats called sharpies, although they probably will not look anything like the *Emma*. For *sharpie*, as I have discovered rather late in life, is a bit of descriptive terminology that means different boats in different coastal locations. A Maryland sharpie, for example, is a boat primarily built to sail as well as row, while an eastern Long Island sharpie would be difficult to sail and relative easy to row. If you become seriously interested in small boats, you will learn that this sort of regional diversity is a challenging exercise in nomenclature. For what is one person's sharpie is another's skiff, and what is another boat owner's skiff might also be called a dory skiff, depending on her lines and where she was built.

Not to worry too much about nomenclature. The wonderful thing about this class of small boats—surely the world's most inclusive—is that function follows form. Just as I was swept away

by the flowing lines of the Swampscott dory I was introduced to in
that empty Maine mill, so will you be informed by the way these
small boats look. Those with the breathtaking lines, the craft that
speak of grace and beauty as eloquently as a lily or a curling wave,
these are the boats you'll want for the sheer enjoyment of their
excellence. Don't ask them to do hard and dirty work; you would
not sweep your front porch with a lily. Ask them to take you for an
evening's row, a trip down the length of Georgica Pond to Mrs.
Wolf's for lunch. Or perhaps a sail across Somes Sound to Northeast Harbor.

Except for the shells designed specifically and exclusively for
rowing, each of the so-called pulling boats, skiffs, dories, sharpies,
Whitehalls, and what-have-you's can be both sailed and motored.
None of these boats needs a large outboard to move along; they are
designed to slip easily through the water. Nor do they require large
sails. Most will do quite well with a sail, mast, and boom (if you need
a boom) that you can carry on your shoulder, just as I carried my
mutton-leg sail and mast for that wonderful Swampscott dory. For
these are boats to be worn like a fine linen shirt, for the luxury of
their being and not their ability to absorb sweat.

You have scores of delightful choices and such a wide range of
marine personalities to choose from, it is relatively impossible to
advise you from a distance. Just be as certain as you can about what
you will ask from your small boat before you acquire it. Then you
will find the one that will surpass your expectations. There are
building plans, kits, and scores of boatbuilding schools like the
Apprentice Shop or the WoodenBoat schools in Maine that will
send you photographs of the skiffs, dories, and Whitehalls created
in their classrooms. There are boats of fiberglass, epoxy, marine
plywood, white cedar, mahogany, aluminum, and more. Just about
any material that can be worked and be made watertight has ended
up somewhere as a small, open boat designed primarily for rowing,
yet able to be sailed or motor powered. And they need not be
expensive if you're willing and able to do restorative work. Remem-

ber our *Blue Peril* and the priceless adventures we shared with her for just a few dollars.

Which brings me to my next and final point. If it's work you're going to ask of your small boat, then get one that's built for it. These are the oldest, the most tried, and the truest designs because the men and women who work on the water have been there for centuries. When they build a skiff or a dory or a seine boat there is no way that boat will ever be compared to a linen shirt. Small, open work boats—the dory is one classic, the skiff another—are a diminishing breed. The men and women who want to work that hard are fewer; the wild sea crops they harvest are vanishing. If you are one of the few who wants to try making a living on the water, then you already know what to ask from your boat.

POWERBOATS I We're leaving the realm of what I call the intimate small boats: the fleet that can be paddled, rowed, sailed, and poled. We enter the kingdom of the powerboat, the small craft designed to be propelled by outboard, inboard, or stern drive (a bit of both) engines, most of them there to turn a propellor, a few to create a jet of water strong enough to push a boat at thirty or forty knots. The powerboat family is a large one, almost too large to be catalogued, and certainly too large to be defined under a single heading. So we begin with the smallest powerboats, the small craft with open decks, no cabins, no consoles, no forward cuddies—nothing but a steering wheel, two or three seats, a throttle and shifting control, and a stern-mounted outboard motor.

Because these small boats are now so ubiquitous, there is an entire generation of folks who assume they've been around a long time. Not so. It wasn't until after World War II that boats designed specifically for outboards made their appearance. Before that, outboards were attached to boats built for sailing, rowing, or paddling.

As you know if you've read the rest of this book, I owned one of the first small powerboats ever mass-marketed. It was just luck that sent that thirteen-foot Boston Whaler my way. If my friend Frank

Webb hadn't wanted a larger Whaler, and if I hadn't been on the water with him the day he decided to get her, his thirteen-footer would most likely have been sold to someone else, someone who knew more about Whalers than I did.

Frank bought that boat new from the company in Rockland, Massachusetts, shortly after it began manufacturing its revolutionary small boats in 1958. The first boats were delivered a year later, and tens of thousands are still being made. I'm certain, thirty-five years later, that the Whaler I got from Frank is still afloat somewhere on the Maine coast. For the pioneering process of filling the space between an inner and outer layer of fiberglass with a high-density, closed-cell foam compound created a hull the likes of which had never been seen before. Unfazed by any of the natural predators of wooden boats, fiberglass is all but immortal. And the amazing strength and rigidity of the Whaler hull configuration protects it from most conceivable abuse. Unsinkable and all but undentable, the new hulls of the late 1950s forever changed small-boat construction and design.

And they are still there and still, dollar for dollar, one of the very best buys on the market. Over its many years of growth, the Boston Whaler Company has added scores of new models and new accessories, but it has never changed the basic materials and design of its open powerboats. With their double-sponson hulls (sometimes called cathedral hulls) beneath the waterline and beamy, open decks above, the Whaler sets the standard in the trade. And because it does, there are a host of "Whaler-type" boats, each, I'm sure, doing a decent job of staying afloat.

I was lucky; I've always been lucky. I started at the top of the open powerboat family. Ironically, I never appreciated how lucky I was. I just assumed that every small powerboat could do what our Whaler did.

Well, some do less and others do a bit more. Again, among the hundreds, perhaps thousands, of choices now on the market, you will find all kinds of materials, including wood, plywood, fiber-glassed plywood, fiberglass, and a number of epoxy and plastic compounds. You'll find V-hulls, modified-Vs, round bottoms, and almost flat bottoms. The Whaler hull tends to pound and slap a bit in short, choppy seas. And thirteen-foot Whalers can be wet. The V-hulls don't pound nearly as much (and deep-Vs tend to be drier). Fiberglass is much easier to maintain than wood, but then wood can be infinitely more beautiful. And I've always believed that because wood, like water, is a natural material, it will react more sensitively to its sister sea. On the other side of that same coin, however, is the undeniable fact that wood can rot. In the warm waters of the Gulf and southern seas, it can decay with surprising speed. Boatbuilders in places like Florida favor fiberglass and other nonbiodegradable compounds and often advertise their boats with the "no wood–no rot" byline.

Whatever make and model open powerboat you choose (or build for yourself), the fulfillment and contentment she provides will flow in direct relation to the accuracy of your expectations. Precisely what do you want the boat to give you? What waters do you expect her to explore? If more boat owners asked themselves these and similar questions—and answered them honestly—before they made their acquisition, the national "satisfied customer" quotient would jump off the charts.

Outboards, for example, should be more closely scrutinized. If a powerboat and its power plant are not properly suited to each other, the relationship is like a bad marriage: neither partner can perform to its full potential. Too many small powerboats are overpowered; big engines may look macho, but they consume too much fuel and add too much weight for the work they are asked to do. Hull designs like the thirteen-foot Whaler's, for example, are extremely efficient and made to move easily through the water. A thirty-horsepower will do the job superbly, but you'll see scores of thirteen-footers with fifties and higher. Check with the folks who make your boat; they'll tell you what works best, especially if you tell them whether you want her for water-skiing, exploring, trolling, fly casting, bottom fishing, or just messing about on the water.

Some manufacturers will modify their models for specific functions. Whalers have been asked to do everything from buoy tending, serving the U.S. Coast Guard and waterfront fire departments, ice breaking, and patrolling the jungle rivers of South America.

Within the past several years, the flats skiff, the newest member of the small, open powerboat family, has seen a jump in popularity that rivals the appearance of the first fiberglass boats forty years ago. Much of the rocketing demand for flats boats is directly related to the concurrent jump in the popularity of saltwater fly fishing. Almost exclusively a shallow-water, saltwater angling platform, the flats skiff is yet one more example of how highly specialized a boat can become. Yet because the market for that speciality continues to soar, flats skiffs that once were seen only in the Bahamas and off the Florida Keys are now turning up everywhere, even in the bays and rivers off New England. And where there once were two or three custom builders producing flats skiffs on order, there are now at least thirty-four, some of them national manufacturers like Mako and Aquasport.

Quite without rails, with its forward flush deck designed as a casting platform, and with its poling stand mounted over its large, powerful outboard, the flats skiff is a small open powerboat obviously designed for an extremely narrow functional range, which it performs masterfully. But for those tens of thousands of would-be boat owners who don't want to fish shallow waters, either salt or fresh, a flats skiff might prove to be an expensive and disappointing choice. On the other hand, if you dream of fishing the flats as often as I do, then you'll be very happy with your new boat.

POWERBOATS II The boat-acquisition decision that crosses the line between the relatively small, open powerboats to the group that can be roughly classified as middleweights is a step from one world to another very different world, with a different scope, variety, complexity, and cost. Which is one reason my experience as an owner is limited, to say the least. I have never been able to comfortably afford a middleweight powerboat; but I have been aboard quite a few and know many middleweight owners—enough, anyway, to list your considerable options.

Among the several classes of powerboats from sixteen to twenty-five feet or so are: the center console group, a contemporary configuration made possible with the arrival of new structural materials like fiberglass and various resin compounds; what I call speedboats or runabouts, the modern descendants of those lovely, powerful, sexy mahogany boats like those built by Gar Wood and seen in movies with stars like Dick Powell at the helm and starlets like Dorothy Lamour in the cockpit beside him. Remember how those engines rumbled, and how the boats fairly leapt from the water when the throttle was shoved ahead and the wind whipped the starlet's hair and the pennant fluttered from the torpedo stern?

Of course you do. And you probably also recall that you never seriously considered owning one. Those exotic speedboats belonged to bootleggers, men like the Great Gatsby or the real Gar Wood, who raced them at venues like Lake George at Saratoga.

Some folks might call those the good old days, and there is a brisk collector's market for those splendid mahogany Chris-Crafts and Gar Woods. But they quickly evolved to the next vastly more popular and more available family of powerboats known today by a variety of names. Each, however, whether it's called a bowrider or a runabout, performs essentially the same function as Gatsby's elegant launch: it's a boat that looks racy, moves very quickly, and, based on every single advertisement I have ever seen, always has a lovely young woman in the passenger seat.

She, however, does not come with any of the boats I know about. So why would you want such a craft? For cruising, which seems to be a prime reason folks buy these boats. With their upholstered seats, wraparound windshields, power steering, tape decks, and stereos, the interiors of a great many middleweight cruisers are designed to be as much like the family car as an eighteen-foot boat can be. The dashboards, instrument panels, and steering wheels often look as if they had been transplanted from a Buick—the point being, I have always assumed, to persuade the person behind the wheel that "driving" a boat is just as easy and comfortable as driving a new sedan. Indeed, much of the advertising copy written to persuade you to buy a V-hull middleweight that "planes faster, corners flatter, and handles better" often goes on to say something like "with multiport fuel injection, your new Water Panther starts as easily as the family car."

This approach has sold a great many bowriders, cruisers, and what-have-you's. And the power plants stuffed in most of these boats extend the metaphor. Whether it's an inboard, stern-drive, or outboard, the middleweight engine is designed for jack-rabbit starts—which helps get water-skiers up on their boards—and speeds that can top seventy miles per hour on more than a few models. One tragic result has been a startling number of boating accidents. The grim statistics seem to verify the notion that a boat built to look and operate like a car will also have accidents like a car. For these are, after all, watercraft. They can be swamped in heavy seas, lost in the fog, run aground on a reef, or may simply end up out of gas thirty-one miles offshore. For no matter what the ads tell you, there's a world of difference between I-95 and the tide rips off Race Rock. No matter what boat you buy, make certain it's equipped with every emergency accessory required by the Coast Guard, and be equally sure you know your navigation basics and the rules of the road.

But if you and your family like cruising, waterskiing, and skipping over the water like a 70-mph stone, then a bowrider middleweight may be just the boat for you. There is, as I've said, an awesome number of manufacturers and builders trying hard for a piece of the middleweight market. It's a competitive arena that works to the consumer's advantage. You may need at least a couple of weeks just to check all your options. According to the latest market research, a million new boat owners a year will be making these kinds of decisions each year for the next decade. If I were you, I'd try for the cruiser that has that lovely lady sunbathing on the bow.

That's if you like boating for play and relaxation. If you want a middleweight for fishing, then you want one of the center console

models, of which there are almost as many choices as there are among the bowriders and runabouts.

But once again, you would do well to begin with a Boston Whaler. If nothing else, you'll be taught just what to look for in a good center-console boat. That's because Whaler not only invented the hull system and construction design that made the thirteen-footer such a small-boat innovation and trend-setter; the same company also pioneered the fiberglass hull, center console, deepwater boat when it built its first seventeen-foot Montauk, the model that inspired a hundred other seagoing center consoles made by almost as many builders.

Unlike the runabouts and bowriders, which tend to favor inboard engines (probably because they pose less of a hazard to water-skiers), center consoles are most often powered by outboards, twins in many cases. Which means plenty of horsepower; two 200-horsepower modern outboards can move a twenty-five-foot fiber-glass V-hull at speeds that would have been considered impossible twenty years ago. Such quickness in the case of center consoles is not just for waterskiing; as the ads tell you, the speed is there to get you

offshore fast enough to allow you to go where the fish are, even if it's a trip of dozens of miles. And as the ads also tell you, you need that speed if a storm begins brewing when you're out there. With 300 horsepower on the stern of your center console, you can beat it back to a safe harbor before the storm catches up.

The center console's alignment with fishing is made clear by features like built-in rod holders, self-bailing cockpits, outriggers, under-gunwale rod racks, built-in live wells, and other similar accessories that only an angler might need. Which does not mean that you should deny yourself the pleasures of ownership if you don't know one end of a tuna rod from another. But because center consoles are designed and built for anglers, they are better buys for those who fish. If you don't, they are still fine boats, primarily because their deep-V hulls are designed to perform well in rough water, and seaworthiness is always—and always should be—a prime consideration if you plan on taking your new boat out on the open ocean.

Which should not imply that every middleweight craft is built for a rough day off Montauk. There are some models that should definitely leave the dock only when calm waters are assured. These are the deckboats, a hopped-up houseboat most often built on a platform supported by pontoons, usually aluminum. There are other hulls, however, including fiberglass, and their configuration can be more catamaran or trimaran than pontoons.

But there is no mistaking the deckboat profile. Some folks call them party barges, and these middleweights do look a bit like a living room set down on a high-tech variation of Huck Finn's raft. Huck and Jim pitched a tent on their raft; today's deckboat fans are much more concerned about all the comforts of home. With a hull that is essentially a beamy rectangle, with a squared-off bow and stern, the contemporary deckboat can be open or carry an enclosed cabin that will have room for almost everything a living room does. Even the open models find space for a stove, refrigerator, wet bar, lounge chairs, beds, and sofas. And although some deckboat models make a stab at adding fishing accessories, most are straightforward about their primary function: to be a platform for families and groups who want to cruise calm waters while they enjoy the view, watch television, down a few beers, and eat lunch or dinner at a table just like the one in their dining room at home. Let's hope they'll have that dinner while their deckboat is anchored in a sheltered cove.

These home-away-from-home boats are gaining popularity in Florida, as you might expect. Whenever I'm fishing on the Gulf side or in a protected channel, especially on weekends, one or two of them will slide by with outboards rumbling, folks gathered on the deck holding a cool drink in one hand and waving hello with the other. They are obviously having a very fine time on the water, which is, after all, precisely what their deckboat is designed and built to provide. However, if the wind is blowing and the seas are choppy, then the deckboats stay in port, as they should.

If you plan on cruising calm waters and you'd like your boat to come as close as possible to duplicating your living room, dining room, rec room, and kitchen, then you owe it to yourself to check out the deckboat family. More and more manufacturers are building them, so there must be a place for them in the ever-expanding

boating market, even if they are a long step away from traditional marine design.

POWERBOATS III   These days they are called walkabouts, or walkarounds, a terminology that's new to me because forty years ago there were no center consoles, no fiberglass, and just two basic divisions for large (more than twenty-five feet) powerboats. The first, commercial, included everything from seine boats to ocean-going trawlers. The second covered all the others not used commercially: yachts, sportfishers, and cruisers. Each had a forward cabin and an open deck aft. The sportfishers had outriggers, pulpits, and, more often than not, a flying bridge built atop the wheelhouse amidships. The yachts and cruisers often had awnings over the fantail, wicker furniture, and much fine mahogany trim along with scrubbed teak decks.

Each of the larger powerboats I have ever skippered or was invited to visit fit the same basic profile, whether it was that splendid Chris-Craft launch of the summer of 1948, the *Captain Kidd* a few summers later, Matty's *Double Trouble*, or any of the deepwater charter boats at Montauk that I mated for or skippered, including Peter Matthiessen's lovely *Merlin*. Although each was built in different corners of the continent, each conformed to the same basic criteria applied to every larger powerboat of the times: enclosed cabin forward, wheel amidships, open aft deck, and an inboard engine, or engines, below decks amidships. Some had pulpits, like the *Double Trouble* and the *Merlin*. Some had flying bridges, like the *Double Trouble*. And some, like the *Captain Kidd*, had none of the above, being built as simply as possible and designed to provide maximum deck space, some shelter for the crew, and a fundamental seaworthiness that gave the boat a wondrous ability to survive hostile waters such as those that have made the North Atlantic notorious around the globe. When you are in a forty-two-foot boat staring aghast at a windblown wave the size of Yankee Stadium curling malevolently just off your bow, you had better hope that the boat's designers and builders gave her the materials and the lines to meet that sea head-on and survive. Which is how they still build boats in Nova Scotia, and why, if I had my pick, I'd choose the *Captain Kidd* over any of the other larger powerboats I've been aboard. And there have been quite a few.

The new boats, the walkarounds and the walkabouts, are built from fiberglass or other similar compounds; some, like the Whaler walkarounds, are packed with a rigid foam between two layers of tough, molded fiberglass, a system which makes for an unsinkable hull. Up to twenty-five feet, most of these new arrivals are outboard powered, usually with twin engines, some packing almost 200 horsepower each. When a boat gets longer than twenty-five feet, however, most builders opt for inboard engines, many of them diesels, which have earned a reputation for reliability and fuel economy.

However, economy is not the flagship of this strata of the powerboat fleet. Once you own a pleasure boat longer than twenty-five feet, you are launched on an expensive voyage. But then, most of these boats are replete with amenities and even luxuries designed to help you feel good about spending all that money. Even the smaller boats, say from thirty to forty feet, offer sumptuous double staterooms, galleys gleaming with stainless steel and burnished aluminum, private heads (baths) with showers that gush hot water, cockpits and salons, backgammon tables, and just about every electronic navigational aid on the market.

Which is one reason why the pages of every boat-buying and trading publication, like the *South Florida Boat Trader*, are clogged with large powerboats for sale. You don't have to be an expert to read between the lines; many owners of these boats on the block had yacht-buying eyes bigger than their bank accounts. J. P. Morgan's advice to a would-be yacht owner is still very much to the point: "If you have to ask how much it costs," he said, "then you probably cannot afford the boat."

There is, currently, another side to that coin. Now that the excessive eighties are over and the back-to-reality nineties are here, there are a great many large powerboats on the market, some at genuine bargain prices. It is, as they say, a buyer's market; if you want to take a step up to a true cabin cruiser from your runabout or center console, then your timing is auspicious. You can, if you look long enough, find relatively sound motor yachts of forty feet or so available for $100,000, sometimes even a bit less. These are all older boats and you'll need to know what to look for. But they are out there in increasing numbers, and if you are lucky you can save yourself the $500,000 or more a new motor yacht the same size will cost you.

On the other hand, you can go to Maine and get a good used but lovely and superbly seaworthy lobster boat for about $20,000. And remember, these are all boats with a forward cabin, wheelhouse, inboard engine, and open cockpit aft, just like the one Humphrey Bogart skippered out of Key Largo in *To Have and Have Not*. It's the small boats that have changed so much, not the larger ones— although it should be added here that Chris-Craft, in business since 1874, is producing some new, large powerboats that look more as if they belong on *Star Trek* than in a 1940s movie.

And if you want a boat much longer than fifty feet, then you probably can afford not to worry about much of anything except having a fine time afloat. There are scores of reliable yacht brokers out there who will be only too happy to help.

SPECIALTIES   There are, apparently, no limits to a marine designer's imagination, nor does there seem to be much of a limit on the specialized functions some boat owners want their watercraft to fulfill. All of which has led to the production of some of the most graceful, the most odd, and the most awkward small boats on the map. There is no need to review them in depth because they each are so specialized that you wouldn't want to own one unless you knew precisely why, how, and where you would use it. In which case, you would know just what the boat would do and where to go to find one.

That being said, I'll continue with a partial rundown of specialized craft. If nothing else, it should encourage you to believe that no matter what your on-the-water needs and interests might be, there is a boat for you somewhere, even if it's still on a boatbuilder's drawing board.

If, for example, you want to hunt waterfowl on Merrymeeting Bay or Chesapeake Bay, or some of the other broad, marshy, and shallow East Coast estuaries that are staging areas for waterfowl migration, then you'll need a gunning float. There are some fiberglass models of these graceful, low-profile boats, but the majority of the few still being built are fashioned from one-inch square strips of cedar, curved and bent as cunningly as an Indian's canoe, and glued and nailed into a seamless hull about twelve to fourteen feet long that looks something like a husky, wooden kayak. The gunner reclines with feet forward under the long bow and sculls with a single long oar off the stern. Sculled expertly, a gunning float appears to glide magically over the water as if she drifted on an unseen current. Apparently, waterfowl mistake her for an errant log or other flotsam and pay no attention, an error that often proves fatal.

Like the gunning float, the airboat is another small craft that is regionally exclusive and is found only in shallow-water swamps, vast tidal flats, and grassy marshes like the Everglades. These boats begin with an aluminum johnboat modified to accept what looks like a giant fan mounted on the stern. With a sound about equal to an aircraft's propellor, the blades turn and push enough air to move these boats at high speeds over grass, thin mud, and places where the water is no more than inches deep. Their engines consume a great deal of fuel and there is little room for cargo on the small amount of deck space unoccupied by the large engine. But there is no better boat for navigating mudflats or the Everglades; wardens, biologists, and other professionals who must have access to such hard-to-reach areas have made the airboat a well-recognized craft, even though there are few recreational boaters who will ever need one.

The same is true for hovercraft, hydrofoils, and iceboats—three more highly specialized boats that nevertheless have become part of the public consciousness. War-movie fans know hovercraft well: they are the rather bulky boats that drag their skirts noisily across the water and/or land, kept above the waves and/or sand by the rush of air pushed downward by a set of whirling propellor fans mounted on the boat's bottom. Thus far, only the military and other government services like the Coast Guard have been able to afford hovercraft, or devise a use for them that can be classified as recreational. Hydrofoils, on the other hand, have made the move from military to civilian life with remarkable ease, considering their high operating and maintenance costs. Mounting two pairs of what look like underwater wings at the bow and stern of a conventional V-hull allows that hull to rise totally out of the water and ride on the wings once the critical speed is reached. Thus freed of the hull's drag, the boat "flies" above the surface at startling speeds—up to ninety miles per hour for the U.S. Navy's hydrofoils used to intercept drug shipments in the Caribbean. On Italian lakes, hydrofoils have been used for the past forty years as ferries roaring across the still waters from one tourist port to another. They are not, however, a family boat, unless your family is very large and very wealthy.

Iceboats, on the other hand, are making enough of a comeback to escape the "specialized" classification, but that's only in the northern latitudes where winters are long enough and cold enough to guarantee frozen lakes and bays from January (at least) through March. Little more than small sailboats mounted on three sets of skating blades—one at each end of a forward cross arm and one for steering at the stern—iceboats reach gloriously high speeds, can be raced like sailboats, and, best of all, give their skippers many hours of exhilaration during the months when most northerners are forced indoors by the cold. If the Ice Age were still upon us and Florida's lakes could freeze, the iceboat would be one of the most popular small craft on the water . . . make that on the ice.

Unlike canoes, dinghies, kayaks, and dories, iceboats cannot be modified to include a motor, nor can they be rowed or paddled or poled, which—in the strictest sense—makes them sailboats, not powerboats. They are, however, very much a specialized sort of boat and belong in this grouping. But because they are sailboats, they begin the transition here to boats that are primarily wind-powered as opposed to motor-driven.

In this category is the smallest of the specialized watercraft, the sailboard, which is the highly sophisticated, high-tech blending of mast and sail with surfboard and surfer. I have no idea who first wondered what might happen if he raised a sail from the deck of a contemporary surfboard, but I wish I'd been there to watch that first ride. The combination of ocean swells, wind, and rigid, narrow surfboard constructed from space-age materials creates a thrilling combination of speed and trajectory. Many windsurfers are airborne, literally, as they ride up the face of a wave and take off from its crest, just like a ski jumper leaving a ramp.

Sailboarders are, almost exclusively, young, strong, and well coordinated. Their sport, and that's what it is, requires these qualities and more. A sailboarder must know how to sail, must have a fundamental understanding of winds, currents, and tides. For unlike a powerboater, sailboarders cannot start an engine and make headway against the winds and tides. A failure to understand this basic difference took one Key West sailboarder of my acquaintance some eight miles offshore in the open Atlantic, where he might well

have ended his voyage and his existence had he not been rescued at sea by the Spanish-speaking crew of an oceangoing shrimp boat. As a "guest" aboard the shrimper until her hold was filled, the sailboarder was asked many times in Spanish what he was doing so far offshore aboard such a tiny vessel. All he could utter by way of reply was to point a finger toward his own head and say, "*Loco.*" Which seemed to make sense to his saviors.

SAILBOATS I, MONOHULLS The transition here from a sailboard, which is not a sailboat, is not as complex as you might imagine. For

the principles of sailing, even though a sailboard has no tiller (shifting your weight on the board does the steering) and no cockpit, it is the wind and nothing else that generates the energy that moves the watercraft. And so it is with all sailboats, monohull and multihull. Which makes them quite a different sort of watercraft. If the wind blows too hard, as it frequently does, a sailboat is at some risk. If that sailboat's skipper is inexperienced, the sailboat is at considerable

risk. If the wind stops blowing altogether, a sailboat is becalmed, as motionless as the sea's unfurrowed surface. Without an auxiliary power source—paddles, oars, outboard motor, or inboard engine— a sailor aboard a becalmed boat has no choice but to wait for the wind. Which can often be a long wait.

In spite of these meterologic realities, and other sorts of challenges, there are millions of sailboat owners, for sailing is a pure and ancient skill. And it is this purity that attracts so many of today's sailors: they want to be part of an adventure that requires intimate contact with natural features like the wind and the waves. Indeed, many modern sailors affect contempt for powerboats. "Stinkpots" is one of their less scatological terms for any boat without a mast and boom, although I have seen few sailboats more than twenty-five feet long that do not carry auxiliary motor power. Their owners can look down their bowsprits at powerboats, but when the wind drops and tides run against them, those same sailor snobs are quick to start their engines.

I don't blame them. I just wish some sailors would be a bit less holier-than-thou about their recreation. Small-boat sailors (like myself), on the other hand, have no room for engines aboard boats like the Swampscott dory and the Old Town canoe I sailed around Middle Bay. But the dory had oars and the canoe had a paddle, so I was never quite marooned if the wind quit. And those boats, along with the two prams and the *Emma*—my first "sailboat"—and the *Georgica Snipe* are the only monohulls I ever owned, although I did learn to sail dinghies, Snipes, and Star-Class sloops during those youthful summers at sailing school.

Which is a start at sailing that I advise for every would-be sailboat owner: go to school, even if it's only a short course, a cram class that lasts just a week or ten days. Because on-the-job training for a first-time sailor can be hazardous to your health and your new boat's continued well-being.

Once you understand sailing's fundamentals—wind, water, tide, current, mast, boom, tiller, rudder, keel, centerboard, jib, main sheet, halyard, windward, leeward, transom, garboard, chine, skeg, and more—you can consider buying your first sailboat. You face a multitude, indeed a limitless number, of choices. Your sails can be marconi-rigged, gaff-rigged, sprit-rigged (like my Swampscott dory), or square-rigged (like the sail I created for the *Vop Vop*). There are catboats, sloops, cutters, yawls, ketches, schooners, and flat-bottomed sailing sharpies that work and cruise in shallow waters from Connecticut to the Keys. There are centerboard sailboats, keel sailboats, outrigger sailboats, and sponson sailboats with dagger-boards.

As you can tell by now, the world of sailing vessels is indeed large, varied, and relatively complex. Anything like a comprehensive review of the monohull family from six to forty feet would fill a book twice as long as this one. But the fundamentals don't change: analyze the reasons why you think you might enjoy a sailboat—racing (and there's a great deal of that), cruising, or simply sailing (which is all I've ever done)—and you'll be a great deal closer to making the right choice.

SAILBOATS II, MULTIHULLS Most folk read the book before they read its appendix, so if you've come this far, you have read about my Hobie Cat, one of the original catamarans designed by California's Hobie Alter some thirty years ago. As you can tell from my story, I thought the world of that sailboat. And based on my reading these days, most of the world shares that opinion. Hobie Cats are now ubiquitous, on beaches and alongside docks in waters that reach from the Caribbean to the Mediterranean, and from San Francisco Bay to Hong Kong and beyond. It's amazing what good design can accomplish.

Catamarans—twin hulls that support a center platform—and trimarans—three hulls, with the large center hull bracketed by a matched pair—are carving a larger and larger niche in the sailing universe, with the largest in the small-sailboat (under twenty-two feet) class. Why there? Because sailing a small cat like the Hobie is just plain fun, no question about it. The small catamaran can navigate shallow waters, sail faster than the wind, resist capsizing, and, because it is made of high-tech, space-age materials, can be easily and economically maintained. With all of these advantages, a cat sailor can put up with the boat's often sluggish response to the helm when she is asked to come about: to change direction by moving her bow through the wind's direction. Jibing, moving the stern instead of the bow, works just fine in a catamaran and it's exciting as well. So is sailing in the surf, cresting breaking waves, and even surfing after they break, all of which are possible in a small catamaran.

These are fun boats, and they represent the most fundamental revolution in small sailboat design since the marconi rig. However, fun catamarans are not meant for lounging, cruising, picnicking, or transoceanic travel. For sailboats that have more livability, you'll need to step up to the larger cruising catamarans or the racing trimarans. During the quarter-century since the large multihulls became a factor in the sailing world—Dennis Conner won the America's Cup with a catamaran in 1988—they have been continually refined and improved. The result has been a natural division: catamarans, with their broad, stable, and spacious deck between two hulls, have become comfortable cruising boats; trimarans have evolved to become the favorite of ocean racers and other rough-water competitors.

However, be forewarned: once you depart the world of small multihulls like the Hobie Cat, you enter a world of relatively expensive sailboats. Large trimarans and catamarans are not built for the budget minded. But then, whoever said boats and budgets had anything in common? Not I, that's for sure.

Some Advice to Boat Buyers

Ann Landers and Abigail Van Buren have made successful careers in journalism by answering personal questions of countless thousands. It's my guess that if they were plugged into the boating crowd and limited themselves to questions from men and women who have trepidations about buying their first new or used boat, there would be no noticeable drop in the number of letters received. For unlike the purchase of a new or used car, microwave, television set, or even house or condominium, the acquisition of a boat is, for the great majority, a process fraught with hazards and shrouded in mystery. Which does little to slow a continued increase in boat sales, but which also contributes significantly to the numbers of unhappy and dissatisfied first-time boat owners.

"I've sold a great many boats," says boat broker Bill Orr from behind his desk at Handy Boat in Falmouth, Maine, the region's largest and busiest boatyard and yacht brokerage, "and I have learned that at least seventy percent of first-time buyers are unhappy with their choice."

Seventy percent translates to more than two out of three boat buyers who regret their decisions. Extrapolated a bit further, the Orr observation means that if you are thinking about buying your first boat, the odds are against you. Why such long odds?

"The trouble in most cases," says Orr, "is caused by boat buyers who have never really decided, or learned, what they expect of their new boat or how they plan to use it. I could sit here all day and give you the names of husbands who called back a month after we delivered their new boat to say, 'Bill, it's either give up my wife or give back the boat. I think I'd better try selling the boat.' Or, a wife calls and tells me how much she wanted a boat to make her husband happy. Then she discovers the last thing he wanted was another major responsibility.

"And don't kid yourself," Orr continues. "I've been around boats all my long life, and they are a major responsibility. Before I got in the yacht trade, I ran an automobile dealership—sold Mercedes, and successfully, too. Believe me, there are no similarities. None. Buying a boat and buying a car are two different experiences. Buying a car is like picking out a new stove; buying a boat is as complex and personal as choosing a wife, maybe more so."

First-time boat buyers, as Bill Orr and every other experienced boat broker I've ever met has told me, should spend some serious time thinking about and discussing: why they want to be a boat owner; what functions they want their boat to perform; how much time (honestly) they can give to their boat; and how much money they can budget, not merely to cover the purchase price but subsequent expenses like insurance and maintenance costs, storage, and major repairs.

"With today's fiberglass boats, maintenance is much less costly than it was with wooden boats. But it's still a fact of boating life, just like insurance, although the cost of decent boat insurance is quite reasonable." Bill Orr takes a breath and reflects. "But it's still the process of putting the right boat together with its new owners for all the right reasons."

As I've attempted to explain in this book, there is such a vast variety of small boats available in today's markets that surely there is one—new or used—that will meet your individual needs, if only you do an honest and thoughtful job of defining those needs. Once you have made every decision that answers the questions about what and why, then the odds for happiness with your new boat will move from two-to-one against you to at least ten-to-one in your favor.

Okay. You've made your decision. Now to find and buy the boat. If its a rowing boat, pram, sailboard, kayak, canoe, dory, johnboat, inflatable, or any of the other boats classified as small and open, the odds jump to about thirty-to-one in your favor. That's because what you see is what you get. There are no hidden spaces on open boats. Set one afloat and you can tell if she leaks. Give her a close visual inspection, topsides and bottom, and use your common sense about the shape she's in. And remember, if you think you have found a bargain too good to be true, you are probably right: the boat isn't the bargain she seems to be. Small boats priced far below their going market value are very seldom marked down because their owner feels generous. Flip through the pages of any of the several boats-for-sale publications you can find on any good newsstand, and you can quickly get a good line on prevailing market prices. Or talk with the folks at your neighborhood boatyard or dealership; they make a living selling boats and are knowledgeable about values and trends.

But small, open boats not only are less likely than their larger counterparts to confront first-time buyers with surprise defects, they also are much less costly to repair when a wrong needs to be righted. Boat buyers need to beware when they decide that only a larger boat can make them and their family happy. By "larger" I mean more than sixteen or twenty feet, with at least an enclosed cabin. Every boat in the larger category has some spaces a first-time buyer can't see; they simply are not available for visual examination. They can be spaces between the inner and outer hull, below the waterline, beneath a coat of paint, or within the core of the boat's most important structural components.

There was, for example, the relatively experienced buyer of a handsome sloop who took his wife and child aboard for the boat's first voyage with its new owner at the helm. The day sparkled, a breeze brightened Casco Bay's lively waters, and every aspect of the voyage promised a delightful interlude. Underway, heeling a bit in the freshening sou'wester, the skipper's new pride and joy cleared the first island and sailed on into the waters of the open bay, where the wind and waves flourished unfettered.

No sooner had the sloop reached open water and heeled sharply in the first gust when there was an awesome crack of destruction, the splintering sound of collapse and the violent end of the "new" boat's maiden voyage. She was, in a moment, dismasted and her skipper had to radio for a tow back to the yard.

After much examination, the cause of the boat's sudden mortal wound was traced to a mainstay that had pulled loose from its belowdecks fastenings. Once the stay gave way, the mast snapped. That simple. And the reason the stay pulled loose was traced to deterioration of the fastenings that held the steel plate to the boat's inner hull, where dry rot had been silently and invisibly at work for several months or longer. Neither the former owner who sold the boat in good faith, nor the unfortunate buyer who had checked everything he could see could be held accountable for the dismasting, which under different conditions could have been a much more serious accident.

Compared to other unfortunate marine histories related by Bill Orr and other boatyard people, the sloop's mishap was but one of many similar sad boat stories. Based on bitter experience, boat owners and would-be owners have learned that the best step to avoid such traumas is to request and pay for the services of a good marine surveyor.

Marine surveyors have just one profession: evaluating and reporting on the condition of a boat, any boat, any size and in any condition, new, used, or abused. Yes, the service costs money, but compared to the cost of most boats larger than twenty feet, it's a small percentage of the total. Marine surveyors (and that's how they are listed in your yellow pages phone directory) have had years of experience with wooden and fiberglass hulls. They know how different boatbuilders design their hulls; they know where those invisible belowdecks and between-hulls trouble spots might be. They can tell, often from nothing more significant than the boat's paint, whether there might be a serious problem in the making.

So if you have decided why you want a "new" boat, how you will use her, where she will be docked and cared for, and what sort of equipment she will be fitted with and what colors she will wear—after you have discussed and made each of these decisions but before you buy the boat—request a competent marine survey by a qualified and experienced marine surveyor. It's likely to be the best boating decision you'll ever make.

One more caveat: marine surveyors often are not internal-combustion-engine experts and they'll tell you so. Most will not evaluate engines; you can request an inspection by a factory representative or by a mechanic you know is familiar with your particular power plant. If I'd spent more time talking with Bert, the Garrison Bight mechanic, about the Evinrude forty-horsepower outboard on the boat Roger brought to Key west, I could have saved myself much time and money. Because he has worked with so many different Evinrudes over so many years, Bert could have told me what was going to go wrong with that motor long before it did. And we could have prevented it for much less money than I eventually had to spend on repairs. Yes, I know it's difficult to acknowledge that you don't know all there is to know about your boat and motor, but I've found it even more uncomfortable (and uneconomical) to admit that it's your own fault, and yours alone, when the inevitable trouble strikes.

Once you've made the all-important and pivotal personal decisions about why you want a boat and how you will use her, look for help from the folks who can best give it. They are out there, in your boatyard, in marine surveyor offices, and in the pages of the many owner's manuals and boat-buying guides your newsstand and library can make available.

And remember Bill Orr's words: "Buying a new boat is as complex and personal as choosing a wife, maybe more so."

He's right, you know.

Index